Hertfordshire
COUNTY COUNCIL
Community Information

Please renew/return this item by the last date shown.

So that your telephone call Is chargod at local rate, please call the numbers as set out below:

	From Area codes 01923 or 0208:	From the rest of Herts:
Renewals:	01923 471373	01438 737373
Enquiries:	01923 471333	01438 737333
Minicom:	01923 471599	01438 737599

L32b

L 33

ABOUT BLADY

ABOUT BLADY

A Pattern Out of Time

LAURENS VAN DER POST

CHATTO & WINDUS

LONDON

Published in 1991 by
Chatto & Windus Ltd
20 Vauxhall Bridge Road
London SW1V 2SA

A CIP catalogue record for this book is
available from the British Library.

ISBN 0 7011 3802 5

Typography by Humphrey Stone
Photoset by Rowland Phototypesetting Ltd
Bury St Edmunds, Suffolk
Printed in Great Britain by
Mackays of Chatham plc
Chatham, Kent

For
Frances Mirrietjie
and her Mediterranean heart,
with love

Acknowledgements

I have always been generously and proudly befriended by Rosemary Magellan de Llorens, and shall always have an abiding sense of gratitude for what she and her family have given me. But here I owe a very special debt to Rosemary herself for putting me on the track of the 'other-ness' of Blady and, in this regard, this short acknowledgement, however special and grateful, is an inadequate expression of what I feel is her due.

And then I have also to thank most particularly Jane Brewster Bedford for helping me to maintain the continuity and preparing the manuscript for publication against all sorts of odds and interruptions which could easily have fragmented the writing if it had not been for her immense contribution.

We all thank, too, Louise Stein who never failed to help when, as often happened, there was more to do than we could contain ourselves.

Contents

I
Floating Things

Although the story becomes specific only in Blady, it does not begin there. That is the trouble when writing about the truth as we have experienced it. Fiction has its own truth. It is a truth which is innocent and flexible in a way that what one so naively calls actuality is not. Whatever conceives and directs the patterns of the stories told from the beginning of human life to this day, the storyteller has all sorts of advantages which the reporter of the truth, with which I am concerned, does not possess.

Take this matter of beginnings. The storyteller can choose his moment of entry into this awesome continuum of time and space and all its relativities, and compel their obedience to the story. He can lengthen or foreshorten time and manipulate its mysterious partner, space, and move freely backwards and forwards in the interests of the drama which must heighten the perception and expectations of the reality of his listeners. He can dispose of fifty years in a paragraph, and prolong for many pages the calm before the storm which he must call forth for the climax of his story, so that what is but a moment of great meaning in the progression of the story feels as if it is lasting for a century, and all that has gone before and comes after, which in real life may take many years to rise up and dissolve, can vanish as if they had been but an instant.

He can marry outer eventfulness with the inner eventfulness of a story that imagination bound to the here and now cannot do, because the truth of life will only yield to the truth attained in a pattern that has been lived. It is never just an outer event. It is always more than the statistics and the appearances in what a Zen monk, in the cool of a great Zen Buddhist temple in

I

Kyoto one early afternoon in the autumn long, long ago, told me was 'a world of floating things'.

Our imagination in this confrontation may tempt us into believing that we can improve on this sort of truth, but that would, as the Zen master expressed it, lead to self-illusion and float away and leave only black holes in the day behind.

There is another great difficulty too: we cannot follow the pattern of our own experience of the truth chronologically, since so much of the truth does not belong to the world of the clock and the calendar but, almost immeasurably, is a 'before' and an 'after' and at our own beginning is already part of an infinite compound which, as our own time becomes more specific, makes us feel as if we were looking into another universe within ourselves, spread out there as the night sky packed with stars presents itself in the southern hemisphere to the senses. Even as a boy I would stand looking up at the night knowing that, among all the brightest planets with their moons and satellites and suns greater than ours, my 'tonight' was not the same night up there, and that across the light years in between, where so many stars were hesitating between their night and ours, there were some that had already vanished forever.

Yet there were also stars whose light would burst in on one's senses in a space where no light had been before with such power that astronomers call them supernovae, their brightness already old when it became newly born in my eyes.

Even more sobering, there were stars and other cosmic bodies, invisible to the most powerful electronic telescopes but already known and charted in the Admiralty map of heaven by their influences on the other stars.

It is the nearest kind of metaphor, inadequate as it may be, for what happened in my own imagination and navigated me, as it were, astronomically to Blady. And what appears to be here, now, the beginning, was a moment when I had to turn astronomer and prowl among the known and visible stars and their neighbours, watching their activity and places of congregation where at some inner sanctuary of the universe the mystery of things is being transformed into a kind of living wonder. And so, by following a pattern in and out of time before and beyond the here and now, one discovers one's own specific sense of meaning which for me would also be lived in and around about Blady.

This, of course, was easier said than done. Some of our easiest platitudes disguise the difficulties of their practice, and certainly one of the hardest to follow is the old English maxim that the longest way round is the shortest way there, particularly in an era which has such passionate faith in the short cut, in the instant happening, and in cutting out all that is imagined to be in the way of instant solutions. There has perhaps never been a moment when the importance of 'being' is so neglected in the general preoccupation with 'doing', and when there is no realisation, at heart, of the unfolding of the human spirit which the truth demands. The truth yields to nothing except growth: it has no method which does not correspond to the 'method of the rose' – which is but to grow.

In the course of time this aspect of the truth grew in importance within my own conscious reckoning. I do not know, even so, if I would have been any good at recognising it had I not learned something about it in my years of imprisonment, including weeks of solitary confinement and days of actual condemnation to death and, ultimately, a narrow escape from starvation. That experience has remained with me in a way which I could never describe accurately but draw upon from time to time as the source of truth and accurate measure of my own and other people's values. It is part, perhaps, of what is most important in human beings and their societies: not their activity, and not ultimately their 'being' alone, but the climate in which both these aspects of living are included. It was this climate which I brought from prison with me, only to go – in a physical state when I could hardly walk, and a drive of just a few miles in a Japanese car made me violently seasick – back into the field for some more war. Yet even there I recognised that the climate had changed and new things were beginning to grow.

And one of these things demanded that when I wrenched myself out of the turmoil in South-East Asia at last, before I could face London again, before I could face my own family

3

and my mother whom I loved without reserve, I had to absent myself from all other human beings and in secret make my way, accompanied only by two haphazard helpers chosen from a group of unemployed among my black countrymen, far off into the bushveld and camp there on one of my favourite (and then still comparatively secret) rivers, the Pafuri, and live alone with nature and the animals for company.

I knew at the time that I could not explain to anyone why I had done this, because it would be too much for their understanding. One of the lessons I had learned at the school from which I had just come was that one had an obligation not to trouble one's fellow human beings with things that were beyond their understanding. One had to learn to respect the capacities of others, whether greater or lesser than one's own. I remember writing at the time a kind of prayer in which I asked that my own gift of light should not blur a lesser one, nor dim the one that came from this area of the supernovae of meaning of which I have spoken. In all communications one had to look for a readiness and a certain two-way traffic of comprehension. After all, there is enough of meaning in even the meanest forms of human being to occupy a lifetime not without wonder in their exchange with their neighbours. I am not trying to say that there are not moments when one speaks out for a truth, as objectively as one can, which collective awarenesses may not only misunderstand but violently reject. But one can only do so then, I feel, through what has been established as of truly objective importance within oneself in the course of the life one has led.

But when asked one day, when I did let out this secret meeting in the heart of Africa between the nature of Africa and myself, why I did it, the answer which came unprompted out of myself took even me by surprise, and I said: 'I have been a kind of Gulliver, not his author, because I am neither a Swift nor a swallow that can never make a summer,' and we all, I remember, smiled at the involuntary pun, 'but I am a sort of bird of passage and in my passing seem to have been through countries which in the great and terrible Dean's book of imaginary travels are symbolically orchestrated. The all-time bounty-hunter of idiots, presumptuous and partial men and their creeds, societies and values, in Gulliver he passes through all four seasons of the human spirit. In the first he is a giant among little men, in the second he is a little man in a world of giants, in the third and most portentous he goes into a floating world of islands, and in the fourth he sojourns in exile for the last time in the Kingdom of the Horses. I too had to make a journey to the animal kingdom of Africa and then come back slowly out of the wars and confusions and the unnecessary wounding and rejection of natural life by the world of men, their clashes of culture, their prejudices of mind and spirit and find, as it were, there on the banks of the Pafuri, the resolution which Gulliver found at the end of his journey to the Kingdom in his own stable and in the company there of his own horses. His stable, indeed, was to him an image of return to "the Garden" as referred to by Voltaire with such precision that his words have become proverbial in the mouth of his Candide: *"Cela est bien dit . . . mais il faut cultiver notre jardin."*

'It was only by living with these horses that Gulliver could persuade himself to venture back into the world of men, first in a state where he could hardly bear the smell of his own wife and family for more than a brief hour or two, and then, by increasing the time from day to day, achieving at last a state in which he could leave the horses and take his place in the world, equipped in mind and spirit to stand firm in what the world of men, and their addiction to the floating world of things, so dangerously called "peace".'

The real significance of this allusion to Swift did not occur to me at the time, although it was clearly an indication that the pattern of Blady was already a profound potential in my unconscious. At the time it just appeared to me the normal kind of association which would occur to any person who loved literature and found himself in my situation.

From this Pafuri moment I ventured out wider into the world of men, and what happened then is, in the sense in which the happenings were of some objective significance, fully described and dealt with in other books I have written. But what does need emphasis here is that – rather like one of the stars which

I have mentioned that exercise a great influence on the movements of their neighbours though they themselves are invisible
and will not be visible until the right and the light of meaning
have been earned – I was drawn as if by magnet to a life which
almost immediately led me to explore immense, uncharted wil-
dernesses in the heart of my native continent, the greatest of
which was the Kalahari Desert, and for some years I devoted
myself to exploring these 'known unknowns'. I did all that – in
so far as I was conscious of what I was doing – because instinct
and opportunity and a love and gift for making do in bush and
jungle and desert matched the opportunities put in my way, and
seemed to be the most honest and worthwhile kind of employ-
ment for a person like me who had to start rediscovering himself
and resuming a way of his own.

I was soon to find that, in exploring vast tracts of country
where no Europeans had been before, the impact on me went
far beyond what my senses conveyed, significant and vivid as
their transmission turned out to be. The simple, overwhelming
fact was that exploring the physical unknown became, from
the beginning, more and more an exploration of an immense
unknown in myself, so that although the journeys themselves
and what appeared to be of interest to a larger world have been
recorded in several books of mine, there were special moments,
almost like phases on a kind of pilgrimage of providence, and
some of those moments – which illustrate this progression over
some six years of my immediate post-war life – stand out now
like the lighthouses I have seen in the dark of the many oceans
over which I have travelled.

The first of these moments came one day when I was lying in
the grass on a mountain top in central Africa with the earth
underneath me warm and alive. Through all my body I seemed
to feel it like a kind of electric blanket holding me warm and
secure as if a gift direct from the caring and loving heart of our
great mother, the African earth. Between the tassels of grass
high above me the sky, as so often in Africa, was a sort of
midnight blue, and a great feeling of exhilaration broke through
me and the thought presented itself, bright and quick to my
slow tongue, and I could only catch it in retrospect on my return

to Europe in words which found a place in my book *Venture to the Interior*. It was a form of certain faith, of even more than the Pauline conviction so beautifully expressed by perhaps the greatest writer in the Bible. It was for me:

> . . . *the not-yet in the now,*
> *The taste of fruit that does not yet exist,*
> *Hanging the blossom on the bough.*

These words expressed a thought that remains constant, and I am amazed how many letters I still get and how often I am asked from which Chinese text that quotation came, or from which poem of Eliot the lines are taken. The answer, of course, is that I merely wrote them down; they came to me out of Africa and the kind of journeying I was doing then.

And its importance has continued to grow and its light in the dark of myself increase because it came out of a bitter experience in prison where, taken out to what we thought could be our own execution, we were made by the Japanese to watch the most brutal execution of others; and, during the watching, an officer, standing between me and a great friend and great prison commander whom we all called Nick, fainted on trembling, thin and weak legs. Nick and I had to support him as he stood there, and in the process we all touched hands and I was startled, because throughout my physical being there was an inrush of what I can only describe as electricity, which was not just a thing of energy but was also charged with a sense of hope, certainty, belonging and life for ever.

I knew then, and the knowledge has grown and not dimmed, that this is what flesh and blood is about and is meant to be, and but for this I do not know how I could have steered my course in the years that have followed even up to today, because the external scene of the post-war human world appears to be stubbornly determined to deny and destroy that one-ness of life we are meant to share.

Perhaps the most important of these moments in the Kalahari came after days of crashing through the bush, and at times forests, between the Zambezi and the Chobe rivers and the great

Makarikari pan, as we hurled our vehicles blindly at an opaque screen of leaf and bush and trees ahead, not knowing what would be on the other side. It was the kind of going that was truly exciting and, just in the going, raised one's spirits into feeling that all was worthwhile. Then suddenly, when I was leading, we broke through the bush and the open Kalahari was before us. We could cease zigzagging, twisting and turning and, to the joy of my black companions who had been lying on their backs with sticks to ward off the mambas that appeared every now and then, birdnesting overhead and, as they believed, lashing out at their faces, we could steer a straight compass course south. Towards evening we went slowly up the sides of a curved dune. There were moments when the sand was so deep that our overheated trucks faltered, yet we were up and almost immediately sliding down the far side when we saw before us a wide pan, bare and firm at the bottom with lines of sedges around the edges and in the far distance a clump, a sort of grove of camelthorns and bushes but, in between, full of animals of all kinds which were no longer grazing but standing still, looking in the direction of this profound rumble that had disturbed them.

There were groups of superb springbok, the most graceful gazelle in existence and the favourite decoration of the long avenues of the blue distances, gemsbok, gnu, hartebeest and eland; and as we went deeper into the pan towards them they seemed totally unafraid, only full of natural curiosity, making way for us politely and gracefully as the animals of nature do when not threatened, committed to make room for one another. And then as the reverberations of our vehicles, moving as slowly and as quietly as possible, reached down into the earth below, jackals came out of their holes, bat-eared foxes appeared and some meerkats popped up, and all joined the watchers.

I cannot put into adequate words what such an intimate glimpse into this undiscovered world of nature did to us except, somewhere, it evoked the 'Garden at the beginning', a world of innocence before man was so successfully seduced by the serpent. It was, as it seemed to me then, not only proof but bedrock of this 'not-yet in the now' feeling I had brought with me to the scene.

All this was confirmed that night when, around our camp, there was a disturbance among the animals on the far edges of the pan and, in the stillness of the night, the sound of hooves pounding the earth like drums. I came out of my mosquito net at once, and then, almost as soon as it started, the pounding ceased and the noise reduced itself to a steady advance of animal feet towards us, until by torchlight we saw that the animals had arranged themselves in close order all around our camp as if nearness to us gave them safety, or at least a sense of increased security. We knew then that the carnivorous creatures of the Kalahari, who are many, some great and formidable, must inevitably, in the interests of the law of proportion, be prowling to invade and feed for survival in this privileged reserve of antelopes and gazelle.

We gave all our camping places a name. This camp we called 'Paradise Pan'. Even friends who have never been to Africa have, by proxy, found this moment precious, and it can therefore be imagined how singularly bright it shone in my own war-darkened mind.

There were many moments too that all became in the sum one moment. Those years on the whole were good years for rain. Kalahari rain tends to be thunderstorm rain except in the north and the northwest, where an intrusion of northern climate brings more consistent and frequent rain. But out there where I was, released from bush and brush, mopani and other forest, between the Nata, the Zambezi and the Chobe rivers, the great Makarikari was gleaming with water and burned night and day with flamingo fire, and even the dust where the birds took wing was quickened into a glow of flame sunk back into its coals.

Sometimes it was so hot that, in spite of the lightning flashing and the rumbling, I would look up at the dark cloud above and could see a release of heavy rain coming down through the air and rapidly diminishing until it was almost impossible to see as cohesive drops, briefly became faintly misty and then was dissolved into transparent vapour. But when after many days the cloud subdued the heat at last and the rains came down, the transformation was magical, because the sands of the Kalahari are fertile. They are part of the profound longing of the great African mother earth to produce and to nourish and to support an immense family of natural life no matter of what diversity and numbers. Plants, birds, animals, insects and reptiles, all were dear to her heart, and I suspect she had no favourites among them. The response, therefore, to what was the equivalent in nature of a deed and act of consummation of male and female was for me miraculous. Everything, from the flowers to the sudden leaf on skeleton-white thorn, the birds singing and building nests, and every living and growing thing filled with excitement of re-creation, was so vivid and unmistakable that a similar process was released in myself. I had no doubt that, in a sense, everything I saw was a natural priest and acolyte, and I had what, in this age of reason and from a great height of contemporary intellect, is referred to as some sort of 'religious experience'. My own reaction was so intense that I thought there could perhaps be no greater task for man than to recognise this vast Cinderella nature of the desert and from somewhere produce constant attention of water and make it alive and full of flower as the rain around me had done.

Even the great Dean to whom I have referred said that 'whoever could make two ears of corn or two blades of grass to grow upon a spot of ground where only one grew before, would deserve better of mankind, and do more essential service to his country than the whole race of politicians put together'.

As so often, this thought of an aspect of the wasteland experience which touches on a reality beyond human day and greater than anything in life, produced an occasion in which the mystery of it all seemed to become substantial.

I would set out in the morning at dawn after having called all my camp to life with a cup of coffee and, with my gun on my shoulder, walk out in the direction of a visible mark I had pointed out to my company and would experience the desert alone until the noise of trucks became distinct and loud behind me, and then I would mount a termite hill or any other mound available and look back in the direction of my little convoy. And how little it would look, with that sea of land and ocean of sky above it. Thanks to the rain, the grasses and the flowers and the shrubs and bush had been so refreshed and fertilised that, as I watched the trucks come through them, they were wrapped in a gold and shimmering veil of pollen. To me it seemed as if the journey and the search were haloed.

There was another occasion; and most of these occasions were small, microcosmic, and yet infinite in their applications of meaning. On the edge of an archipelago of camelthorn country, far ahead of their own abundant region in Kalahari country, we came to one of my favourite scenes, described in the *Ivanhoe* which was part of every boy's library in my youth as 'a glade'. From this first encounter with the description of a glade I was amazed at the role glades played in the records of knight-errantry. They seemed to have a kind of pre-Raphaelite hold on the imaginations of the writers who dealt with these things in those days. We stopped for a while in the shade because our trucks needed cooling. As usual, we were tired after coming a long way and were very still. And then at one side of the glade there stood a bull giraffe in the full pride of maturity. He was not looking to the right or the left or listening with his ears to the natural sounds around him, he was looking in front of him and his whole bearing was that of a being obsessed with a great singleness of purpose. He strode forward, slow and measured and swaying slightly from side to side, and for some reason I thought of an adjective used by the Spanish admiral whose fleet destroyed Sir Richard Grenville's *Revenge* to describe the manner in which the doomed ship made for his fleet: it came towards him, he said, '*galliardandino*'.

And that was not all. From the opposite side there stepped another bull giraffe of the same age and maturity, similarly bound and obsessed. As both giraffes came where the sun fell bright like a giant spotlight on the centre of a stage, their coats seemed transformed into coats of shining mail, and it seemed to me that as they approached each other there was something almost like a nod of recognition coming from both of them. When their heads were almost together they turned about and arranged themselves side by side until they were almost touching, carrying out the manoeuvre with such fastidious precision that they looked each other's stance all over from the tips of their ears to their hooves on the ground so that they were, I am certain, parallel and even, almost to a millimetre and with very little space in between. One looked the other over with great disdain. The other responded in kind. They did this three times until the meaning of it all burst through me and I knew it was the giraffes' equivalent of the exchanges between Marlborough and the French at the battle of Malplaquet when one commander is supposed to have said: '*Monsieur, les anglais tirent les premiers,*' and the other countered, '*Mais non, monsieur, les français tirent les premiers.*'

And then suddenly it came. One giraffe brought his head as far as he could arch it sideways, and then brought it back with a thump against the head of the other that, even if it did not make the screen on my truck tremble, certainly made my senses jump. The other replied in kind and so, with brief pauses for a breath in between, the glade became a duelling ground or, as portrayed in so many anecdotes from Malory, a clash between two knights errant. They did this not just for seconds or minutes but half an hour went by and we thought one of them must soon be concussed or fall over with dizziness. But they were made of some special giraffe mettle, immune to this kind of feebleness. In the end we just had to leave them, until the bumps became a distant thudding and the usual desert sounds took over. I was relieved to be rid of the noise because somewhere, deep down, it had begun to rankle and unsettle me profoundly.

It was not difficult to know why: this was the pattern of war which underlay the horrendous orchestrations of the world wars in my lifetime, when powerful countries mobilised and betook themselves to vast areas of the world, specially selected under the cover of all sorts of rationalisations, for the purpose of facing one another as the giraffes had done and then butting at one another with all that modern technology could give them until there was plausible ground for dividing them into vanquished and victors.

All that remained, the next morning, was to carve on the side of a camelthorn, with its bark so thick and succulent that the juice ran like blood from the letters, the name of our camp: 'Giraffes Errant'.

In the course of the day that followed, the pollen lost for the moment its power of symbolism and continued to be so heavy that the bonnets of the trucks were yellow and the radiator vents clogged with a sort of pollen mud, and our vehicles overheated so that we had to make camp early, at a place where the grass stood so thick and high that we had to clear a space for our camp with spades.

There came the moment when we sat round the fire and listened to our Irish mechanic, Harry Bennett, sing to us and to a listening wasteland. We had no musical instruments with us, only his lovely tenor voice. He had an immense repertoire of Celtic ballads and good songs from the opera, and once, sitting round the fire, when strange little gusts plagued our camp and no matter where one sat smoke got into our eyes and bothered us greatly, Harry stood up and removed the irritation by a wonderful rendering of 'Smoke Gets in your Eyes', and then continued until a goodnight rendering of the 'London-derry Air'.

He had just sat down on this occasion when everyone suddenly began to sneeze, and sneezed on and off in the most uncharacteristic way. I told them then that the cause must be pollen, and told them how lovely they had all looked in the morning, travelling each in their own private and personal halo of gold, whereupon Harry said: 'All I can say is that this camp must be called "Hay Fever".'

From Hay Fever camp we zigzagged west, south, east, north and, after almost a season, one afternoon came to the beginning of tree country. There, as we were about to pitch camp in the early evening – and so many of these special moments of meaning I am concerned with occurred at that hour or in the early morning, because at other times of the day the wasteland world was asleep – the calm and stillness of so remote a place was suddenly broken with a rush, a scurry, a confused turmoil, and then, through a screen of bush, like some animal through a paper hoop in a circus, appeared a most princely zebra.

Once clear, he looked swiftly around and behind him, and

immediately began to walk, first fast and then more slowly and, picking his steps with great elegance and poise, made his way without looking left or right. He was one of the loveliest zebras I have ever seen, and he held his head like an aristocrat who might have been going to the guillotine, and not just escaped the wasteland equivalent of one, as I was certain the zebra had done.

Immediately my impression was confirmed, because from the top of his mane and all along his left flank and the middle of his body up to his shoulder, it looked as if a scarlet blanket was flapping there, until we realised the blanket was made of flesh and blood, the skin still dripping wet. It was proof that the turmoil we had heard was his tussle to break out of the grip of either a lion or a leopard and, in the course of breaking free, had this mark of the price he paid for delivery laid upon him. Yet he bore himself as if no injury had been done. His head was high, and every now and then he seemed to lift it slightly and flick it at the frustrated enemy in the bush behind him, as if to say: 'What sort of a zebra did you think I was?'

It was a most moving witness to so many of the values I believe natural to all living things, from insects up to the most brave and well-bred of men. My first association, indeed, was of unknown soldiers from the far-flung islands of Indonesia whom I had seen being marched to decapitation and bayoneting alive by the Japanese, many of whom shook themselves free of the hands of the soldiery who were gripping them as if they would try to escape, and then quickened their pace of their own free will to the places of their death and, before reaching it, held their hands precisely in that way.

It reminded me of how often in war the gallant officers and gentlemen with whom I served, and who had such exceptional pedigrees for soldiering and acquitted themselves so well, would make people feel it was due to their breeding and superior education. I do not despise these conscious contributions to natural patterns of these kinds in all forms of life. But, for me, the greatest and most moving demonstrations of conduct without fear in the killing fields of the world have come from men who had no especial breeding but who had never been educated out of their contact with their natural selves, and who as a result, no matter what happened to them, always had a source of natural breeding to see them through their end and, I believe, on beyond.

This immense memory of all the life that has ever been to help the life that is, never fails, and provides the greatest university of endeavour and behaviour to whatever training schools societies have in these matters. Above all, it demonstrates, as this zebra prince demonstrated, that, no matter on what terms, life is the greatest gift of all. It is always worth living, and one fights life for life's sake until life decides, through its own experiences, that the time has come to bring the fight to an end.

I can only say that, silently and in awe, we watched the zebra walk off slowly into the west, in and out among the trees and grass up to his flanks, until first the red blanket badge of his courage was invisible, and then he disappeared into country just as dangerous and unpredictable as he had left, into the added danger of the hour of nightfall with the hyenas and jackals around and about looking for whatever is vulnerable in the desert to devour. We named our camp after him: 'Zebra Prince'.

There occurred also an experience which had immense outer and inner consequences for me, and that was a happening which took place when I had gone down deep onto the bed of one of the greatest of those dry watercourses which tend to run across the desert from northwest to southeast in a wide bend slowly tilting north of east. It was amazing how fast we could travel there, where once river waters had flowed at a height of seventy or ninety feet above our heads, and where at times the blue above was so clear and so dense that we could easily have had an illusion of travelling, not just along an ancient riverbed, but underneath the surface of an Atlantic blue sea. One evening we came out of the riverbed to go over the top and explore the raised wasteland around, and came to a pan which had obviously held some water and just gone dry. There, in the clay, we found nineteen separate and distinct footprints of men, women and children. They were like casts in the clay, and they were clearly the footprints of the first people of Africa, a Bushman clan on the march. The hair at the back of my neck went all atingle, and a shiver of the most complicated kind, of profound tensions, hopes, expectations and as yet unborn desires went through me.

That was perhaps the most significant and yet the briefest of all happenings in the desert. This spoor was to pursue me night and day until it led me in time to the consummation of a pact I had made with myself as a young boy and written into the only diary I have ever tried to keep (a diary lost, alas, in the bombing of London), to the effect that when I grew up I was going to look for survivors of the Bushmen and beg their pardon for all the wrongs we had done to them.

The only parallel to what I was experiencing then, as I turned my back on those footprints, I believe, was what happened to Robinson Crusoe when, after many an island summer, he found human footprints in the sand. I thought of myself as having been a kind of Crusoe and how, for good or evil, his exile was over and once again he was neighboured.

Naturally, we called that day's camp 'Crusoe's Camp'.

There were the bad years too, in between good ones of rain, when the desert was more of a desert even than the Sahara I had known, simply because it had once looked so fertile and well covered and alive with animals and now looked as if it had died and all its children with it, except for the stragglers we saw: springbok so thin that they looked as if one of the increasing number of whirlwinds and dust devils would blow them over, and all the other antelopes similarly emaciated and elongated. Even the elephants looked thin, wan and near their end – something I had never witnessed before. There was no leaf, and where there was shade of skeleton trunks and branches it was only a paler form of burning sunlight.

My instinct and my reading of history insisted more and more fiercely that all this had happened before and all would, sooner or later, recover, but my heart was deeply afraid and the blood in my veins, instead of singing, seemed to be moaning in my ears with despair. We all seemed to lose our appetites and felt as sick in stomach as in heart. We did not, perhaps, realise at the time how we participated almost mystically in the condition of the desert. Eliot's *The Waste Land* speaks of the desert of the spirit, and often on the journey I marvelled at the power of his imagination that could, without the physical experience, convey the double wasteland through which we moved.

Even my guide, who was born and bred in the desert, began to murmur that perhaps we should call off our exploration and wait for the rains to come. But then suddenly it was as if we had reached an *Ancient Mariner* moment in the life of the earth. The wind began to rise, and the emaciated life of antelopes and gazelle seemed to quicken and all to turn about and slowly, feebly set course for the northwest. In our camp that night, as I watched the sun go down, without any accompaniment of cloud but just full of angry flame, and the dark come up swiftly as if on the wings of the blackest bird of prey, far below the burning horizon there was a flicker of light and lightning started to play. It was clearly great thunderstorm lightning, hurled not only at the earth but at the unyielding sky. The next day the movement of the animals had slightly quickened, and that night the lightning was a good deal higher in the sky, but it was a week later before we heard the first rumble of thunder It was thunder that spoke and proclaimed: 'I am here and I am coming.' And finally it rained.

For anyone who really wants to know what drought means to someone born in Africa I would only say that my words are not enough. Go out and experience it for yourself.

It was, of course, miraculous then, a miracle that speaks for itself without any words, because there is no imagination so poor as to be incapable of imagining the abundance and the beauty of that dead world resurrected and alive again.

But, what mattered to me, there began to appear – not in vast herds but as single spies – animals from the far north who had no normal business in that country. We saw, for instance, and I could never forget him, a lone old eland bull, member of a breed who lives and moves in families and clans if not in herds, all alone, taking the vast unknown expanse upon himself because he knew there was grazing and water at last. After him came a lone old wildebeest, also walking off into the night, and then, in due course, a gemsbok, the oryx of fable and heraldry. And one day as we halted at the base of our first scarlet dune and I walked away while camp was being pitched, I saw going up the side of the steep hill of sand slowly to its summit, not once looking to the right or the left or back, a big lion, though old, still with a thick mane of unbleached titian hair. He himself was almost as tinged with the red of his scarlet setting as his hair. From the summit one had a splendid view of a sea of scarlet dunes travelling in waves towards the sunset. He did not pause to take it in but vanished down and out of our sight.

Finally, I think it was two days later, we saw a lone, black, immense old elephant bull, unbelievably asleep at noon, or perhaps just resting.

And then I had it. I had proof of how false were the observers of nature who had only a kind of Freudian, biased interpretation of this phenomenon and held it to be evidence of the fact that the young bulls combined to throw the older ones out of their herd, harassing them so constantly that they were forced to go off on their own. I am certain that all vigorous animal males have their equivalents of athletics and Wimbledons and steeplechases for deciding who is the fittest to ensure survival of their breed. But this is only a phenomenon of the mating season. The loners I am describing are phenomena one encounters in all seasons. They are, I have no doubt, the 'sanyassin' of the animal world of Africa. I had many experiences of this pattern in India and the memories are all there, vivid, to sustain the impression. I had met numbers of sanyassin, men who had taken to the roads and the byways of the vast subcontinent in an instinct that, by walking alone through the great natural scene, they would find the food for the greatest of all the hungers flesh and blood can feel. They would have left behind them all that they had of worldly possessions, often rich and thriving businesses, and just trusted the road, and the people to whom the road belonged, to meet their physical needs. Each lone animal I had seen was a searcher with his animal soul compelled, when he had done all his duties by his herd and helped to fulfil and ensure the life and physical future of his kind, to find a reckoning of his own before earning his discharge from these splendid parades of living things and plants I had had the privilege to see.

The elephant in particular seemed to me the greatest and most mysterious, the animal spirit most gifted with length of life and possession of the longest of memories, a priest, as it were, who would always demonstrate the great reckoning not 'in a little room' which Shakespeare so movingly describes for Elizabethan and European man, but in the vast room of this palatial wilderness of Africa.

All this may sound silly in rooms full of books and chairs and the noise and the rumble and the fumes of modern cities, but these encounters and the memory of them in the evenings beside the fire of a desert camp, with the stillness of the vast desert all around one, became holy moments.

The wise men of Africa in my youth used to say one must always have a place beside the fire for a stranger who might come through the gates of distance or just through the entrance before the kraal is closed for the night. It was a cause of some sadness to me that one such place kept vacant in my own mind was never filled on this journey, and I was comforted only by a feeling that it would surely be filled one day. It was simply that a great animal character had been left out of my desert experience: I did not see a rhinoceros. It seemed to me that the company I had kept needed a rhinoceros, needed the unicorn of Africa to be complete. I would often rebuke myself that, after all, I had been so rich in these encounters and was being greedy, not satisfied with more than enough and demanding perfection.

I was, and I remain, afraid of seekers after perfection. I am afraid of total symmetry and perhaps even proportion. These totalities may be desirable and may have to be sought on a purely provisional basis, but in the foundations of life it seemed to me that such a long-term longing was proscribed because it would create a standstill in the processes of creation. It would be a kind of hatred, in a loving disguise, of the dynamics of life and its changes and endless renewal. Again I thought of my encounter in my youth with the Zen Buddhist in charge of the temple garden that gave me most in Kyoto, the so-called 'Abstract Garden' which moved an old Japanese lady to tears and speechlessness on the autumn afternoon when I first saw it. I remember the priest saying to me, among other things, that the heart and spirit of man was asymmetrical, and, as he said it, he put his hand upon his heart and stressed how lopsided was the situation of the heart, not in the centre of the human body but way out on the left. He would not say more, but I turn to this as a parable which, I think, justified my asymmetrical, unfulfilled longing for the rhinoceros to have been part of my experience.

I was aware too that the Kalahari had once been great rhinoceros country. This I knew not from records of great explorers and hunters who probed with their killing into remote Kalahari regions, but from an intuition within myself which arose because on my journeys I had discovered in some sacred hills a vast treasure of prehistoric paintings, and among these animal processions on the rock there were rhinoceroses, including the precious white rhinoceros whose extinction had only just been prevented in my native country. This sense of the vacancy his absence caused was sharpened by the encounter with the elephant, but, happily, elsewhere in Africa I had encountered his rhinoceros counterpart, the lone rhinoceros also taken to the road and with the same cause and destination.

And then there came the last moment of all, the dreadful ambiguity between the sense of a double mission fulfilled and a profound reluctance to let go and return to a world which stared starkly at me just then like some kind of prison. We were at that time going through my most beloved Kalahari country. It is a country that I still think of with some pain at heart, because I have not seen it since the 1950s and I know that I will never see it again. It was a country of the tree which I have already mentioned more than once: camelthorn country. The tree made that part of the desert like a parkland, so well made as to give one a feeling that the architect of the universe himself had planned it for his own delight. Nothing could have been more open and frank and welcoming, and in such contrast to the clogged forest screen I had had to break through hundreds of miles to the north, and on this final day I think that not only I but all of us were joined in a feeling that ours must be a very special camp that night, if it were to match what we had experienced first in Paradise Pan and to do justice to all that had occurred since then.

So I chose a camp early and, as always, consulted my company, particularly my indigenous company. On these journeys, whoever fate puts in charge of the company is judged and accepted not least by the kind of camp he chooses at the end of every day. So I would always, after our break in the dead hour of the day, remind everyone that I was open to any suggestions they had for a camp, and we always accepted the condition that the camp must be chosen while there was enough light of day to help us in its preparation for the night.

There was another condition for the final camp. It had not only to be suitable in every normal way but had to be situated around the biggest dead tree we could find. Happily there were many good candidates, and it fell to the leader of my black drivers, John Mosothouane, who had proved his capacity as a judge of good camps, to spot the place and the tree.

It was so good a choice that we all teased him, perhaps to disguise truth as jest, and said: 'We shall now have to call this "Mosothouane Camp".' He instantly became as shy as a young girl and held his hand over his mouth to disguise the smile at the pleasure this act of recognition had given him, but then he shook his head and a deep '*Aikona*', that lovely final 'No' of Africa, broke from him. And after a while he added: 'It would not be a good thing. Only Chiefs can give their names to places.'

While the trucks were being unloaded I walked with Mosothouane towards one red dune that showed among the yellow dunes in the distance, and I marvelled, as the Bushmen did, at how the red dune with its sand like powdered Parisian rouge could stand so red and unmixed by all the yellow dunes around it, and so touched on a mystery that plays greatly on the imagination of Bushman and Hottentot peoples who have had contact with the dunes since the days of prehistory.

We did not come back until the camp was complete and the base of the dead tree was stacked high all around with dead wood for our evening fire. As soon as the sun was down and the darkness took like a swift to the air, we lit the fire and sat down to eat around it. We watched the fire climb from the ground slowly in Gothic flame, stage by stage, into the sky until it stood there like a great cathedral of flame with the last flame of all on the summit flickering among the stars.

We did not talk much that night, which was most unusual, but Harry sang for us and I found myself thinking of something St Augustine had written; St Augustine who, since he was the Bishop of Hippo in North Africa with whom I had already perhaps been over-familiar by calling a very large and rather troublesome hippo night visitor in the swamps in the north 'St Augustine', came more solemnly to my mind with these words:

> To myself a heart of steel,
> To my fellow men a heart of love,
> To my God a heart of flame . . .

and I asked myself why, at the completion of every journey I had made in this desert, I had felt we must end with fire just like this, though it had never before been so great or so high. And the answer came that it was in the instinctive belief, from as far back as consciousness can go, back at that awesome moment when creation decided there had to be light, that one of the greatest properties of fire was its power to transform, to remove the impermanent and perishable from the permanent and the imperishable, the false from the true, and let these move on and grow into the future.

I found myself thinking of how, on the Hindu island of Bali one night, I had watched an aristocratic funeral as one of the great equatorial sunsets made grand opera of the hour. The dead aristocrat's body had been placed on top of a tower of dead wood and the tower securely lashed to a big raft, and the timing, as the final ritual demanded, was in harmony with the tides of the sea and the raft launched as the tide turned and the placid water full of opal sky withdrew out to sea. The priest waded after the raft until the water was up to his shoulders and set the pile alight. He joined us all standing silent on the shore and we watched this tower of fire go slowly out to sea. The light left the sky: it became dark. The stars came out, and still the fire flickered in flame further and further out to sea. I do not remember how long it took but I do know that suddenly somewhere behind us a bantam cockerel crowed and the fire vanished and we all made slowly for home.

Early the next morning I took the camp chopper as well as my hunting knife and gun, and thought I would go out and blaze a name for the camp on a tree, but as I walked to what seemed a tree grown to be blazed, my mind, though full of feelings for a name, could find none. I became quite desperate, but every name I thought of seemed not so much to be wrong as to diminish all the feelings I had about the camp. It was almost as if the camp had become a personality and was warning me not to presume to give it a name. Finally, with an immense feeling of relief, I decided that I would not give the camp a name. It would remain a 'something that could not be named'. As I walked back towards my camp, there, on the rim of a yellow mound of sand, I saw the silhouette of one of my dearest friends who had done all my Kalahari journeys with me, whose gun had fed us and, when necessary, protected us. It was Brian Currie, who used to ask me never to mention his name in any of my writing but to use a pseudonym, saying: 'You must please not mind me, but I am too superstitious for this sort of thing.'

I thought that he would understand why this camp should not want to be named and at the same time I knew that it would embarrass him to talk of these things at the beginning of the day. Perhaps – and even then only perhaps – one could try it out if necessary after dinner and coffee round a campfire with a lion or two roaring in the background, but certainly not now. His silhouette, with the red of dawn wrapped like a blanket around him, his pipe in his mouth newly lit and the smoke like a little cloud, transparent above it, made me think of a Red Indian.

I joined him in silence and watched what he was watching. Just as the sun was about to show a tip above the horizon he turned to me and said: 'Special, isn't it?'

I agreed, and we had another pause, and then simultaneously turned about and walked towards the camp where the trucks were already being loaded ready to leave after an early breakfast. And he said, slowly, as we walked: 'It is strange, but I have never camped anywhere in Africa where I have not felt as I left it that we all have left something of ourselves behind.'

And by the evening of that day we had crossed the Molopo

River and immediately there was a hotel. Beside it there was what is called in England an 'off-licence', doing a brisk trade with a mixture of races of all colours, some clearly showing traces of Hottentot and Bushman blood and some already unsteady on their feet. Over the dirt road east to Mafeking the dust stood high in the air, raised by the motor traffic speeding along it, and I knew that we were back in a world where everyone was in a hurry and men were too busy to live. It was as if we were facing a new form of imprisonment and, fast as men could move and displace themselves in the world before them, no speed seemed to me to have been so great as that which had taken us from that moment of total resolution when the morning star, the Hottentots' 'Foot of the Day', had first shown itself above the acacia tops, to this scene around the off-licence of human disintegration.

2
'F' and 'F'

I have not been back to that place without name. It was not that I took a conscious decision not to go back, nor for that matter that I did not have the opportunity to do so; but there are many circumstances to explain why it would have been difficult for me to go back. My return from the Kalahari was really as near as I could get to return to my total self, and all the partialities I had had to follow as a result of the war and its consequences seemed to have been dealt with and given their relevant human form. Above all, it had brought me back to a more acute awareness than ever of the total interdependence of the world without and my own objective world within. It was something which I recognised in hindsight I had possessed naturally, and intuitively, and I had in a sense been educated out of it by what passes for education in our time.

As a result I was busier than I think I had ever been. I went back to my writing, which had always been in the main what I wanted to do since I started writing poetry at the age of seven. But that was not the only thing. I have always had a keen sense of obligation to the life of my time which did not seem to me discharged by sticking to writing alone. I shared, from as early as I could remember, something of what in inspired measure Dante explained as 'the necessity to be a good citizen'. He did not mean by that any of the perverted meanings the terrorists of the French revolution attributed to their depraved concept of *citoyen*. The city, to Dante, was a symbol of the best that men assembled to a common purpose and a common good could build to and before their Creator. It was expressed in the image of a city standing four-square on a hill and marking, in a way that no other product of pooled human activity could match so completely, a fulfilment of creation in humanity. It is an image that he carried with him down into the depths of hell, so far down that the going down became a coming up until he emerged in a new hemisphere packed with stars around the Southern Cross, and from there on and up the Mountain of Purgatory, across the waters of Lethe and the other miraculous rivers and lakes towards the absolute of creation until he was among the community of the Creator himself, and as far as he could see around him the universe was stacked with layer upon layer of cherubim, seraphim, angels and archangels, and yet they were not just another exalted collectivity because wherever he looked he saw that each one of these souls was uniquely itself, and at last communities had become congregations.

So in my small way it was not regard for the kind of democracy of which the ballot box more and more seems to be the final image but a personal and private pursuit, seeking a way of transforming the vast collectivities and overblown masses of communities into congregations around the highest and the most complete and total values of which human beings are capable. I think it was expressed in a letter that I wrote to two people when I decided that I would abandon a career in the army and start another kind of life. I wrote to the Prime Minister of the day, and to Stafford Cripps, with whom I had to work closely during my time in South-East Asia, that I did not want to return to a life of private profit. I felt that we all owed Britain so much for having saved the world from eclipse by evil in standing alone for so long against the totalitarian darkness of the hour that I would like to go on serving my country.

As I write it I realise how naive the words sound in a new age when any feelings connected with one's country are instantly suspect and, if not just causes of embarrassment, subjects of severe condemnation, as chauvinism of the most dangerous kind. But in the midst of writing some twenty books I did just that, happily most of it anonymously.

Yet, more occupied in this regard than I had ever been before, the 'place without name' continued to haunt me. I dreamt about it. I thought about it at all sorts of odd moments when no such associations could have appeared more remote. I once had a vision of recall, travelling on a bus, that made me ache all over with longing for return. But somehow this longing, which is still there today as sharp and clear as ever, never prompted me to revisit it. I could have explained all that by a general reluctance to go back to the desert. Indeed, it was not for another thirty years that something compelled me to go back to the Kalahari – but it never occurred to me to extend the journey to the southwest, and I think as a result I have come to look at that last night of some years of exploration in a different way. It was a unique and a timeless moment, 'not-two' as the Japanese would have put it. Had I gone back and made it the occasion of another experience by another version of myself caught up in a totally different context of time, I would have violated the original experience and dishonoured the meaning it gave to me. I would often think of that great cathedral of flame we built and see it again, climbing from the scarlet earth, flake by flake of fire across the pile of dead wood and up the smooth trunk of the dead tree until it reached so high into the sky that the last flame of all brushed the stars. As always, these moments of recall included the awesome feeling of being in the presence of fire in its true Promethean role, where it was not only light and warmth in the physical life of man but also a profound process of metamorphosis in the human spirit where, both in his physical self and his innermost being, what was imperishable was being removed from the perishable, the truth from the error, and both released to travel on beyond.

This is a subjective rendering of the event, but it had, I believe, objective consequences in that it seemed from then on that the extra something which had been added to my awareness in those years of exploration acted rather like an early warning system, a kind of radar, of what might be massing beyond the furthest frontiers of life as we knew it and would sooner or later come to join in the increasing turmoil of our day.

One of its consequences was that it led me in rare moments of leisure to a reappraisal of my life and, in the most unlikely and mysterious of ways, without my knowing, brought me to one milestone after another on the road that would lead, one day, to a Blady whom I did not yet know existed.

27

As so often in this enigmatic pattern weaving in and out of time, the going forward was rather obscure and at a first glance could have appeared as a going back to something old. It came about as a requickening of an interest I had always had in the role of plagues and sicknesses in history. I do not know when precisely this interest came alive, but I do know that when my mother first read to me from Genesis and told me of the last of the great plagues which sent the Angel of Death to devastate the homes of Egypt and compelled Pharaoh to let Israel go, it was already so much part of my imagination it seemed to me singularly apt that only this plague could accomplish what all the other plagues of Egypt had failed to do. It was there as a special sort of signpost for me on the long road between Genesis and Revelations, and although the spiritual journey was immense, it seemed only a short time between the night in which my mother told me that story from Genesis and another occasion when she told me of the role of pestilence in Revelations.

I was still very young – for some reason I am convinced that I was barely three – and as a statistic of the event it does not tend to make the conviction more probable, but it was one of those rare moments as a child when I was alone with my mother, and even to this day I remember it with astonishing clarity and have rehearsed it so often in my life to find it unchanged in any detail that I accept it almost with mathematical certainty. I remember the dress my mother wore. I was always immensely interested in my mother's dress and this was one of my favourites, and she sat in her favourite chair in our drawing-room on an afternoon that was singularly blue in my memory. Her chair was turned sideways and her face was clearly outlined against the french windows which gave onto the garden, gathered into the L-shaped wing of our home. Just outside the french windows there was a large sunken pond, and between the pond and the L of the window were vines, heavy with leaf and grape, trained like creepers over special trellises to throw a shade under which we often dined in the hot days of summer. And beyond, towering over the gabled rooftops, there were tall Lombardy poplars, their leaves trembling and shaking the late afternoon sun, flake by flake, from their leaves.

She had paused in her reading from the book of Revelations and was simplifying the biblical account of the past phases of the story of man, and the sombre decline towards the day of judgement with its dynamic and enigmatic imagery, told in words with a texture almost of fire, like those of the horsemen of the apocalypse of our Armageddon, of the sound of a trumpet introducing the final phase before the dread choice was to be made between the quick and the dead and the twilight as of gods seen when pestilence ruled the land. In a sense it is a story of horror, and in looking back I have often thought almost with sympathy of the Calvin who did not want it in the Bible and called Revelations 'a dark and dangerously obscure book'; but somehow the way my mother read and interpreted the words gave them a feeling of necessity and of being the only words to describe an outcome that was inevitable, and a sense of it all being cosmically fair deprived its impact of any enormity.

The result was that when the tempo of Revelations changed and the first note of resolution was struck, the sweetness and the reassurance of my mother in those early years – still as real and acute today as they were then – was joined to a sense that in the end all was happy and meaningful, and hurt and injury, tears and all that, were abolished and one was held whole and secure, from the opening statement, 'And I saw a new heaven and a new earth' on to the final 'Alpha and Omega, the beginning and the end', in a feeling which nothing could ever shake that ultimately life and creation had a happy ending, that it was, as Dante put in the title that flies like a banner over the account of his great journey of exploration, a Divine Comedy, a feeling so certain that it saw no contradiction but merely paradox in the fact that there was an awful amount of suffering to endure between the first plague and the last vial of seven pestilences which figured in Revelations.

This train of thought, even though I had no inkling of where it would be leading me, was later confirmed by an experience so commonplace that it had no obvious link with what was buried in my past, except that I harboured this suspicion that our body ills were not just the physical symptoms that most people took them to be but also an expression of an equal and opposite condition of spirit.

If it had been merely something that had come to me out of my books, even out of such a book of books as the Bible through which I was guided by so remarkable a feminine spirit as that of my mother, it may not have survived the onslaught of an increasingly rationalistic education and the incorrigible extra-verted trend of a whole age. But I was to find that from the moment I was able to do my own reading I was being increas-ingly supported by my own experience, and without any other aid was drawn into a process of sustained speculation about an affliction which was minor but as hateful to me as it was inexplicable.

It happened in the interior of Africa where I was born. Mem-ories of the persecution of my forebears in France by the power-ful Roman Catholic establishment of the day, and rejection of those who fled from it for freedom to Africa by both the Dutch and the British who followed after, were as acute as they could be. It predisposed everyone of my generation, I believe, not only to anticipate hurt and rejection from others but even to see it where it was not intended. What made it worse was that I have a childhood memory of burnt-out farms and other evi-dence of damage inflicted on the Boers by the British forces in the district all around us, like silent witnesses and perhaps reminders of the sense of injury, charged with the historical task of seeing that these things should not be forgotten. This kind of climate of a whole country, despite a liberal and unsoured upbringing by parents with an enlightened sense of the world and the wider plan of life and its modern realities, had a most inhibiting impact on my choice of friends.

There was, for instance, an English boy whom I liked immensely, and I was delighted to find that he was as keen on being friends with me as I was on being friends with him; but although my own bilingual parents did nothing to discourage the friendship, this climate and collective emphasis of dis-approval from our neighbours was so strong that our friendship became too self-conscious, too contrived and in a sense too fur-tive to have a decent chance of growing.

From the moment that I had to accept the impossibility of having natural relationships of my own free choice in my own life, I began to have one series of severe headaches after the other. They were totally unpredictable in their timing, and our Scottish doctor, whom we all trusted and loved, could find no physical cause to which he could attribute them. For some years he thought it might be a result of a severe fall I had on a rock and which has left a long scar in my scalp to this day. The extent and depth of the gash and the shock had made him persuade my father to take me to the Cape for consultation with a specialist, but the specialist could find no relation between the injury, bad as it was, and the all-pervasive headaches that at times affected even my stomach, and all the comfort we derived from him was a pat on the shoulder and the remark: 'He is young and strong and will no doubt grow out of them.'

For years, though, I did not grow out of them. On the contrary, they became worse and must have been rather like the intractable migraines for which modern medicine has, as yet, found no cure. I do not think the word 'migraine' existed at that time, and, although I was taken to all sorts of other specialists, those headaches continued to appear and disappear at their own unpredictable will.

In the meantime, as my own feeling for history and its meaning developed – and it did so at an early age and remains one of my greatest interests to this day – I found the collective attitude to our past, and in particular to the English, more and more wanting and ultimately totally unacceptable. At that point the whole matter was resolved for me when I went away to a public school, where half of some hundreds of boys consisted of English and the other half of country extraction like myself, and there, without any conscious effort on my part, this taboo, this profound racial impediment seemed to vanish, for when I went back for my first holiday and this friend who had never been allowed to be a friend arrived back from his own public school, instantly and without a jar of any kind we became the friends which our community had prevented us from being before. What was perhaps most remarkable was the feeling we both had of accomplishment in succeeding in breaking through

31

something almost evil and pioneering something in human relationships which the future would take for granted. We had such a feeling of having, in our small way, made history that we decided that we should design an heraldic badge for each of us to mark the happening. So we designed a green shield with a gold band across it, and on either side of the gold band engraved and painted two golden 'F's. We pledged ourselves henceforth to wear these badges but never to reveal their meaning.

Perhaps the most important ingredient of what we had accomplished was that neither of us had been influenced in this by anything we had heard or read. It had come spontaneously to us out of our natures, along with the conviction that it must, in the first place, be secret. Yet in no sense was it 'secrecy'. It was, I believe, an intuitive anticipation of what I know from conscious experience today to be a fact: that in breaking through into a new area of oneself and life, or in beginning any new enterprise which comes to one's imagination, one must not share it with the world until it has grown strong enough to stand and contain itself. The time would come when I thought of this kind of secret as an equivalent in the human imagination of putting a seed into the earth, covering it over and watering it until one day in the course of its own lawful process of growth, it chooses to show itself above the ground, and the world can choose either to join in its nourishment or, as it so often does, try to trample it down.

This sense of having a living secret between us grew so much and became such an interest that we thought we should have a secret place of meeting where we could celebrate its existence in the way in which all these bonds and relationships have been honoured over time: with its own form of dedication.

Most of the ring of hills around our village had reefs of rock – 'kranses', as we called them – with gashes in the cliffs full of bushes and herbs and plants of the most aromatic kind, and in one place in particular an outcrop of blue shale which led to a little plateau on the top. On this plateau there were great loose boulders, and we chose one of the greatest of these boulders, dug a kind of cellar deep into the gravel beside it and used it to hide several tins of Mazawatti tea. These painted tins with tea from the Far East were like magic lantern slides to us and provided the esoteric element which the special sense of communion demanded. We kept them full of rusks and biltong and delicious dried fruit from the Cape and, when we had finished one of our celebrations, covered them over with a strip of tarpaulin which in turn was covered with earth and had a flat waterstone over the top, so that in so secluded a place it was immune to discovery.

From then on we would go there on our ponies three or even four times a week, scramble to the top of this great boulder which gave us both such a sense of assurance and stability for our enterprise and, once seated, we would seldom talk for long but would sit there munching in silence. Even at the time, the eating of food from a secret hoard peculiarly our own seemed to be part of the essence of the ritual we were evolving. Even now, in spite of the great distance of time and events in between, I remember when we were at our ease on the rock and had removed the painted lids of the Mazawatti tins, how silent we went and, for two boys who were normally as lively as we both were, how filled with a solemnity of which we would have been suspicious had we observed it in others of our age. Yet there was nothing whatsoever contrived about it. It absorbed us utterly, and I cannot remember that either of us was ever afflicted with any unease that we might just be playing another boyish game and not doing something that was both natural and serious.

It was remarkable too how the view of our little village down below in what was an old pass through the hills, leading from the great river to the south of us towards the remote and unexplored interior in the north, seemed designed for these special moods. So still was it that we could hear the church clock some two or three miles away strike the hour.

That stillness is perhaps the element which conveys most of all how special those occasions were, because it was a stillness which I believe it is not possible to find in the world today. There is nowhere now, even in that part of the interior of Africa, for great stillnesses to speak the profound language of silence. Everywhere there is, however subsonic the disturbance, an unease of sound trying to be born in human ears from the constant vibration all over the earth of the great engines of technologies, of aeroplanes rushing across the sky, bulk-carriers and tankers thrashing the oceans, trains and trucks and motor cars dashing across the vast distances of even uninhabited places, stirring the great cauldrons of silence so that, even if sound is not heard, the precision of the silence is lost and its voice is blurred.

To give some indication of the kind of silence which was such an intense form of benediction to the two of us, I remember how the shepherds on my grandfather's farm some eight miles away would tell me that on Sundays they could hear the church bell calling the dark-clad Calvinists to church. The oldest among them, an old Griqua Hottentot, described to me, in his language full of aboriginal metaphor, how on the day of my father's funeral, when the bell tolled stroke by stroke the number of years of his life, as was the custom in that remote interior, they could hear it mixing with the bleat of the newly born sheep, and then when there was no bleating and the stillness flowed in again the sound of the bell hung suspended over a well of soundlessness like a distant wind-hoverer on wings that were so distinct as almost to be visible, before fading and the sound fell away.

Indeed, the last visit we paid to our secret boulder and its treasure of food was made almost unbearably poignant by the quality of silence pressed to the extreme. We had been caught up in our packing and goodbyes before leaving for school at two o'clock in the morning of the next day. We had got there at sunset and on this occasion did not draw on our supply of food. We seemed to have lost the need for a ritual meal that day; the sense of the last was too dominant for anything else. We had watched the sun go down over the village which, with the twilight coming down on it, looked like the description Anatole France gave of a township in France which he loved, saying that the houses were there gathered around their church like chickens around a hen. The evening light was still so clear that we could follow, on the hills beyond, the spiral of the tracks cut deep into their ironstone flanks by the British gunners in that war which had unleashed the emotions we were there to contain; and the whole view was blue and implicit with an unutterable feeling of history before the arrival of European man. Some of the hills even had ancient Hottentot names that pointed to that history without revealing its secrets. For instance, there was a great hill the Hottentots called 'The Mountain of Mercy', but mercy for what? There were two other perfectly shaped little hills standing on the horizon like twins of time which were known as 'The Hills of Weeping', because they were the location of some unspeakable happening in the lives of the first people of the land. And so on and on in the long level light, which was slowly turning the fringes of small islands of cloud into reefs of rainbow coral in a sea of blue, until we saw, some twenty miles away just on the edge of a lift of veld, a line where the day went black and the light coloured the tips of the great trees around the place called 'The Fountain of All'.

I know of no natural phenomenon which makes one feel so deeply involved with the forces and temper of creation as an African sunset, and this sunset which was unfolding its mythological pattern around us just then was special. It seemed to me that in looking back on the short history of our own journey between the boulder and our normal life in the village it was almost as if we had come to a little wayside shrine to perform what struck me then as our own form of eucharist. Even the crude experience in the village of guarding our secret from our own peers lost its vulgarity and coarseness and was transformed into an essential of what our secret had given us. We had soon become accustomed to village taunts about what the 'F/F' represented, such as the 'Filthy Fags' which the village bully had hurled at me one day, causing the two of us to have a fight which excited some forty boys very much, but which I afterwards regretted. These taunts had made us only more resolved to keep our secret, because they were an indication of the laughter and the scorn that would have surrounded us all through our precious vacation if we had told them that the F and F stood simply for 'Forgive and Forget'.

But as we walked to our ponies, because the black was gathering fast, the whole experience was somehow made immune and a theme of orchestration that continues still, not least of all in this dimension of the interdependence of what Manley Hopkins called 'the inscape and the great landscape'. It grew dark so swiftly in the direction of 'The Fountain of All' that, before the hooves of our ponies sounded, abnormally loud, in the high street of our hushed little township, total darkness came over us, and the black snuffed out the light as utterly as the silence quenched the sound.

There is no black like that black left anywhere in the world today, because the busyness and unease which has deprived us of pure silence has robbed us of the same quality in the dark. For again, everywhere there are almost as many lights attacking the black over the earth as there are stars in heaven. Even below the remotest horizon of the deepest bush and desert there is a ceaseless vibration of light of all kinds, not illuminating any essential road for the human spirit or being, but depriving it of the healing rest which the perfect black over Africa gave it in my youth.

As a result, the more remote that little experience becomes, the more profoundly do I realise how happy I was to have the intuition that brought me to it confirmed so absolutely by the meanings entrusted to the sharing of that incorruptible silence and darkness.

So in the course of the long random years that followed the agonising and irreversible progression to another world war, through the world war itself and then a return to Africa and the desert, I was increasingly aware that it had all been a leaven in my imagination and that, without it, I would not have been led to so steep a heightening of perception of the profound relationship between the human body and the mind, the spirit and the heart, the within and the without, not only in the life of the individual but also in that of his time. I marvelled more and more how throughout history these inadequacies and fallibilities of spirit, and the inflexibility of both individual and collective awareness towards the calls for renewal of life and not a narrowing but an enlarging of consciousness, would sooner or later draw attention to themselves: their impatience to be expressed in flesh and blood would show itself more and more, not only in distortions of our ways of looking at reality but through afflictions of the human body and in the end, if they were not heeded, a breakdown in the order and coherence of society.

Indeed, in the years between my departure from school and the war, this little experience, coupled with the old interest from childhood in the great plagues and sicknesses of the past, seemed to have become a basic assumption or hypothesis of my attitude to life, so much so that it figured prominently in my first book, written in 1930. I was still in my early twenties and not aware of any outside influence to bring me to the writing of this book. I was only aware that I seemed suddenly presented in my mind with a pattern which I had to obey. The book I am referring to is *In a Province*, and the title came from a quotation in the Bible (Ecclesiastes v.8): 'If thou seest the oppression of the poor, and violent perverting of judgment and justice in a province, marvel not at the matter.'

Significantly, and perhaps with a feeling of being vulnerable and alone in my endeavour, I turned also for support to a French writer whom I came across on the French island where I was writing the book, just as I was finishing the story, and I quoted him: 'For the first time in ten thousand years,' he wrote, 'man is to himself totally, and without any semblance of knowledge, a problem. For he no longer knows what he is, and he knows at the same time that he knows not.'

But, most important of all, *In a Province* was the first book written by someone born in South Africa as profoundly concerned as a solitary, inexperienced young man could be concerned, with the tragedy and the potential disaster of the racial and colour prejudices of his world. The main character, in fact, experiences the pressures and the challenges which these clashes of races and cultures provoke and which the establishment of his society refuse to recognise or heed, at such a deep level that he can find no meaning in his way of living and less and less meaning in the society that contains it, until finally in the climax which precedes the tragic resolution of the story all these unlived forces in him break loose and stampede through the corridors of his blood and being as a dangerous physical fever and a hallucination of his senses.

I was not aware at the time that there was a much greater and inspired exploration of this very theme in Thomas Mann's *Der Zauberberg*, or *The Magic Mountain* as it was called in its English translation. I had already read Thomas Mann's book, *Buddenbrooks*, which interested me greatly without stirring me deeply and in a way left me with no marked desire to read much more of him. I was perhaps influenced in this by the fact that the world of literature and those aesthetes who seemed to be in command of the London I knew in the late 1920s – and liked so little that I left it to write my book on a French island – almost unanimously denounced *The Magic Mountain* as much as they praised *Buddenbrooks*. Mann was held to have gone too philosophic and turgid and Teutonic in *The Magic Mountain*, and the general climate of opinion for some years seemed to be that he had 'dived too deep and come out too muddy', as one Bloomsbury prophet put it.

I did not read *The Magic Mountain* until a Dutch fellow-prisoner of war in a Japanese camp turned up with a battered German paperback of *Der Zauberberg*. I read it then and instantly felt, as I still do, that it was one of the most significant novels of the twentieth century. The reassurance, too, that it gave me in my own way of looking at the world was immense, because from beginning to end it was a recognition of the symbolism evoked by the appearance of a largely incurable sickness on the human scene.

The validity of its symbolic grasp of reality stood out for me to such an extent that I saw what I had missed in the period I spent in the London which rejected it – that it was a reflection of the world which scorned it and, in its ultimate import, a mountain in the mind of man and certainly a mountain in the spirit of my time. The tuberculosis and the isolated sanatorium in the mountains on the frontiers of Switzerland and Italy, with its community of sick men and their endless discussions of the art, the philosophy, the humanistics, the ideologies, the social order of the day, all strangely and uneasily joined by their common physical plight, reflected so well the aesthetic nunnery and monasticism of the Bloomsbury spirit which made of aesthetics and art and its rare and refined intellectualism a new kind of holy order. There was nothing that this world disliked more than discomfort of the spirit and the dimming of the lucidity which was worshipped and pursued without knowing that the greatest lights of the mind cast the darkest shadows. Any fluttering of the dark shadows massed increasingly angry on the rim of the clear, exclusive focus of the élitism and strange privilege conferred on them, provoked the fierce rejections which revealed themselves in their endless dialogues.

Every time I read *The Magic Mountain* in prison, it seemed to me that the principal character of Mann's story was fatefully twinned to the main character of my own book. Both are so clearly victims of the civil war in the heart of the time in which they lived. Both are condemned to experience this sickness of a whole age, a contagion of a plague of unfulfilled history, as observers rather than afflicted. It seemed that, even in this, Mann's imagery did not fail me, because if his hero had been afflicted himself he could not have helped being an instrument of what he was trying to observe. He could not have helped looking behind the mirror of his age for a reflection of his own face in the world around him and so forfeiting the objectivity demanded of him. So his hero, and the main character in my book, are both in such close and continuous contact with an affliction that they can see it almost as if they themselves had experienced it. Indeed they have become so involved on that secluded mountain of the mind – for that finally is the abiding image left by Mann's world – that they find release from an arrested process of meaning and time inside themselves only when the disaster which has been building up as a lethal illness within humanity spills over into the world order, and life seeks to purge itself of the irrelevant, the ineffectual and the loss of instinct in man by asserting its archaic priorities in war.

Although I had written my own book so many years before I encountered *The Magic Mountain*, when I came to the end where the strange, moving and lost person, his hero, who goes under the extremely ordinary and unheroic name of Hans Gastorp, is thrown out of his asylum into perhaps the bloodiest of wars the world has ever seen, I felt there went not only the people of *In a Province* but, by proxy, all of us.

Mann's choice of tuberculosis to represent a condition of spirit lethally inadequate also had a special meaning for me. All my reading of history and experience of art and literature left me with an acute impression of how vital an element tuberculosis was in the climate of life and time behind us. Great as the role of plagues and illnesses had been, with their names – the Black Death, leprosy, and so on – attached like sinister labels to desperate stretches of time, tuberculosis added a new and subtler element to the nature of disease, because its role was such that one could hardly tell where it began and ended as a state of mind or a state of body, since through its working in human life and imagination these two things seemed from the beginning present and interchangeable. As far as I was concerned, it seemed almost the perfect sickness to qualify as the chosen instrument of an inflexible, inscrutable and implacable fate.

I came out of the war with this impression intact. I went through those years of fourfold exploration and returned with it still intact and without any awareness that tuberculosis had any rivals or even upstart challengers in this role until, in order to recover from some years of malarial infection and reinfection, I took to skiing. I found myself staying not far from where Thomas Mann had found his prototype of the sanatorium for *The Magic Mountain*, and indeed my hotel had itself been a luxurious sanatorium. It was still so new in its role as a skiing hotel that in the evenings, when it was battened down like a ship for the night, it had almost an odour of the sanatorium, as churches have an odour of sanctity about them. It was as if there were the faintest traces of ether and medicaments in the air, and one was rather startled to meet smart waiters carrying champagne in buckets of ice rounding the corners of the long, carpeted corridors instead of hospital attendants and doctors in their white overalls. It was only then that I realised that tuberculosis had completely lost its terrors for modern man and that something else must have moved into this role in the theatre of fate which it had left vacant.

And thereby hangs the story and begins a slightly more defined hint to a trail towards Blady, although Blady had not yet appeared on my conscious list of characters.

3

The Great Uprooter

Although this preoccupation of mine was of such long and persistent standing, it did not dominate my imagination and awareness in the years that followed. I had some twenty books to write and many other interests and demands to keep me busy, but all along at all sorts of odd moments I began to notice that, in public obituaries and within the circumference of my own life, one heard more and more about cancer. It was an affliction, of course, which had already drawn to it distinguished researchers and doctors, but as far as the so-called ordinary people of the world were concerned it was remote and only to be feared as one of a number of other terminal illnesses. In my own life, for instance, up to the time I left Africa I had known numbers of people who had died of tuberculosis, but none of cancer.

Indeed, up to the outbreak of war, I remember that I thought of it only in connection with the United States of America, and was struck by the extent to which the fear of it showed in the space devoted to its incidence and character in American news-papers and magazines.

But now, as the post-war years advanced, the incidence of cancer seemed to come nearer and nearer to my own world. Here and there someone I knew, an old friend, some public figure, died of cancer, and every year the number seemed to grow. I sometimes thought of it in terms of an image that our gunners had in the war. Where they targeted their shells, at the exact point of impact there was a deadly zone which they called the 'effective beaten zone'. Round it was a 'beaten zone', much larger, and where the explosion did not inevitably kill; and then there was the 'outer zone', where the chances of being killed were much lighter. This image increasingly came to me, because it was as if my own life had already moved from the 'outer zone' into a 'beaten zone', and the speed and the spread of cancer into my own world became horrendous. By the year, more friends and acquaintances and people known to me were afflicted by cancer. In one year alone, seven of the dearest and the best people who had been in prison with me died of cancer.

And then something happened which had a great deal to do with bringing me into the target dimension where, without knowing, I was going to find also the roundabout trail to Blady.

Notice of its origin, if one could presume to set a precise moment of beginning to so mysterious a phenomenon, was served on me and my family in such an obscure way that we did not have the address of the court of fate, the name of the judge or the sentence it was to pass, but for me the announcement was portentous enough.

I was telephoned by my son John, who asked me if he could see me urgently. When he came he told me about a recurrent dream which perturbed him so much that he sometimes doubted his own sanity. With slight variations the dream was, as so many of the most significant dreams are, short and to the point. He was somewhere by the sea, watching the rising of an equinoctial tide, and wanted to turn about and run from it but felt himself fixed in that position and could not turn for all his trying. So paralysed, in dream after dream he would see a black head emerge from the phosphorescent swell and 'insinuating waves' of an ocean heaving through its own motivation and not because of any wind or other disturbance. The head turned towards him and slowly, with immense deliberation, began to come closer until an enormous black African elephant bull stepped through the swell and began to move remorselessly towards him; and always, at this point, he awoke in terror.

The terror surprised me because he knew elephants in their natural surroundings in Africa and had always expressed a special love of them. Moreover, one of the first things we had done together when I came back from the war was to go deep into the bush to live with the animals, for the sake of my own debrutalisation from war and the naturalisation of a relationship that had separated us for nearly ten years.

I had to ask: 'But what did you associate with this elephant to make you afraid?'

'I knew,' he said, 'it was not just a normal elephant. It was an elephant bent only on uprooting trees.'

And then some of his fear communicated itself to me. I did not know precisely why at the time, but I knew from friends who were special authorities on the nature of the dreaming process that it would be wrong for someone like me to try to help him understand such a dream. I myself had never had the sustained analytical experience of dreams which I believe is essential for a proper understanding of their role in men. So I suggested to him that he could go and talk about his dream to a great friend and distinguished doctor and psychologist, Alan McGlashan.

For some five years John had the company of this man, who had ended the war in 1918 as a pilot in several clashes with von Richthofen and, after a dog-fight in which both had exhausted their ammunition on each other, they had dived back behind their respective lines with a chivalrous wave of farewell. I knew that Alan McGlashan from then on was an enormous help and comfort to my son. I never asked what happened between the two of them except, one day, some years later, when he mentioned the elephant again and said he still could make nothing of the dream, I asked him: 'Did Alan say anything to you about it?'

He said, 'Yes.' But nothing apparently had been clarified. Alan McGlashan's association seemed to have been: 'It suggests bookends to me.'

I immediately saw how, and in a sense why, this image had come to Alan, but I did not know what his own interpretation of it was. There was, after all, a time when bookends were common enough, and elephant heads carved into the wood were used to keep rows of books in place on shelves in many a suburban home. But the fear inspired by my son's dream, and the fact that the image had occurred to someone so sensitive and experienced as Alan, added to my anxiety, and I began to wonder if my son might not be far more seriously ill than the doctors whom he had been seeing for some years thought he was, and whether, coupled with the vivid association with a great uprooter of trees, it was not telling us that this is where a life as we know it finishes, where the tree is uprooted and the story comes to an end.

All this occurred during a time when my son had been feeling a great unease of body and mind, and although he could not specify precisely what it was, and could only say to the doctors that he was feeling far from well, all those close to him were increasingly troubled over his condition because he had never shown any traces of the hypochondria which some of the physicians seemed to suspect. Indeed, only three weeks before his own cancer was diagnosed, a consulting physician told him that he thought he should consult a psychologist rather than a doctor. I do not say this to bring the doctors he consulted into disrepute. They were all honourable and dedicated men and were, I am certain, doing their best. But this aspect needs stressing because it shows how enigmatic and how subtle so deadly a sickness can be. Even after he had undergone an operation, the surgeons were so pleased with the result that they said they did not think it would be necessary to see him for another six months, and that all he needed was a holiday. If it had not been for an X-ray, totally unconnected with the operation and taken for suspected sciatica, no one would have known that the cancer had spread to other parts of the body and established secondaries in areas where they were declared to be terminal.

Despite this diagnosis, despite the images of the dream and the analyst's associations, the hope, the will and the courage to overcome, in both my son and Alan McGlashan, were most moving. We all, and there were many of us, were fearful but somehow never gave in to the fear. The battle went on to the last hour of John's last morning. Even on that last day there was no medical prediction of the end. Alan McGlashan just said he had seen too many last moments become first moments, and it was a matter for life to decide and not for rational speculation.

A week or so before the end my son, in great pain, had insisted on taking me to his favourite little church at Binsey, which was close to where he lived in Oxford. The church had once been in the keeping of Nicholas Breakspear, the only English priest ever to become a pope, and was, of course, most significantly for me, the place of Gerard Manley Hopkins' poplars. As we came out of the church and looked on the day again, my son said: 'This is where, if I am to die, I would love to be buried. But, of course, that would be impossible because Oxford is full of influential people who have already claimed for themselves all the earth that is vacant.'

I took heart from this 'if', and we walked slowly back, in an afternoon clear-cut and cold but full of a long yellow sunlight, so dense and sweet that the birds beginning to home seemed not to fly through it so much as to be swimming in a kind of honey. Then he spoke again: 'You remember that dream I brought to you nearly six years ago? I know now that that was the precise moment the cancer entered my body.'

The brief moment of relief brought on by his 'if' passed swiftly. We were back in his own private and personal field of battle, and I watched the light as Manley Hopkins must have watched it, thinking of his dismay when, on another day of similar sun, he saw his beloved poplars had been felled in the night: those poplars which 'dandled a sandalled shadow that swam or sank on meadow and river and wind-wandering, weed-winding bank'. His words came to me as if on a lift of air, cold and precise, evoking Hopkins' anguish of wondering whether human beings ever knew how, when they 'delve and hew' and 'hack and rack the growing green', even where they had intended to 'mend', they end something 'tender and slender', and aftercomers would never guess the beauty there had once been. Words and images followed one another delicately until the final stroke of havoc which felled the poplars for ever nearly a hundred years before left 'the sweet especial scene', as Hopkins called it, 'unselved'.

So clear and compelling had this evocation of the poet's poem been that it was intertwined with the mood of both of us and the overall feeling so special to the afternoon. Inevitably a question came, with the finality of the instant logic of the heart which had commanded the poet's reaction, and I asked of myself and of the day that if the felling of poplars, however dear and real they were in the poet's senses – poplars, moreover, that could be replaced – evoked such anguish and unselved a scene that was beautiful still, tranquil and radiantly making its way san-dalled again through the gloom towards the dark, how would I deal with the unselving when the person who walked tall beside me, his shadow lengthening in the sinking sun, was gone, and the uprooting of the tree of which he had dreamt six years before was fulfilled, and the book ended? What then?

I have seen much of death and dying and have even lived alone under what appeared to be an irrevocable sentence of death, but there was something new about this kind of dying, as if it were carrying deeply encoded within the process an urgent message, desperately trying to tell us something 'most immediate', as we had labelled messages of the greatest priority in the war behind us. Of course we knew, deeply, that his dying would be unique, and he could not be nearer to it at that moment than I had been to my own, so strangely deferred. I knew the country he was entering, as it were, from just across the border, within sight of customs and immigration. I was the last of seven brothers and had lost both father and mother and four sisters and, of course, had lost many, many others dear to me. I was, in a sense, as well prepared as a human being can be, yet I felt lost and unarmed, except for a kind of still but insistent voice from beyond the furthest star whispering: 'Ask and ask, again and again, until it speaks. Importune until door or window flies open and reveals some intimation of meaning that will trans-form and redeem.'

And perhaps, in the little left to us for importuning, enough was done to firm us for the end of the pattern which appeared to have started with a dream, so that it could end with another dream. Apart from a natural predisposition to take the dreaming process in life seriously, there were good reasons why I had to take these dreams more seriously than most. Ever since my son came from Africa to Europe he had, out of his own regard for totality and the wholeness of truth, taken his dreams to heart and mind, and it seemed right and of absolute import, therefore, that just before his death there came a final dream. Brief and vivid, it must be one of the closest intimations of the end ever to be recorded. He dreamt: 'I was back in the Cape of Good Hope. To my amazement the sun came up on the wrong side.'

I know that those who are in the business of dream analysis and who help others and have gone through it themselves, and who know far more about it than I know, would hesitate to pronounce on any single dream, least of all when they could not ask the dreamer for his own amplification of the dream. But the dreamer was gone, and out of touch with us, or perhaps, more precisely, was in touch only in a kind of new and inexpressible nearness, and one could not ask him, in what passed for language between us, for his own associations. But I felt that there was more than enough evidence from history to give us the relevant associations, particularly in regard to a person who knew his Cape and its history as well as he did. Besides, whatever it is that dreams through flesh and blood would have presided over these dreams, true and free of anything that is false, as it had presided over the centuries behind us.

The Europeans, especially the Portuguese, who probed along the coast of Africa from the north to the south, fearfully around the Bight of Benin, past Guinea, the coasts of gold and ivory and 'the white man's grave', onwards south for year after year under the Southern Cross, would always see the sun rise on their left – until one day, centuries later, there came the strange, blessed but awesome morning when the sun rose on their right. They sailed on, fearing it could be an aberration or an illusion or perhaps just a distortion of the coastline they had followed for so long. They watched it almost in unbelief, day after day, but it kept on rising on the right until they accepted with a great inrush of joy that what had been called the Cape of Storms at first had suddenly become the Cape of Good Hope, and that the way to 'the East' where the new day begins was open to them.

It seemed to me no message could be clearer, that both before the uprooter of trees had appeared and after that strange sunrise, the master dream, of its own accord, began the uncoding of the message we had longed for and stated clearly that there was more to the life of which we had just lost sight.

I stress the word 'began' because the process of wondering started by these two dreams, one at the introduction of the cancer into flesh and blood and the other at its exit from the here and now, led me to realise, without any feeling of bitterness or condemnation, how inadequate were the hypotheses and the points of departure of scientists and doctors in their approach to something so mysterious as cancer. I have so often heard doctors say that if only people had come earlier they could have dealt with the cancer. But how can one be early enough when the process itself may not be accessible to human perception until, having crept in on tiptoe and caught one asleep, with no conscious reason to protect one, it moves in and takes hold of the imagination, as it had done with my son? What did surgeons achieve when, to use one of the most ambivalent popular phrases of the English language, they proceeded to 'cut it out', when they were dealing with something that was not just physical but also dream material? Even if doctors did, as one hopes they will one day, use dreams and their decoding as an essential part of their diagnostic equipment and perhaps could confront cancer at the point of entry, how are they to turn it aside, unless they are humble enough to keep their instruments in their cases and look for some new form of navigation over an uncharted sea of the human spirit for a way to resolution of this fateful affliction?

But at that moment all was forgotten in the resolve to see if my son could be buried at the place where he had longed to be buried, and in that small dimension to defeat the negations of which the illness was part. John had been right: Oxford was full of people who loved Binsey so much they had reserved burial plots there. Nonetheless, the priest and the remote little church council who had these matters in their keeping, showed complete understanding when they heard the whole story, and I think they had a glimmering of what I was already calling to myself 'the great without' in the sense that the symmetry of meaning demanded such an ending to my son's story. So John was buried in the fullness of another Binsey morning, there on the fringe of the unique little hamlet hard by Breakspear's and Hopkins' church, within the sight of some picture-book cottages wherein, for him who had loved music so much, there was somebody who made it heraldic by playing a harp, just for the love of playing.

But from the beginning there had been an orchestration of the theme. Almost at the time of my son's dream of the uprooter of trees I had been in Switzerland. I was working at a book in the mornings and evenings and came back one afternoon from skiing in the mountains. It had been a day of what felt like creation for me, with an afternoon of skiing deep in fresh snow among those old hills, which I always think of as elder statesmen of time, and I was making for my hotel on a roundabout journey through woods, in and out of the shadows, the trees silhouetted dark and still against the steep decline of light of the day. Every now and then the shadows were lit with flicker and flame of deer coming down to their grazing in the valleys, and twice I saw chamois, still and serene, contemplating with ease the abyss on whose edge they stood nonchalantly on their toes.

I could not have felt better or happier, until I sat down to go over my morning's work and was interrupted by a call to the telephone. It was the voice of Jessica Douglas-Home, a voice usually so clear, fastidious, precise and charged with spirit, but on this occasion a voice I hardly recognised because it was shaken and blurred. She said: 'It's Charlie. He's got cancer. The doctors say he will not live much longer.'

So where there had been only one of my own, now another of my most intimate circle had made it two. What went on in the deeps of my soul needed days of unravelling, but among my dominant emotions was a strange kind of anger I had never experienced before, perhaps the anger we all feel when we are assailed by doubt and fear so real that we refuse to acknowledge them. Besides, I felt that, with my son already attacked, even the measure of fate was being exceeded. I heard myself say, almost fiercely, as if I accepted totally the doctors' verdict: 'We shall not allow it. We will tell God that he cannot do this to you and Charlie.'

From then on we pooled all we could of experience, resources and all that I had already gathered on my own way. We sought advice from all the major research centres, hospitals and experts in Europe, America and even Japan. We went outside the realm of medicine and science, crossing cultural frontiers in our search for what could help, and came to a point where we thought we were trying everything that mankind could possibly try in search of a cure. We encountered enormous diversities of approach, strange and unlikely prescriptions for healing, but, divided and often contradictory as they were, they shared one assumption. They all said that, as far as they had been able to arrest or even cure, there was one indispensable element without which nothing would have been possible, and for this they used just a single word: 'Fight'.

They meant it as a call to battle not just to the afflicted but to all who surrounded the afflicted, because that was essential for creating a climate that somehow might be predisposed to transform the dark, inscrutable pattern of destruction. I was troubled by the implications in so small but powerful a word. I had a suspicion that merely to fight back against anything, even so mysterious a force as cancer, might expose the person in battle to becoming in some backdoor way the very thing he was trying to overcome. It seemed to me something that went beyond cause and effect, action and reaction. Something transcending both was needed, but what was that? Where was it to be found, and how was it to be mobilised and made specific in the problem which confronted us? That seemed to me inevitably to point to 'the great without' which my son implied when he said that the cancer had 'entered his body', which in a sense is ambivalent and not meaning merely a particular physical body but including a sort of overwhelming overall something which encompassed all the withouts and withins we could experience. Inevitably it seemed to me to mean the area of life from which dreams came, from an area where something dreamt through us.

As time went on, my imagination turned more and more to that dimension. How, and to what extent, began to reveal itself as the story drew others into its theme. For the moment all we had to do was inevitably focused on the immediate day, and the reservation I had about the call to fight was in a sense diminished by the fact that my son already had committed himself to the other dimension and had unusual trust in the commitment.

Although by profession a scientist, he was by nature an artist/ scientist, more interested in what used to be called pure science, and deeply regretting always the extent to which he was side-tracked into its immediate application. He saw no conflict between the non-rational element of awareness, which science increasingly seemed to reject, and his own discipline. For instance, much of his dreaming self went into the design and work with a small team on what was the prototype of the Harrier jump jet – 'the flying bedstead', as they dismissively called it amongst themselves. I remember him bringing the first model of the engine to show me one weekend in London, and it was truly a thing of beauty. It was like a Leonardo da Vinci drawing translated three-dimensionally into gleaming silver metal, so much so that I said: 'When you have done with it, could I perhaps buy it and have it with my bits of sculpture here at home?' We laughed with the fun of the thought, but I really was in earnest.

So, one way and another, I was not troubled that he would get the fight wrong, and in the beginning, thinking always of that side of his nature, I was more hopeful than I had perhaps any justification to be. And to start with I was more troubled about Charles. Yet I knew that, although Charles had begun his career as a soldier and had an immense knowledge and interest in military matters and the history of war, yet he would not take what was happening to him literally. He too had worked for many years on this dreaming dimension of himself and indeed was actually living it out in his work and writing. What worried me most about him was that it appeared he had had the cancer much longer than my son had done – to judge by the look which for some years I had seen on his face and in his eyes. It may not sound very much, it may even seem totally unlikely, but by then I had had so much experience of the fall of cancer among friends and acquaintances that I had come to believe advance notice was served on me of something profoundly wrong in the base of their being by a look they all had in common.

In Charlie it appeared in a convincing form some eighteen months before when he 'phoned to ask me to come and see him in hospital, where he was recovering from what the doctors had diagnosed, as in the case of my son, to be severe sciatica. He told me then that he had hurt himself more severely than he had known in a fall from a horse while out hunting some months before and had been warned by his doctors that a sustained rest in hospital was the only way of putting a stop to these painful recurrences. It was then, as he spoke, that I saw this subtle shadowy warning I have mentioned.

As a way out of great unease I tried to tease him about his love of horses, which I fully shared, and particularly his casual approach to hunting. One of the many things I loved about Charlie was that it never occurred to him to be anything other than his natural self. He seemed to be always what his nature disposed him to be. Hunting, which he loved, did not need to be ritualised in him or require a traditional habit, however attractive. I was told how many times he had mounted his horse in such a hurry that he just wore what was nearest to hand, and once was seen appearing in the sky above the steepest hedges looking as if he were flying rather than riding because he still wore his dressing-gown and bedroom slippers. I always had a feeling that he would have been safer dressed this way than wearing prescriptions for a traditional occasion. I suggested that the fall must have come about when he was too smartly dressed for his natural self. He denied the charge vehemently and then said, with a smile of affection for the object of his observation: 'It was the horse. Silly creature! That is the trouble with horses. Of all the animals in the world, in proportion to their flesh and blood they have the smallest brains in existence. They have tiny little minds,' the smile broadened as he added, 'tiny, little Chinese-y minds.'

We laughed and I said, 'Yes, I know. But they have great spirit and great greatness of heart – perhaps the greatest of animal hearts.'

I was about to change the subject but found myself adding something almost before I knew what it was going to be: 'And they are very musical too.'

He was somewhat startled at that because he was profoundly musical himself, and then looked at me slowly and said, as he sometimes did, 'What an incorrigible old native you are.'

As he was speaking, from far away a memory stirred in me of something from a time when I was too young to have words to describe it, and which seemed, therefore, to be all the more powerful for the lack of anything but emotion to express it: it was of a moment towards nightfall just before the upside-down bats launched themselves upright in a twilight hour and cut with such speed through the air that it seemed to squeak with pain. Then another sound broke in with a cavalry clatter, a horseshoe struck the cobbles of flint in a stable yard so that sparks flew like fireflies and one knew one was home, and in an empire of stillness with a long corridor of night and the glow of a lamp at a door to a world of light. Yes! A horse was around before my verbal beginning.

Charles was soon out of hospital, but the pain in his back never left him and the difficult months went on. After what must have seemed an age to him but was only some eighteen months for us, the hypothesis of sciatica was abandoned and replaced by the diagnosis of cancer; the warning look which had alarmed me was confirmed, and the long campaign began. Knowing that some of the treatments that he would have to endure would be so severe that they would, in the short term, alter or even distort his physical appearance, he amplified his wardrobe with clothes that might be needed to serve any changes in appearance. Even the baldness which often accompanied one of the treatments was foreseen and a wig made in good time. These preparations in their sum were so meticulous that few people were aware of the fact that he was suffering anything more than the severe consequences of a hunting accident, and to the end that was how Fleet Street gossip portrayed his illness and explained his absences from the office.

Indeed, to those of us who knew how gravely and desperately he was fighting a two-pronged battle, one for his own life and totality and the other for the rehabilitation of what had been left in his hands of a sick newspaper, the lampoonery to which he was subjected in the gossip columns and the London equivalents and efforts at anglicised *Canard-enchaîneries* seemed heartless, uninformed and malicious.

Jessica's role in this was as heroic as his own. She seemed to me, from the day it began, the woman of all ages accompanying her man through a war, and she seemed to me to do this with a spirit which drew on something that was not purely English – or European for that matter. Indeed, ever since I had first met her I had had the impression that, in spite of an appearance which proclaimed an essential Englishness, there was another important ingredient that I could not connect with Britain or put a name to. With it went the impossible feeling that I had known her somewhere before – but since this feeling occurs so often in human experience and one is seldom able to discover the cause of it, I accepted it as one might accept the scent of a flower one cannot see and does not know when one walks through a country lane in spring. Then some years later it came unexpectedly and vividly alive and identifiable. I met her father for the first time and, to my surprise and delight, found myself confronted with someone who looked like a Javanese gentle-man. He told me then that his grandmother had been a Javanese princess, came to live in England and, gifted and musical, became a distinguished and popular hostess in London. And then, of course, I knew that it was the Java in Jessica – not in her appearance but in temperament – that had been trying to get through to me, the Java in which I had spent nearly seven momentous years of my life, in particular the Java of the aristoc-racies of the ancient sultanates of Djokja and Sodo, of complex Malay, Hindu, Buddhist and Muscat elements which had pro-duced a people of a delicate and beautiful mould of mind and bone, speech and movement, grace and passion, ordered and moving with apparent harmony through the life of an island without seasons and where it might have been always afternoon, and yet, when provoked, as their earth and clear-cut mountain summits were, by tensions at the centre of their world, so still, abundant, resolved and bejewelled under clouds like temples and immense wheels of sunlight, they broke out with a power and ferocity of earthquake and volcanic eruption not experi-enced anywhere else.

The sum of all this in Jessica, however, never shattered her capacity to contain, and it was most moving how it all expressed itself in our search for a cure. Yet often, as I looked at her, as we met or I saw her coming into a room or walking down a street, something that had happened to me in Java and concerns a woman of the aristocracy with whom she was allied by blood, flashed into my mind and was all the more poignant because I would realise that the two women, who had never met, shared profoundly of the same spirit.

It all went back to one very depressing moment in Java in 1942. Everything we were doing to try to establish a base in the jungles of Bantam was going wrong. I myself was at my headquarters on the mountain which, high as it was, was yet part of the great jungle of Sunda. It was called Djaja Sempoer, 'Mountain of the Arrow', and it stood in a valley called Lebak-sembada, meaning it was 'well made'. I had just, that morning, received a message from the peoples of the valleys below that the Japanese forces were massing around the base of the mountain and that soon there would be no way to escape. I was discussing this with an officer, a Swiss volunteer whom I had recruited because of his love of the people of Sunda and because he knew the jungle as they did. He had, in fact, a home of his own close to a sultanate not far away.

Suddenly a sound from one of the sentries below made this officer jump up, turn around and look down the narrow track along the saddle of the mountain. Some Swiss words of astonishment that I did not know broke from him and then the cry: 'Srie!' This was a woman's name, and as I looked along the path, a woman dressed in a sarong of beautiful batik came out of the shadows into a patch of sun, walking uphill barefoot, her long black hair streaming behind her, effortless, graceful, and not like a person going steeply uphill but more like some Atalanta running a race in the Hesperides. Behind her came three women, all carrying bundles and following her with equal ease. She was the daughter of the Sultan – and the mistress of this man. She came both to warn him and to join us, because she said it was no longer safe for her to be in the valley. She not only joined us but, even when I walked into an ambush and was captured, she stayed on with my group for months until they too were caught by the Japanese.

This, in a flash, was the metaphor evoked by Jessica at that moment, of the woman joining the man in the inevitable war. The image, the efficiency and the tenacity which Jessica brought to the years that followed had this kind of ancient historical immediacy about it, and never changed from beginning to end. Moreover, she and Charles lived in such a way that he went on working at one of the most exacting vocations in the world until days before he died. He was never away from his desk for long. Always he came back and went on working, doing perhaps some of the finest and best work that had ever been seen on his paper. The irony of it was that his appointment to the editorship-in-chief of *The Times* coincided almost exactly with the diagnosis of cancer, so much so that it seemed a basic part of the pattern that fate had designed for him rather than of his personal seeking. He had, in fact, decided to leave *The Times*. Not long before, he had telephoned me in Switzerland and told me, and it made such an impression on me that I know still that it was a Monday afternoon, almost at the same hour of the day that Jessica had telephoned. At the time he was not the editor of his paper but had sufficient authority to feel unusually involved with the direction of the paper, and he had come, sadly, to the conclusion that he could no longer work with the paper in the way wherein it was managed and run, and he had resigned. On the Wednesday after, he telephoned me and told me that he had just been offered the editorship and wanted to take it. It was, he said, something that he had always wanted to do, otherwise he would not have even considered taking on so great a responsibility, which was going to be also extremely unpleasant before the job and the newspaper became what they should be. So all through this he had, as it were, both a body and a paper to cure of affliction, and these two exactions to be kept equal and parallel to the end of his time.

The spirit with which both Jessica and Charles had accepted as axiomatic this universal exhortation to fight back at the cancer which had been hurled at us from all over the world was matched by the dedication Charles brought to the rehabilitation of what had long been an ailing newspaper, whose great role had for years been increasingly imperilled by an inferior administration. He brought to it all the gifts of a truly vocational journalist and a fine individual and moral integrity. Moreover, it was something that as a vocational journalist he had wanted to do all his life. His own gift and interests he knew committed him to serve the word in a tactical rather than a strategic sense. His own taste and love of history made him aware of how long-term service of the word was rendered without haste or busyness by art and literature, but aware too that, in a democracy, there was instant need, from hour to hour, of the word devoted to informing people as fully and objectively as possible on their lives and affairs.

Few knew that over the years the pain he was suffering was so intense that the strongest drugs could not suppress it. I can remember times when I went to see him at night so that Jessica could have some relief. It looked as if the pain could tear him apart and, in desperation, I would suggest to him that he should do what we did in the war at times when our wounded had nothing to still their agony; that he should groan as hard and as long as he could, because it could make a rough music of the pain and diminish it accordingly. And, strangely enough, there were moments when this was more effective than the drugs to which he had become habituated.

What worked best of all, though, was not rough but real music. As the pain mounted gradually and remorselessly towards its Everest, a gift from Alfred Brendel appeared in the form of music to match it. He had just completed his great rendering of all the Beethoven sonatas. He was a close friend, and one of the first things he did when he had recorded the full cycle of sonatas was to send Charles the recordings. Often at night, even when the pain had driven him to be in one of many hospitals, and he felt at the end of his resources, he would ask the nurses to put on one of these recordings, because he had discovered that they would calm and soothe in areas which no drug could reach.

There came a moment too when the limitations of just 'fighting on' intruded, and we discussed what else should be done. In this, as in other discussions about this awesome and mysterious affliction, we came to use a language that in the calm and regularity of the everyday scene, which is so good at concealing its own abnormalities, may well sound contrived and affected but at that moment worked and was the only recourse. We talked of making friends with the pain, almost as if it were not just a blind force but a kind of personality. It was extraordinary to me, and infinitely inspiring, how Charles did make friends with his pain, so that very often, when others might have clung to their beds and refused to be moved, Jessica and a nurse would help him dress and take him to the office of *The Times* where for hours on end, late into the night, he would carry on with his work.

Some of his best leading articles were written when the pain was intense, including one which I think, within its ration of daily newspaper space, is among the finest contemporary statements of what Christianity is about. It was called 'The Way of the Cross' and was a devastating reply to the sociology which the highest establishment in the churches was purveying as religion. There is a fashion nowadays that editors of newspapers should not concern themselves with writing leaders but concentrate on the general direction of their papers. But Charles knew, as all great editors have known, that the kind of newspaper work which is essential for the proper exercise of democracy cannot be done without total commitment to its purposes, and the heart of an editor's and a newspaper's commitment is, or should be, in its editorials. At a moment of grave crisis in the Falklands War, when there was a very real danger of Britain taking the wrong course, he wrote a leading article which had a decisive effect on the government and brought all the confused waverers back on course and made a proper conclusion of that infamous challenge inevitable.

Perhaps of all his leaders the greatest was the one he wrote on the Christmas Eve before he died. He was back in hospital again for another variation in his treatment and I spent some hours with him just sitting in his room while, in between doctors and nurses, he wrote it, and as he wrote it someone from his staff stood by to take it to his office. Re-reading it today one can see the cracks in the writing where the pain broke in and tore at the continuity and he would deal with the interruption, pull the parted seams together and write another paragraph, and so on to the end.

In the months that followed there were moments when we thought he would die, but over and over again he would recover and carry on, until, on a lovely late September morning, I had a call from Jessica and she said that he was dying. I was just leaving to go abroad and cancelled my flight to join them in hospital. I had never seen Charles look so peaceful and serene as he was then, and Jessica so contained and so at one with him. We hardly spoke: the three of us held hands and sat for long, mostly in silence. In so far as I took in our physical surroundings, the things that made an impression on me were small and, to the world without, insignificant. For instance, what was a large box of *marrons glacés* doing on the table beside his bed? It could only mean that, at a moment when all taste for food had left him, some emotion connected with a favourite delicacy in the nursery had broken through so clear that it still demanded satisfaction and in the process produced its own moment to outwit the pain and feed the ultimate feeling that, despite the suffering, all was and would be well. It was important enough, somewhere, even if I explain it badly, nearly to unman me, because it was a sign from a world so young to a world old and spent, and a vindication of how first and last in the end were joined, and the years in between made timeless.

Yet hard on it something of the quality of the mood within that room moved to the forefront of my feelings. Already the cancer was behind us. Whatever it served, whatever it was trying to tell us, the purpose was utterly fulfilled, and the instrument in the shape of Charlie was fully prepared and, as his soldier self would have said, at the ready. I thought again, as I had often thought in war and prison when I saw these moments come in the lives of men I had never known and whose names I would never know, how distinct and clear-cut they became and how, at one moment when three unknown Ambonese walked to their deaths barely a yard away from me as if they were going to a wedding, I thought there should be an heraldic order for anonymous valour in the unknown multitudes who displayed it, to rebuke and redeem the brutality about to shatter them, and to ennoble their end.

Certainly there was no air of defeat in our room: rather a great calm of fulfilment, and though someone like myself could only convey it in feelings and not words it was, I believe, carefully noticed and recorded at the monitoring post of life at the exits of the world as we knew it.

Jessica made a silent sign that she thought the time had come for me to go and I leant over Charlie's bed to say goodbye and found he was looking at me with wide open eyes and the suggestion of young mischief in their look. He smiled and said once again: 'What an incorrigible old native you are!'

Outside in the corridor by the door Jessica said she thought that was the end. She said it, again without hint of defeat or personal pain, rather like someone called upon to bear witness to the beginning of an end that was also the begetting of another beginning, and of cosmic importance. Yet, some days later, someone close to both Charlie and myself telephoned me in my hotel abroad to tell me that Charlie had only just died. He was a good friend and had been to see him over a period of some days after I left and was amazed to find him in a kind of St Martin's summer of himself. He said he had never known Charlie so lucid, so stimulating and so abundant in spirit as he had been then. As I put the telephone down, an image of the story of Charlie's end, which had been trying to form itself from the moment I left the hospital, became clear and I saw it as I have often seen life towards the end, like one of those torrents which, in its last descent towards the sea, finds on the golden beaches sand enough to pause and form a reluctant lagoon and builds up slowly water enough to mirror heaven before breaking through the final bar and joining the Homeric white horses of the sea.

With all this, and more, that I felt and saw in Charlie's death, I wanted to put something into words as a memorial to him, but on this journey of mine there was no room for writing and I had to dictate a summary of many complex things on the telephone to someone in the office of *The Times*, who served me well, but I would have liked to have done much more. And to this I must add, not because the facts have any meaning which was not in the story of the deaths of my son and Charles but merely as evidence of how the phenomenon of cancer was proliferating in my own circle of life, that within three months I had to dictate two more such memorials to friends, both of whom had died of cancer as well.

Meanwhile, the story of Charlie's life in this world came to an end with an act of public recognition which I personally had not foreseen. There was a service of farewell for him at St Paul's, and it was in a sense a surprise only because he had never advertised himself or made any great to-do about his aspirations. There, as in all else, he was in his own eyes merely following his natural self and had little consciousness, certainly no trace of self-consciousness, of ever having done anything remarkable. I myself, and I think both he and Jessica, just supposed that he would be buried quietly in the country, in communion with nature and the earth which he loved. Yet somehow the quality of what he had done vocationally as well as in his own personal battle for sanity and wholeness had penetrated to a far wider world than I had realised. It happened without contrivance and so naturally that it gave his going a symmetry which would not have been there if this final salute at St Paul's had not been included. It was, in its own low key, something of a Churchillian occasion. Heads of Governments and Opposition, ambassadors of European countries and representatives of all the elements of what is called 'the establishment' of a great society, as well as intimate friends and family, all crowded into Wren's cathedral.

For me, perhaps, most moving of all was seeing in the cathedral Charlie's favourite Cockney driver whom I thought of always as one of the last ambassadors from Dickensian London. I had travelled in his company on a number of night journeys between my home and some clinic or hospital. He was a person who did not speak very much and told one more of himself and life through what he was desperately trying to say with his limited vocabulary. But his total acceptance of the importance of driving a car properly for someone he admired and for whom he had acquired an affection far beyond his powers of expression, made the function and the man both extraordinary and great.

It was an indispensable element of the many others that made the morning so representative of humanity that I thought of the Russian poet who accompanied me to Pasternak's grave outside Moscow one May morning, not long after Pasternak had died, and the poet recited his own poem, some inspired lines which expressed in a sense the beat of the buried man's pulse:

> *We bore him to no interment;*
> *We bore him to enthronement.*

So far from any extravagance of traditional display which the occasion could have been, it became a spontaneous and deeply human event with which all sorts and conditions of us could identify, and the shape of it was, as my Australian soldiers would have said, 'Too right'. It was right that Prince Charles read the main lesson, and read it as well as he has always done these things, with his own unique sense of the music there is in the real meaning of words, joined to his capacity for participating in art and life and the reality of others. It was right that Charlie and Jessica's sons were there to greet all who came and to join in the reading of the lessons. And it was right in its choice of music, and perhaps most right of all that Alfred Brendel was there, after the pain, to play something of such delicacy and concern for creation that those who did not know the piece would not have believed that Beethoven, who has such power and authority in his music, could be so delicate, so tender and so still, with an implication of even his inadequacy to do all that something so shy, sensitive and urgent to be known demanded.

For me this Beethoven-Brendel moment seemed to transcend all the paradoxes that tend to tear the heart and mind apart when concerned with death, particularly the death of someone so young and so full of promise. Even the acoustics of St Paul's were overcome in that moment. They have many negative associations for me; they tend to spoil the best of the great music which I have heard there, and have acquired a notorious reputation in that regard over two centuries of music. Even on this occasion some of the musical outlines at times were blurred and somewhat interlocked with one another – except when Brendel played this piece. Although, inevitably, it too had moments when the sound had to soar, it never entered the danger zone where this law of the acoustics of St Paul's applied, but was played in such a manner that even at its summit it was below the level where it might have been distorted by rebound from arches and ceilings. It seemed to unfold in a strange, privileged order where there was only this almost slippered progression of the music to be heard. It was a singularly beautiful rendering in which the subjective and objective elements were profoundly at one.

As often when moved by music, I found that I had to close my eyes to stay with the sound, and suddenly it was as if, through the music, I saw something, nearly intangible and imponderable but never to the point of irrelevance, join the assembly of things within a permanent memory. It was an image – I hesitate to call it a vision, because that sounds too loud and substantial – and it was as if there had come along with the music a glimpse into a field of grass, just stirring in the wind of morning, leading to a succession of fields and hedges, hedges and fields, on and on to where they contracted in a line of a blue which stopped just before it went over into black under a Madonna-blue sky. In the foreground there was a horse, which had a head I seemed to recognise and a mane that was abundant and long, and someone young with his back towards it, the level sun like a halo around them both. This young person picked up a halter from the grass beside him, took the long leather thong and made of it a rough bridle which he put in the mouth of the horse. Barefoot, he mounted the horse bareback, put it into a slow graceful walk, timed, it seemed, to the pace of the music. He rode away straight without looking back or to the right or left. Near the point where his silhouette was about to join the last hedge the horse seemed to go into a canter and then rose above the last of all impediments to the view, like the last fence in a final point-to-point, up and then down, and out into the blue. Almost at once the sombre funeral theme moved to its close, but with time enough for me to re-connect with the strange associations that came to me when Charlie and I talked of horses, their hearts and spirit, at an early sickbed. Yes! There it was again: this horse and its bareback rider were riding out and away from a moment in St Paul's but into a world uniquely my own and related to that winged moment between the brown and black of the day where a hoof struck fire from a cobble, a bat squeaked and then, across a pool of night, a door went amber and there was light and a sweet promise of shelter and rest, like a golden comb of honey at the exit of the dark.

Joined to this music of such surprising supplication and inter-cession, this image has retained the power to shake my memory at the most unexpected moments, like those little gusts without ostensible cause which move through the blue and precise cool of autumn to make the leaves all over the trees tremble, and somewhere one sees from the highest of all branches a leaf detach itself from a quivering tip and come down, reluctantly, sideways to the earth, and one knows that the process of another great separation in the seasons has begun and summer is about to be amputated and the winter move into its place, an act of separation which demonstrates, as it were, that there has to be separation and separateness if there is to be creation and recreation.

When I came out onto the steps of the cathedral the day was still clear and the sun shining, but the rush and the noise of the traffic and the speed with which the overwhelming everyday world took over was brutal, if not sinister. Yet even with the vast spill-over of the numbers who had been in the cathedral slipping into their functions as if they were part of their dress, that slight, visual experience evoked through music remained firm and redeemed the rest of the day and still recurs in similar moments of the autumn. It harmonises naturally with the fact that Charles, after this monumental farewell, was buried in country he loved and, as Housman in his *Shropshire Lad* moments might have put it, wears forever 'an overcoat' of green earth.

As the days went by, with a sense of tragedy so heavy that they seemed at times to have lost their will to walk and were almost brought to a standstill with the weight of it, the emotions involved, especially for Jessica and my son's family, came near to the unbearable. But in a strange way I was helped by a feeling of how partial and inadequate a word 'tragedy' was to describe what had happened. All certainly was not withdrawn. Into these dear, vacant places something else had moved that once more seemed to be desperately trying to tell us something. All certainly was not tragedy. It was as if they, or something close on their heels, were about to deliver some message of tremendous import, and this feeling rose like a river about to flood when, before long, this pattern of the two was joined by that of a third. Edward appeared on the scene, and at once the pace and thrust and volume of time quickened.

Edward was the son of one of my old friends and is part of one of the many island stories that have played a significant part in my own life. It is odd – and perhaps even sounds highly unlikely, if not totally implausible – but even as a child in the heart of one of the greatest continents on earth, my imagination was inflamed by the thought of islands. The first of many was the island of Robinson Crusoe, of which I had news first from my mother at a remote time when I could not read. But from the moment I went to school to learn to read as soon as possible and I heard of such a phenomenon again, and in my first geography lesson I was taught the basic definitions of wonderful things like continents, subcontinents, archipelagoes, capes, bays, gulfs and islands, the definition of an island as 'a piece of land surrounded by water' struck me as one of the most magical and eloquent of poetic statements I had ever heard. And then, of course, there were others in literature, as for example the Coral Island that followed soon after, all contributing to a perception of life in which, among the many civilisations of the world, two island peoples, the British and the Japanese, so totally different, were to give me personally most of all.

I also used to have a recurrent dream in which there always appeared and reappeared a vision of an island, in a wine-red sea of morning, where the dreamer was drawn – hushed and somewhat fearful – by a whisper on the wind that behind some forbidding cliffs there was a place of water and reeds where at midnight a great flower opened with a sigh, and closed with another at dawn.

Over the years this feeling of special relationships with islands grew in substance and significance to such an extent that I instinctively parted company with Donne – a poet I loved – over his remark: 'No man is an island, entire of itself; every man is a piece of the Continent, a part of the main.' I was convinced beyond doubt that every man is an island but joined to other islands by the main, which is the sea.

It did not seem to me so strange, therefore, that before I came of age there came into my life one island which I was to meet and re-meet constantly to this day, which when I first saw it might have been a variation of the island which had haunted me in my dreams; and that was the island of Madeira.

It is, of course, still exceptional to this day, but it cannot compare with the impression it made on me more than sixty years ago when, after nineteen days at sea and a long farewell to the interior of Africa, my ship, with its lilac hull, gleaming white decks and red funnel and all the signals in the yeoman's locker run up to the masthead, dropped anchor in the roadstead of the island. The flags hardly moved, the sea seemed spellbound in stillness and, after the hysterical clatter of the anchor and its heavy chains, there was no sound to be heard coming to us from the shore. In that moment the island chose to be ambassadorial in one of the most delicate and nostalgic scents on earth; the scent of wild freesias, first like whiffs and whirls of an almost invisible smoke and then enfolding the ship all over and penetrating even down into the public rooms and cabins.

For me this island was sheer magic. This, I knew from history, was still a vestige of the ancient outpost of Europe before we came in the fifteenth century to destroy it. Why we did it and how it happened is not known; all we know is that this island, from the tip of its toes to the top of its mountain head, tall and well-clad in the Atlantic Ocean, caught fire and burned for years until there was not a tree left and all the valleys and steep gorges, covered with orchids, exotic flowers and, above all, freesias, were utterly destroyed and only a cindered earth and secondary growth took over. It was perhaps, in hindsight, an awesome kind of warning of what the destruction of the natural world, which was a consequence of frantic European exploration, was to do to life, and yet there was hope in the fact that the most tender of its ancient plant life, the orchids and the freesias, came back and thrived, and on my first visit there they were, to speak of the indomitables of creation entrusted to the smallest and tenderest things on earth.

I celebrated the enchantment of that encounter by coming back to the ship in the dark with my arms full of freesias. They overflowed the basin in my cabin and their scent saw me safely into Southampton.

That evening as I took my seat at the Captain's table I found myself sitting next to a beautiful, middle-aged lady with a naturally commanding, but not obtrusive, manner. We seemed to take to each other naturally. She was Edward's grandmother, and from that moment started an island relationship that developed steadily over the years and continues to this day.

I made a habit on my many voyages between England and the Cape, since the ships I sailed in always included a stop at the island, of going ashore and spending time with the family. Often I would gladly jump my ship and spend a week on the island and then continue the voyage with the next. Not only did this become a rule but all sorts of coincidences crowded into life to confirm the validity and meaning of these visits.

For instance, when the war broke out I found myself on Victoria Station, posted as a private in the army to my first training establishment, at exactly the same time as the second son of the house, John, who had become my closest friend. On his island, where for generations, much as they loved their Portuguese context, they had continued to be quintessentially English, this Englishness demanded that John should immediately rush to London when war broke out and join the army. We must have had the same impulse at the same moment, a moment so naturally synchronistic that when we reported to the quartermaster for our kit that evening, we found that John and I could only be fitted out in Boer War cavalry jodhpurs and puttees, which was to make us the object of battalion jokes for some months to come, as we were the only two.

Then, on my return from nearly ten years of war, when our ship called in at the island, there was John standing in the bows of the pilot's launch coming to meet us, in order to be the first aboard. In these and many other ways this continuity never failed our relationships, and in due course included my wife Ingaret, who became as great a friend of Edward's mother as his father was of mine, and we all formed a close bond with the children; my wife particularly with Edward, and I with the others, Richard, Michael and my god-daughter, Rosemary.

My wife, whose imagination all through her life was quickened by the hint of trouble in the spirit of people whom she met, was particularly drawn to Edward because he had so profound a stammer. On outings they would always join hands and walk apart from the rest, and on one of our more adventurous expeditions when we climbed the peak which dominates Madeira, she and Edward got there before the rest of us and I have to this day a wonderful photograph of the two of them sitting, not triumphantly but with a prophetic sense of achievement, the wind blowing scarves and hair sideways. There seemed to be always with us, in the island and wherever we met, a profound feeling of past and future meeting, with the 'now' only a link between the two — the more so on that day because I remember in the evening John sitting at the head of the table, the wine in ship's decanters with narrow necks and very wide, cut-glass bases, in the room more like the cuddy of a flagship in the force of warships under sail of which John's grandfather had been an admiral and his mother had travelled as the admiral's daughter and so came to Madeira. Behind him there was a painting which Nelson had given to another ancestor out of gratitude for what the family had done to help him repair his ships after the rare battering they had had from the Spaniards off the Canaries. There was almost nothing in the room which did not have some history of this kind to bring in the past, which added a greater poignancy to the unusual presence of all the children, alert and bright with anticipation of the future.

To complete the sense of celebration, John said he thought that this was an occasion to test 'that Madeira'. And 'that

Madeira' I knew, from two previous occasions which came roughly a decade apart, was the Madeira originally bought for the British Government to stock Napoleon's cellars at Longwood on St Helena. Napoleon died with only half the Madeira drunk. It was so good a Madeira that the family bought it back, and it was becoming so old that there was always a fear that the wine might have gone past maturing and be about to decline, since it had been bottled in the year the Bastille was stormed. I always sipped mine reluctantly because I felt the wine so much a testament of irretrievable history. The bottle was broached and the wine found to be better than ever, and so was left to continue maturing, except that we were given some bottles to take back with us to England, with such awe that I still have one bottle left and am waiting on providence to announce some happening of sufficient significance to warrant gulping two hundred years of momentous history.

That day and that evening seemed to take Edward's relationship with Ingaret into a new and more urgent dimension. They met now not only on the island but regularly in England, first when he was at a public school, then at university. This happened because Ingaret and Edward together had decided that they should look into the pattern and the message they felt was encoded in his stammer. To an imagination hovering with hindsight, rather like a bird, over the total scene of their relationship, and aware of its relevance to what is to follow, although I could not see at the time, it was of critical importance. I had described Edward's stammer to myself from the beginning as a 'Mosaic' stammer, the stammer behind which Moses had tried to hide when he was summoned by 'that which cannot be named' to go back to Egypt and deliver his people. I did this not merely instinctively but because by then I had known well three other men who had similar stammers. They had all been exceptional characters. Two of them were killed in the war without achieving worldly renown, and one is still alive and seems to me, as the others did, to live with an especial quality he may not have been able to achieve without the stammer. I say this because already I suspected the stammer was more than an impediment and was, in one sense, a measure of some totally inexpressible abundance of insight into the nature of truth and reality, something that seemed to come before, rather than with, the Word.

So it was not surprising that when he and Ingaret started to survey it psychologically and, above all, through his dreams, they did not seem to set out with the idea of removing the stammer, which was unusually profound, so much as in a belief that somewhere in the exploration simultaneously of their inner selves, a predisposition of mind and circumstances would be created wherein the stammer would have a chance of being transformed. In due course there was evidence that this possibility was beginning to exist even if it had not been there before. There were moments, without warning, when it vanished and Edward would telephone with a joy that almost made the telephone itself crackle with excitement, and report that he had just come back from an exacting debate in the Union of his university and, on impulse, had spoken without notes and without a stammer for half an hour, and then answered questions without any impediments for the rest of the evening. Yet the next day the stammer was back. There were other occasions too when he discovered an eloquence that none of his contemporaries could outshine, but on the whole these moments were rare and unpredictable and the stammer seemed to prevail. It was typical of them that neither regarded it as a defeat, because their exploration in every other way seemed to them both so overwhelmingly rewarding. Even I, who had no part in the dialogue between them in that area, could tell just by looking how rich and eventful an experience it had become, so much so that I had a feeling that the matter of the stammer had become almost irrelevant, if not a confirmation of the significance of what they were doing.

That feeling always brought me back to what I had called in the beginning a 'Mosaic' stammer, and the thought of the three friends I have already mentioned. I was tempted to conclude that, however useful and convincing as an excuse for avoiding a challenge of obedience to a larger duty, it was rather like a kind of birthmark, an image of a destiny unlike that of other men – perhaps even a badge of an intuition so acute of potentials of life that it was almost like a direct line to creation, bypassing the need for words.

Just as Moses in the biblical beginning was filled with an awareness which could not be named, and as a result overwhelmed with so much meaning and so many implications of what his role meant that he came near to speechlessness in his inability to find adequate words for its expression, the stutterer was condemned to use only the easiest sorts of everyday words as proxies for those that total meaning demanded. The more Moses failed in this regard, the more he was bound to be obedient to his prompting and thereby, in some mysterious fashion, was enabled to be the leader, the guide, the bridge between his fallible but seeking nation and their Creator.

I had barely begun to think along these lines when some substance was given to the thought by what happened on one of Edward's voyages between England and Madeira. He and his two brothers were travelling home in a crowded passenger ship when the ship caught fire and was plunged into dangerous confusion. Edward, helped by his eldest brother Richard – both of them still schoolboys – extracted themselves from a cabin black with smoke, and from then on played a great role in leading people onto deck and organising them into parties to go into the lifeboats until the first rescue ship arrived. Once aboard the rescue ship, his little family group went on helping the crew of the inadequate tramp ship to care for the exhausted survivors. Afterwards he and his family took all this for granted and no great to-do was ever made about it, but the incident explains how Edward came to be so much loved, found so many friendships and brought to whatever he was doing in life a special quality of a life lived, rather than spoken.

He finally found Georgie, a young woman who matched his quality. They were singularly happy and soon abandoned London in order to go back to the island where he inherited his mother's house on a sleepy volcanic buttress of Madeira. He had hardly done that when cancer struck him too, as it had already struck and killed his remarkable mother.

He tried all the cures, some more up-to-date than those my son and Charles Douglas-Home had tried. He went naturally even more deeply within himself where he and Ingaret had already been very far down and sought a cure in a world of faith and spirit in reaches of the human psyche where few others had been. He did not neglect the world without for the world within but willingly underwent the succession of operations which leading specialists prescribed. If the specialists and their kind had known the answers, of course, they should not have failed after all he went through, because they could not have had a more positive patient; but fail they did. Again and again, after moments free of pain, the affliction broke back. Finally an operation was advised which the surgeons admitted could not cure but would merely buy more time. Something within Edward snapped and he announced that he would have no more, and defended his decision against the clamour raised around him by answering back without a stammer.

Then suddenly the progression of the cancer seemed arrested of its own accord. His life seemed full of light and peace and calm and a sense of enrichment which was the most indescribable of the many indescribable things that had haunted his imagination since childhood. He felt somehow that he should pass on the experience, and thought of Ingaret and myself. He cabled unexpectedly from Madeira that he was coming to see us in London, and hard on this followed a letter to Ingaret in which he referred to 'the experience', and described it with a metaphor – especially striking since his stammer ruled out the use of metaphors in his conversation and he had to confine himself to the stark necessities of meaning. He said it was as if his life had found a water full of light and stillness and reflection of the blue of heaven, close to the great Atlantic Ocean which, night and day, pounded his island home and made the greatest stillness of which that region of the world was capable – the sound of the sea. That nearness to the sea, he said, gave him an intensity of nearness to the earth and the sky and human beings which was the most precious thing imaginable. It was all so beautiful and so still and felt so permanent and rewarding that, no matter what should happen to him in future, this moment made all more than worth it, and more than he had ever dreamt he could deserve.

We had not seen him for nearly two years and were afraid of what the illness might have done to him, yet when he walked into our drawing-room he came in with an air of great well-being. If it had not been for his eyes, I would have concluded he had never been better. He always had fine, wide-open eyes, alert and full of feeling, and so they still were. But there was a look I knew, with its implication that his own time within had been altered: the seconds forgiven and the hour advanced.

He had just come from more consultations with his specialists, had been through another series of tests and been warned that, in spite of his feeling of wellbeing, the cancer was merely suspended and he would do well to have more treatment. Yet he remained firm in the conviction which made him refuse their knives and medicines and radium the last time he had seen them, and stressed that he could find no greater answer than had already been found in himself.

I left him and my wife to talk alone, which they did for some hours and I had never known either of them so resolved. Later I watched him walk away and down our little Chelsea street towards the river like someone going to a feast.

He returned to his island and we did not hear from him again until Christmas, when he always wrote. The letter added nothing to what he had already told us, largely because the fact that his wife was expecting a child had moved all else into the background of his thinking. After that there was no more news from him direct, but suddenly his brother Richard wrote me one of his very rare letters to say that the cancer was back and that this time there could be no doubt that Edward was dying. He said I would be glad to know that Edward was dying the Edward way, a way that made them feel they were witnessing not an end, and not even a beginning, but a continuation of something everlasting wherein all that was happening to him was a form of supreme privilege, and they all privileged to be a part of it.

So where there had been two, now there were three. Three, I felt, somehow ought to be enough to put me on course to resume the search which had begun in my imagination with that strange visitation of the headache of my childhood.

Three has never been to me just a number. It has always been an imperative of sorts. All numbers up to ten, and perhaps even zero itself, had always seemed more than just statistics. It may be possible that numbers beyond ten are also more than statistics and, as it were, signposts in the world of high algebra and mathematics to a self-contained meaning of their own. I would not know and can only have suspicions. But three has something, beyond doubt – intercessionary, almost mystical, and absolute. It is so in folklore and fairy tales, and patterns of parcels of threes seem to run in all dimensions of life and time, always with an extra charge of meaning. Everyone knows that the postman, not just of the Royal Mail but as messenger of the gods and fate, knocks thrice. And it is no accident that there is the awesome trinity in religion, where it is not only affirmation of what can be derived of abiding achievement from what has gone before, but is implicit with the four, about to become the square, which in turn provokes the transcendent compulsion to be rounded.

So the sombre third which Edward's death made of my experience insisted that a phase of the search was over, and a reappraisal of what it had meant was necessary before one could move on.

Foremost in this reappraisal was Edward's sense of 'privilege that transcended all'. There had been more than a hint of this already in the way in which Charles had searched for a release from cancer and finally found his way to his appointed end. Both he and my son had lived lives which in no way contained the elements which the specialists claim induce or provoke cancer. Their lives were not brutalised by the archaic collective which is sweeping like the shadow of an apocalyptic storm over the life of our time. Each in his own way had sought individuation and a wholeness of spirit and body, and yet, particularly in Charlie's case – which I mention because I observed his progression over the years, and was confronted with my son's only near the end – I had already felt that in his own way his life had parallels in history, and I had begun to draw on the story of Job for an outline to follow and to contain new dimensions of thinking and being.

Job, after all, suffered his fate not because he was rejected and unrewarded by life and God but precisely because he was the most loved and exemplary of the Creator's servants on earth. So that one had to accept that, in essence, his tragedy was tragedy in the midst of exceptional privilege.

One says this in connection with three such loved and comparatively young people with hesitation, out of fear of the fat presumptuousness of our age where, in great comfort, we watch nightly on our television screens and read daily in our papers matters of death and suffering parading more and more as kinds of entertainment. It is only too easy to make philosophy out of the pains of others and to prescribe to them idealistic courses of behaviour which one could not live oneself.

But I felt that here the grief, the capacity for grasping suffering through participation – something to which our age seems increasingly impervious and incapable of accomplishing – was like what my black countrymen so movingly called 'the stringing of beads'. In this ancient and beautiful Bantu metaphor, each tear of sorrow shed is a jewel that has to be strung on an unbroken thread of feeling into a necklace, which one can thereafter wear as an ornament of grace around the image of one's spirit, and so prepare the way for the final metaphor: 'Let in our sister, Grief, who should always have a place by our fire.'

And this repeatedly brought me back to the way the story of Job had presented itself to me when I was a boy. Ever since I first met it I have found it perhaps the most provocative story ever thrown into the pool of our deepest imagination, casting ripples of a troubled speculation which continues to travel from generation to generation over that vast sea, so wide that 'God Himself scarce seemèd there to be', on which Coleridge's old sailor found himself alone. It is a story that would not, and I believe will never, go away, and whenever one thinks of being rid of it and at last ready to walk on unburdened, one finds one has hardly started to turn about and face forward again when something about it tugs at one's coat of mind and heart and holds one back as if to say: 'But then, have you thought right through all of this?' and the wondering breaks out again. And always one has to answer the question why someone so good and true and loyal to his Creator could be so cruelly punished – as it seemed on the first occasion to me.

The rationalisations with which interpretations of the story try to deal with this seem plausible rather than convincing. It did not make sense to me that all that had happened was done merely to prove to the Devil how great and how loved the Creator was. It seemed more of a reminder, if not a rebuke, to man, that it was not all about material rewards and compensations and justice, with only a sociological or, as it is now put, a social scientific moral. Early on already I wondered if the contrary could not be true and if those whom the Creator truly loved, and would ultimately reward in ways that surpassed all human understanding, could be called upon to suffer most and should be looked for not among the rich and prosperous but among the cruelly deprived in life. This indeed was the point so admirably made by Froude in the abundant and prosperous days of the great white Queen, and whose essay on Job I came across in my last year at school. For him the main point seemed to be that the story of Job was a pointed and devastating attack on the morality which regarded material prosperity and social recognition as providence's reward for a life of civic and conventional rectitude. It was obviously not the main message to be extracted from the Book of Job, but it was clearly part of the meaning to be derived from so profound and enigmatic a testament.

The important thing for me was to think of Job and the immense dimension of suffering with which it was concerned as the orchestration of a great symphony of meaning. To take it literally would be to destroy all entrance to a great and imperative unknown to which it was pointing, and the question gradually arose, why those who were nearest and most loyal and most obedient to the exactions of the patterns of creation in life were called upon to realise that their Creator, in so far as he could be spoken of in an image accessible to us, was also a profoundly suffering Creator, and that the love of which he himself was a subject demanded that those he loved should be taken into an ever closer partnership where flesh and blood would have to endure not only the joy of helping to bring more light in the darkness that was in the beginning, but also the suffering of the everlasting battle for more light out of chaos and old night. Only those who were nearest and dearest to him would not be destroyed but enriched by a glimpse of the great and terrible enormities of creation which would have been unendurable at all levels if they were not part of a cosmic battle for life subjected to the love where feeling and intellect truly join, or what Dante called 'the love that moves the sun and the other stars'.

An interpretation on some such lines as these seemed to me implicit in the process of evolution of the human spirit, introduced with the dream of Jacob's ladder. Suddenly man is no longer merely someone to be ordered about by his Creator but, through his dreaming self, has a means of communication with his Creator and his Creator with him. It is the first great hint that there is to be what today is called 'two-way traffic' between man and God, a suggestion of partnership, which is greatly extended through this story of the most profound confrontation between man and God in their battle against darkness which, put into contemporary terms, is a battle against blind, unconscious forces, a battle for greater consciousness, a battle for awareness, in which both are engaged.

The more I lived with the sense of this loss of the three, the more important it seemed to me to go on following all the Job-like imagery which seemed to float in whenever I pursued this kind of wondering. Through the discipline of the sense of loss and suffering there was no presumption or exaggeration, and there was even comfort, in believing more and more that the three had been greatly and most mysteriously favoured. And there was no limit, no horizon to the wondering, because ultimately all that could be known was in terms of an acceptance of an overwhelming unknowable that could never be reclaimed by words.

Even Job, the archetype in symbol of a pioneer in the world of the spirit, after all the eloquence that flowed between him and his comforters, between him and the suffering which threatened his integrity, had to 'lay his hand upon his mouth' and, in the act of confessing his defeat, the knowledge came to him:

'my redeemer liveth'. And at that moment, emptied of words, of all argument, of all resistance and attempts to deal purely out of himself with his suffering, into this terrible vacant place within himself there moved something for which I can only borrow the old theological word: grace. A process of metamorphosis immediately took over, and something that in this field of cancer is called a 'remission' occurred, and all that Job had lost, and more – even in a worldly sense – was returned to him.

There is admission in all this of a dynamic known unknown, a knowledge that belongs utterly to the future, and yet is magnetic in the present in the area where world within and world without meet and are interwoven. There, at that point of remission, there is no longer any doubt. Metamorphosis is a fact. Perhaps the most terrible physical affliction which has ever assaulted human life is strangely transformed or, as Job might have it, redeemed.

No one any longer doubts the reality of remission in cancer. There are so many proven examples now that they justify the epithet, used in the jargon of our day, of being a 'scientific fact'. They can no longer be explained away, as they were for many years, as cures of an affliction which had never deserved to be diagnosed as cancer. They cannot be dismissed even as rare occurrences in an eccentric area, so rare as to justify the cavalier attitude science tends to have towards coincidences, and be excluded from our reckoning as accidentals. All should know by now that they are part of an area subject to laws of creation of which we are inadequately aware. Even the physicists who find themselves passing through the divide in their split atoms emerge into another universe beyond, for which they too have no words any more and run out even of mathematical equations to describe another segment of the great unknowable, and in desperation borrow from the vocabulary of poets and psychologists to define the new confrontation.

Edward's case for me was most significant in this regard, because it was prophetic. He experienced the happy ending, as it were, the grace, before his body had done with its suffering. He was an example of the potential in the sufferer, of the 'not-yet' in the now. This, it seemed to me, was the Mosaic element in his make-up which I had from the beginning connected with the stammer; just as Moses could lead others to the Promised Land, he himself, his bodily, worldly self, was not allowed to enter it, but had to content himself and make his great peace with it in a vision from a mountain top of his spirit – gleaming and abundant across a formidable shimmering and taut waste-land – and that, for him, of course, was more than enough. I was certain too that those moments of terror from pain which no drug could still, and which Charlie, in the dark nights alone in some clinic or hospital, could only resolve by listening to music, those too were similarly Mosaic.

This was the final image which haunted all the abundant images and thoughts that came to me out of my experience of the three, and it seemed to me that I had no sooner become aware of tragedy as a singular and disguised form of privilege than I was told of a remission of a terminal cancer in its starkest and simplest form from a source I could not doubt.

I heard of it from Professor Meier, a close friend and for forty years one of Jung's closest collaborators. He himself had qualified in medicine and surgery in Switzerland, Paris and Italy, and as physician and psychologist had a unique experience of life in this dimension where the two great objectivities of the inner and the outer meet in the human body and soul. It was a story most telling in its simplicity and totality. He said that when he was a young surgeon at a hospital in Zurich and work-ing with one of the most famous surgeons of his day who specialised in cancer operations, a farmer from a remote valley who spoke only his own local patois came to the hospital, des-perately ill. The surgeon performed an exploratory operation, made the sombrest of faces and declared the man had cancer in so advanced a state that the kindest thing to do was to seal the incisions and send him back to die among his cows and his friends in his valley.

Several years later Professor Meier found himself in the valley from which the patient had come. He was sitting outside a hostelry in the summer sun with a glass of wine and the local valley cheese and bread and suddenly found himself thinking of this man and wondering how and where he had died. When he

80

went to pay his bill he spoke to the owner and his wife and asked them if this man's name meant anything to them. They said it was the name indeed of a well-known farming family in the village. He told them how sorry he was that a man from that family had, some years before, come to his hospital and that they had been unable to help him and had to send him back to die. At this the couple were amused. They said they knew the man, and all the village remembered the great surgeon who had cured him of his desperate illness and sent him back so healthy and able to resume his life as a farmer. The man was still alive and had never been better and had become one of the most progressive farmers of the valley.

'Now, what the hell do you make of that?' Professor Meier laughed. 'You certainly cannot dismiss it as sheer coincidence. It is a fact, and the only way I can explain it to myself is that the cure was brought about by faith, by a simple and profound faith in the healing powers of this great surgeon to whom he had come for help and in whose powers he utterly believed, rather as the peasant in the dark ages believed in the powers of Merlin.'

He thumped the table for joy because, healer as well as scientist that he was, he liked nothing better than seeing what he called 'hidebound practices kicked in the pants'.

Robust as Professor Meier's concluding remarks had been, they reminded me that this was precisely what Edward had done. I seemed to see him as I saw him last, walking down towards the Thames, a river which is no ordinary river, because for me it is so much more than water bound to rejoin the sea it had once left as vapour. It is a river full of history not only of outer events but of the human spirit. As I looked at it on that day, there was the tower of the old church flying the flag of St George, and, hard by, the rooftop of the chancelry from which Sir Thomas More was taken to the Tower for his ultimate execution. And there were all sorts of other reminders of artists and philosophers, and gardens in which the healer in men had sought cures for the ills of the flesh throughout centuries of a great city's evolution. These associations which I have with London began for me when I first came to it in the 1920s. As I

looked at its skyline from the highest vantage point on its northern boundaries, there was not a single thing in that gentle view
to contradict its history. From where I first saw it, the composition of the town was the most organic compound I had seen
of man, his home and social building, and his love of grass,
trees and gardens. All was there, laid out as if in a blueprint of
the human spirit which thought of a city as its fortress and light
on a hill of the soul. As a result the skyline was for me the most
beautiful I had ever seen in a city, and it was not so much broken
as uplifted and sent soaring by the spires of its many churches
like arrows bearing messages to heaven. There are smaller cities
in the world which may have a greater number of churches, but
I know of no city anywhere going about gigantic contemporary
business that showed such aspiration to heaven as London when
I saw it first.

Now I was suddenly jerked out of all these associations and
appalled by my inner comprehension of how it had all changed.
My unawareness of it seemed unpardonable, and even more
unpardonable my lack of recognition of what this change was
telling us all. The message was stark and brutal: London itself
had cancer.

Judging by the failure of a century of research to discover
what cancer is, this special affliction of our age might even have
its cause and origin in the spirit, or in the dimension of the
great unknowable where terms of mind and body, spirit and
matter express merely different points of observation of a
phenomenon which transcends all; the great unknowable whose
language is that of the dream, and what dreams through us, and
which had come to my son as a dream and had prompted one
of his last remarks on the subject, that the dream came to him
'at the precise moment the cancer had entered his body'.

And wherever I looked at the city I saw – and still see – cancer
in concrete: in the sprawl of the city and the way of life that
went on like a recurring decimal, merely repeating itself and
refusing to take part in the resolution of their sum and make
possible the decent division which is differentiation, and rejection of repetitiveness, in the interests of renewal and creation.
I went back to the definition of cancer which a remarkable

research biologist had given me in my youth. When describing it in the human being, he defined it as a lawful process of growth that had got out of hand. Normally a cell had to renew itself to replace wastage in the economy of the body and promote its overall renewal and progression into its lawful future. But with cancer it appeared that a cell would defy the general law of increase and move out of its lawful orbit, bent on renewing only itself at such a rate that it invaded one vital area of the body after another, ultimately killing both itself and its host. He called it proliferation.

Thought of in this way and in terms of the natural images that it evokes in the human imagination, the behaviour of the single cell in the human body which acquires such a degree of self-importance and such a lust for power and hatred of discipline within the complex of an infinite whole, is obscene. It is, perhaps, the most archaic and the most brutal single image of the emergence of the hubris of the ego which, through consciousness, has discovered power over less conscious forms of life and sets out to use them for its own particular ends.

Now everywhere I looked there were eruptions of proliferations; horizontally and vertically cell was joined to cell and piled upon cell, increasing its domination of the city. What had been growth and a harmonious composition serving man's relationships with his earth, with his neighbours, with his country, with nature and with his own spirit, was being eroded, and where there was replacement it was another rearrangement in right-angled patterns of multiplications of the cell. There was no longer any sense of cities growing, but merely of a mass of buildings without any discernible centre or heart advancing to all the points of the compass.

I remember when, with the loss of the three still fresh, I sat at dinner beside a man who was said to control one of the great financial empires of the world, and heard him tell how important it was for his organisation to keep expanding because the moment it ceased to expand it would lose its dynamic. I wanted to protest and say that this for me was a dynamic of death. This was so great a defiance of the laws of proportion that it could only lead to disaster. There must be a point at which enough was enough. Nothing in the dialogue which followed between us could remove the fact that, at heart, there was a confusion between 'expansion' and 'growth'. They are not the same. They are not even substitutes for each other, because this process of expansion out of control, which the skyline and the sprawl of London suggested that man was caught up in, was death to growth. Indeed, I had no doubt that expansion could only end in the death of growth in terms of a life of increase and wholeness.

What made it even more depressing was that this masquerade of the part, and the partial, as the whole of what man needed to build for himself and his societies, was already in command of terrifying areas of contemporary life. It was there, for instance, in the increasing phenomenon of the 'takeover bid' in the marketplaces of the world – an illustration that no longer needs any clarification. It was there in sociology and politics, where conformity was regarded as an imperative of unity; yet it is in fact a grisly kind of unity which in its turn becomes a source of weakness and death to the spirit of creation, because it eliminates all the infinite options of life and diversities of motivation which can be contained without loss of identity in a harmonious whole, which is the only unity that is a source of strength.

It is there in the increasing peril of numbers, stampeding with a mad geometrical progress over all forms of life, compelling societies to select and produce from the infinite variety of nature only that which satisfies and pleases its own provisional needs of the moment, and rejecting and eliminating all the other forms of life and environment that impede so partial a view of existence.

Already the numbers are so great that the world scene regarded purely in terms of human survival reveals how fast the earth is losing its capacity to feed the proliferating millions, how fast the atmosphere is running out of air for the millions to breathe and stay alive. Even the life of the sea can no longer multiply at a rate to satisfy this hunger and, far from increasing or even standing still, sees its own forms of life diminishing and about to vanish altogether. It is as if procreation is become anti-creation and constitutes the most formidable attack that has ever been mounted on the totality of nature and the wholeness of man.

More profound and subtle – and far more dangerous – is the peril of men in such numbers that each man is induced to become a number himself and is steadily losing the vital differences on which his integrity as an individual depends, and substituting a kind of common denominatorism of the spirit in areas which were once his own and highly differentiated, enabling him to exorcise conformity and make a contribution uniquely his own to the life of his time.

This process seems to me to be manifest most glaringly and energetically in our attitude to time. There too the unit is taking over from the whole, and I am fearful in saying this because I am speaking of one of the greatest lifegiving mysteries of all. We do not know what time is. We have no words ultimately to define it. The great and awesome equations of relativity and the theme of a space/time continuum help us ultimately as little as the classical concept of the Platonic year and its seasons. All we know is that creation came out of time. All mythologies speak of time. It may not have been there before creation. It may be a product of creation stirring in the chaos and old night that was said to be there in the beginning, but it certainly came no later than the creation. It was already there, enfolding all, and equipped with a law which was beyond appeal, even when the forces of creation became symbols, and the symbols images, and the deified personages appeared on Olympus and were worshipped in the valleys of the Nile in Thebes and Babylon, along the rivers of the Ganges and the Yangtse, and in the foothills of the Himalayas. There was already time, and an acknowledgement that the role of time, however mysterious, had to be recognised and had a role to play in the human spirit that no other reality had.

All that seems to me to have changed, and time itself is under attack. Not a day goes by without my hearing someone say somewhere, 'I am just killing time' – time of which we have so little and which in any case kills all in the end when it is no longer right for them to live, and will kill them even sooner when they have forfeited, as they are forfeiting now, their right to live.

The rebellion against time shows itself perhaps most in the compulsion to make life faster. There is not so much a love as a lust for speed, for doing things quickly, which totally ignores the fact that time is nothing if not measured, and that every plant, animal, organisation, stone, star and cosmic system has its own unique measure of time and this measure demands obedience to the rhythm of seasons and renewal. We, however, improve on the 'killing time' mentality with the slogan that 'time is money', speeding up all the processes not merely of traffic and travel, which is perhaps the least harmful of all, but processes of growth in plants, in flesh and blood, in reaching deep into the mystery of the ultimate genetic units and beginning to manipulate life for our own busy ends so that in systems everywhere 'being' has been taken out of life and a compulsive and frantic 'doing' and busyness put into its place.

The seconds have become so important that it is regarded as economic justification enough to cut fractions of seconds from the speed at which men and horses can run, and other instruments of travel can perform a journey from A to B, and even there a conformity already has moved in to kill, so that one hardly can speak as algebrists do of an A and a B but of moving only from one A to another form of A, the lifegiving differences have gone, felled by the same process that lops off the seconds. So today the importance of the second is moving in on the place once occupied by the minute, the minute moving in on the hour, the hour on the day, the day on the week, the week on the month and all on the years, serving ultimately a hubris grown so great that, as always in the past, fate will inflict on life disaster great enough to restore it to its proportions and give time back its measure.

There is also the worship which follows logically from the love and increase of numbers, and that is the love of size, the proliferation of ounces and inches, and hence a state of spirit which worships giantism and has lost all contact with the small, the invisible seed of creation on which all creation depends.

The list is endless, but increasingly to me these could only be described as symptoms of a sickness of spirit, a sickness which in its very small and ludicrous way was a headache in my boyhood and which today for me is part of the totality of cancer. And here I find myself like another Edward, overcome by a stammer of my own, the totality too large for my powers of expression and powers of awareness. I was certain only that the hypothesis on which all the research into the phenomenon of cancer and all the dedication devoted to discovering a cure was based, was totally inadequate. There is too much excluded from the basis on which men attempt to explain this affliction. The great unknown, if it were to yield more of its mystery, had to be approached from many other directions, so that it would be possible for them all to meet in the master dimension and serve the totality of the onslaught. Why not, for instance, begin as I had had to begin and look for it in the dream, and in what dreams through men, because that was the origin of the first intimations that I can vouch for? And that is the dimension to which the relief from pain, and Edward's sense of privilege, and the metamorphosis of Job's comfort all point. There is, somewhere beyond it all, an undiscovered country to be pioneered and explored, and only a few lonely and mature spirits take it seriously and are trying to walk it – although the recognition is already there in the child and his nurse, who take nothing more seriously than what the grown-up dismisses as a sentimental whimsey; this land of dreams. There, on the frontier of that land, I had no concepts, I had no ideas, I had no knowledge that could take me further, but through the three in the main, and many others of my acquaintance in part, I had been led to accept that the whole answer to this dark totality was there for the duration of our asking. It seemed to me that cancer in its paradoxical role was there not just as an instrument of the great reaper, or the great uprooter of the dream – it was extraordinary how only platitudes seemed to serve these ancient images – but also as a desperate attempt on the part of creation to make man and his physicians whole themselves, the healing that was once the 'making whole', that led to 'holiness'.

There I had to leave it with a tired brain and a tired pen, and as I left it to grow wherever it wanted to grow out of the as yet

unreceived imagery from my spirit, there came another experience to make a four. At this I felt a quickening of heart, because
if the three were about to become four-square in the spirit, the
four themselves could be circled.

This then was the four. As usual, it came, however interest-
ingly, in a matter-of-fact way which did not suggest anything
extraordinary. Eva Monley, a close friend and a well-known
producer of films, told me that she had been invited to work on
the development of a film about a professional jockey and a
horse that had been condemned and would have been destroyed
if the jockey had not taken up its story. She was, she said,
somehow attracted by what she had seen of the screenplay but
would tell me more when she had read it. In retrospect it seemed
only hours later that she spoke to me again with some excitement and said that the story was far more interesting than she
had thought, because not only the horse but also the jockey had
been condemned. He had been found to have terminal cancer
and was told that the chances of his survival were so small that
he was as condemned as the horse. Like the three before him,
he refused to accept the diagnosis as final. Somewhere at the
back of his mind he said: 'I am not going to die before I have
won the Grand National.'

For those of us interested in horses there can be no race in the
world like the Grand National. Everyone who knows anything
about it knows that anyone's chances of winning it are almost
in the region of the chances that one has of recovering from a
terminal cancer. Very few who pitch themselves against fate on
this racecourse in a lifetime of trying ever succeed in winning
the Grand National. Some are physically broken in the course
of their careers. One or two have even been killed and a lot of
horses have died in this point-to-point, as it were, of life and
death. The horse had been put out into a stable where it would
be properly cared for and given every chance of recovering,
which many doubted it could. The jockey himself took to heart
as deeply as anybody could the exhortation to fight the affliction. He did all that the specialists advised him to do. The
medicines prescribed for his particular cure were so dire and
their consequences so awful that halfway through the cure he

did not want to live and, even when that reluctance was over-come, thought that he would die of a combination of drugs and the affliction. But he won through, and at the end, although he was declared well again physically, he had changed so greatly in appearance that he did not recognise himself in the mirror, and those near to him only had to look at him to be upset. He had lost all his hair; his muscles and reflexes were atrophied; the body ached perpetually because of what he had been through; and he was told even in his convalescence that when fully restored he would never be able to ride professionally again and, what was worse, would never be able to have children.

All this was superbly put on to film, and there came a Sunday morning when my wife and Jessica and I were invited by Eva to a showing of the film in the Haymarket. From the beginning I was gripped as I have seldom been gripped, which is only par-tially explained by the especial history that pre-conditioned me to an extra involvement with the film. As I saw the horse, whole and well, begin the story on the screen, running full out, its mane in the wind, it had all the power of a plenipotentiary of all the horses there had ever been in the life of man. From there the story developed and finally ended with the condemned man and his horse reprieved, in partnership at Aintree, and winning the race. If it had been make-believe, it would have been well enough done by my friend and her director to be accepted as valid and even great fiction. But it was more than fiction. It was more even than fairy tale. It was in some way myth in an area of the mythological in us all where myths are facts, and facts are myths. It was true in the way things and events are only truly transcended when they and the story which they are called to live become one, and the ending is not only happy but full of meaning. As I listened to the applause that broke out all around us in the cinema, and afterwards came out onto the steps and faced the London traffic again, I was back on the day of Charlie's memorial service at St Paul's. In my mind I had retreated to that moment when I was listening to Brendel and Beethoven's music and seeing the horse, bareback and his bare-foot rider move out to where, with the last chord of all, they took the horizon as a last fence in a Grand National of the universe, as if to say, 'Look! You may not always see it like this in the here and now, but ultimately all endings are happy endings. The human comedy finally is divine.'

And at that moment Eva took my arm and pointed and I recognised the man, Bob Champion, whom I had just seen winning his Grand National on the screen. There was a young woman with him and she carried a baby in her arms. I did not need my friend's prompting to recognise that here was the threesome, and his horse had been the fourth. In this area from which the fourth came, I seemed to recognise the element that made a four of the three as they walked in a burning fiery furnace far back in a Babylonian moment of history.

I found myself left with the thought that it was the jockey's love of the horse and faith in the horse which gave him access to all the enormous energies which are in the province of man's immemorial associations with the horse, and the horse with man. I was utterly convinced that neither he nor the horse would have run the race so triumphantly, neither of them indeed would have been healed as they had been healed, if fate had not made them keep so strange and significant a company. I had a feeling as if my imagination was intruding in an area where it should cross itself, although there was nobody in the world with which the horse and jockey were involved who would not have thought it preposterous to make such an association with so popular and worldly a sport. I myself was amazed, in trying to analyse my feelings, at the energies available at such an ancient level of man and horse in partnership; at this element which made Job lay his hand upon his mouth and remark that he knew only that his redeemer lived. It was clear to me that, even in the soberest reflection, what had happened to this man and his horse was a form of redemption, of 'punishment' redeemed, a suffering that was a privilege and led to increase and new meaning. Both horse and man had been bonded in suffering, both had been deeply wounded, condemned and, even when uncondemned, rejected. And yet they had run their race and run it well because they were bonded in a depth that only an experience of cosmic suffering could have produced. It seemed to me that, whether he knew it or not, consciously or unconsciously, the man and what was instinctive in the horse were joined in love and trust, and had it not been for that love of the horse, the love of something totally beyond himself, both man and horse would have perished and another fateful race would not have been run.

I was suddenly aware of how unconscious I had been of my interest in the man and the horse and their prelude of being condemned, and their suffering, and that my interest had been quickened because, far back in time, I had a horse of my own, and a life around the horse which began a process of thinking and feeling in me which, unseen and untended, had continued and prospered until this instant of recognition; and there hung a tale far greater than I knew at that moment.

4
Bird of the Wind

And so there then was Diamond. He was there so suddenly and vividly that I was startled at the enormity of not having thought about him for so many years. This aspect of it was expressed for me by a Negro song that Paul Robeson had sung when I first came to England, 'Oh Waterboy, where have you bin hidin'?'. Everything that I associated with that song – originally uttered by a chain gang of black people in the American South, driven, parched and overworked to a fatigue that was acute pain, and to whom the waterboy came literally and symbolically as a deliverer – came back to me, and I found myself going through the words of the song silently with: 'Oh Diamond, where have you been hiding?' And hard by Diamond, just as suddenly, there was Windvoel, literally Windbird, or rather Bird of the Wind, as the English idiom demands.

The emotions of this recall were so intense, despite the seventy years of silence in between the experience we shared and the present, that I felt more sure than ever that the race against cancer at Aintree could not have been won had it not been for similar emotions and energies of spirit stored up in the soul of man by his timeless association with the horse. My life in London suddenly seemed unreal and singularly impoverished and colourless compared to this world where I rejoined Diamond and Bird of the Wind. There they walked and communed together as if in some privileged empire of the universe, still full of the magic and the magnetism as it had issued warm and trembling from the fingers of our maker. To my contemporary self nothing could have been more strange than that the three of us should have been so closely linked together; but to the other me, whose hand I took so firmly with my own just then, nothing could have been stranger than that I should be where I was at that moment of recall.

Yet there was one element of strangeness about our threesome even then that should enter into the reckoning before I go on with Diamond, and that was Bird of the Wind. None of us knew anything much about his origins or pedigree. I think that, in part, accounted for his name. He was a person that had come to us like a bird on the wings of the wind from some lost world beyond the furthest horizons of the interior of Africa. My old nurse, Klara, who loved Bird of the Wind, would always warn me and my family about him. She described him in a metaphor of her own that meant 'an inspired rogue', and implied that his was a form of genius which one had not to despise but to love. My grandfather said she was right, and in one of his rare ironic moments said that Bird of the Wind made him think of our Lord's injunction that man had not only to be as cunning as a serpent but also as gentle as a dove. He thought that, in mixing all the elements that went into the making of Bird of the Wind, his designer forgot above the dove.

Yet my grandfather too loved him dearly, as we all did, because this inspired form of cunning was also at our disposal, a form of ancient primordial wisdom essential for survival in an unpredictable Africa and an instrument, as far as we were concerned, always of love of the family that sheltered him. It did not matter that the cooks and servants continually complained about a steep rise in the consumption of sugar, which was a rare luxury, or that my father wondered why the cigars in his great silver cigar box appeared noticeably fewer than when he had last opened it for his guests, or that a bottle or two of brandy or wine had suddenly gone missing from the cellar, and all these strange visitations were blamed on Bird of the Wind. Yet he was never punished for any of these digressions, as anybody else, even we children, might have been. The most he suffered was some outburst of exasperated abuse which would make him look so forlorn and misunderstood that he was soon mollified with a gift of some delicacy which no exercise of virtue would have earned. This would be followed by a solemn shake of the head, that one could not expect anything else from such a creature – a description which lacks the affection implicit in its indigenous equivalent, '*skepsel*', which for me implied that he was a mere morsel of creation and could not therefore be expected to be anything but '*skelm*' – perhaps the best word in any language for roguery without malice.

Many people took him to be a Bushman, but Klara, as a Bushman herself, rejected the proposition with ardour. She admitted that he undoubtedly had Bushman blood, but her theory was that he was born of some nomadic moment during the long retreat of both Bushman and Hottentot before the invasion of their ancient lands by both black and white nations, although there was a long time as a child when I thought from the air of mystery which surrounded the way she spoke about him that one of the elements in his making indeed might have been the wind.

My grandfather seemed to favour Klara's theory as well because, when he bought his own vast lands from the Griquas, the last coherent fragments of Hottentot people in southern Africa, Bird of the Wind was already among them as a young boy herding a mixture of Hottentot and European sheep and cattle. He himself could not add to our knowledge because he found himself already in a Griqua context in their search for shelter deeper in the interior, and with a wave of the hand somewhere towards the great southwest he would indicate that he had come from 'yonder'. He had no knowledge of the past in a form that we could understand but an imagination clearly enriched by a mixture of aboriginal sources that made all he told us as colourful as any of the great rainbows seen after thunderstorms in Africa.

It came out, above all, in the endless stories he told us in which the principal characters were seldom human beings and made no sense to the grown-up people around me, but to me, who accepted the existence and principle of a magic which invested and transformed all living and even inanimate things, made more sense than many of the things I was taught at home and at school. And when there were elements which seemed to defy comprehension, the explanation seemed to me entirely convincing: one could not possibly understand the behaviour of some of the plant and animal heroes if one did not know their language.

According to Klara, Bird of the Wind earned a great deal of tobacco money by providing lovesick Griquas with herbs which he gathered in the veld at night, and which were said to be effective only when they were gathered when the moon and the stars in their constellations were in certain places. It was whispered even that one of the foremost pioneers in our community consulted him in all sorts of circumstances where fortune-telling, prophecy and magic ointments from some root or tuber were combined. I myself had an inkling of this side of him when I started accompanying him on small missions. For instance, my first recollection is of one occasion during the excessive heat of the day when he stopped in the veld and between the bush and the grass pointed to what looked like a very small curl of green shaped rather like a little pig's tail, thriving in a tiny patch of its own. He gave a little bound of delight and pulled out his knife, went down on his knees and very carefully began to dig the earth around this tiny growth. With great care, as if he were an archaeologist expecting ancient treasure to appear at any moment, he widened the circle of this little excavation far beyond what the sprig of green seemed to require, and as Bird of the Wind ultimately dug down deep enough to put his hand in and lever whatever was hidden in the earth with his fingers, he pulled out what looked like a sweet potato almost the size of a football. He cleaned it and then cut it into slices for us to eat. It was surprisingly full of a thick white juice, with a taste that was nutty and tart but wonderfully soothing in our parched mouths and throats. I remember as we sat there munching on our heels how he smacked his lips with satisfaction and waved his knife at the world and said that there were many, many more things like it hidden in the earth around us, and that even if all our cattle and goods were taken away he would keep us alive with the food that he could find underground. I did not doubt him then, and over the years he introduced me to so many other forms of what we came to call veld-food that I had implicit faith in the claim.

It was not surprising, therefore, that with such an imagination he had a very special relationship with the earth, the plants, the insects, the birds, the animals and even the weather, and confidently claimed that he could hear the hunting cries of the stars which packed the night sky, because the stars, although we may not realise it, were the greatest hunters of all. I recollect many moments when all around us felt enchanted, and somehow all the multitude of patois of the world and the universe were at his command and, as he spoke to things, they replied in kind.

This was apparent even in the prosaic details of service on a great and complex pioneering farm. For instance, I remember the wagons loaded with wool setting out on their two-day journey to the nearest railhead for shipment to the coast. Each wagon was drawn by a span of eighteen oxen, and my grandfather's farm by then was so well established that each span of eighteen was composed of oxen of the same colour and the same wide spread of horn. Each ox had a name, and would respond to it when Bird of the Wind's keen eye and intuition thought it was slacking; and it was noticeable how all the team in his charge were so responsive that, even if they set out last, they would usually arrive first at the railhead and be the first wagon home. We would know almost to the hour when the wagons would be coming home, and it seemed to me that long before we caught sight of them winding slowly towards our upland and the hills around home one could hear Bird of the Wind's voice and, like a punctuation mark in the grammar of transport, the crack of the long oxwhip lash as it flickered over a delinquent head to add emphasis to his exhortation. These exhortations had something of the Old Testament about them in that Old Testament country – as that world of sheep and cattle and occasional water seemed to me. And this exhortation, the louder it came, was transformed by its fervour into something of a sustained hallelujah when he saw the roofs of home and his oxen got the sniff of water and the smell of trees and the unyoking awaiting them after a long journey, just there beyond the curve of one of our hills.

Long before I was born it was discovered that Bird of the Wind's inspired gift of communication with all that was natural included what was for me a very special and mysterious affinity with horses. There was no history of partnership between man and horse in southern Africa. Neither Bushman nor Hottentot – who had a more sophisticated culture and possessed sheep and cattle of their own breed and selection – had seen horses before the arrival of the European in southern Africa, and yet there was Bird of the Wind who seemed to know horses, and horses to know him, in the way that not a single one of us did. Indeed, even pooling all that we knew about horses, it seemed to me very little and strangely functional and unsubtle compared to the extraordinary and magical intimacy that existed between them and Bird of the Wind. As a result of this gift he was already the equivalent of what on a farm in Britain would have been called a head carter, and was responsible for all the horses in my grandfather's establishment.

I do not know exactly how many horses that involved. We always had anything from eight to twelve in the stables for daily use, but there were many more turned loose on the veld and brought in from time to time, for special occasions, or to be selected for breaking in as riding horses, or trained for pulling various carts and transport vehicles. All in all our horses were an impressive bunch, and seemed to possess a singularly happy blend of the wild and the tame in their natures. Just as we would put on our best clothes and behaviour to go to town, so they had the same happy knack of becoming 'horses about town', without any loss of identity.

Bird of the Wind was said to be by far the best breaker-in of horses. To see him ride a horse was an extraordinary experience. He did not seem to mind whether he rode bareback or in a saddle; once mounted he seemed to be part of the horse, and even the rawest recruit among the horses going through its first day of being broken in seemed to take to the exercise far more readily than when one of the other farm riders was in charge. Often I watched Bird of the Wind riding on a horse which he had only just brought in from the veld simply by beckoning it; and the horse, before allowing him to lay hands on it, would lower its head and sniff all over him from head to foot, as a dog might when it wants to get to know another being totally. Once that was done, the horse would allow Bird of the Wind to slip a halter over its head and would stand at ease, almost welcoming what was to follow. Bird of the Wind would leap lightly onto its back and ride on to round up the other horses as if in possession of all the accoutrement that other riders would have demanded for such a mission. And, watching him, I had the strange illusion that for a while horse and man were one and that I was witnessing what I had already seen in my books on Greek mythology – the primordial man-horse or horse-man, the Centaur.

All these sorts of impressions were singularly warming and reassuring to me in a way that I took for granted and even to this day have never tried to explain, for how can one explain all the many things in nature that please the eye, are tasteful to tongue and palate, bring joy to the ear and especially to the touch of the hand – that oldest and greatest language that there ever was for expressing something that all the words which we have found since the beginning of time cannot yet express, and is indeed so precious that in the world of today, where this language of the touch of the hand is fast diminishing, it is almost as if some vital food for the spirit is being denied to us and unless we recover it in time we might vanish because of the lack of it?

One of the earliest pleasures I discovered for myself had to do with these horses when they first were stabled. It was as if Bird of the Wind thought it essential to make a feast of the occasion. Two days before they were brought in he gathered buckets of yellow Indian corn – the golden 'mealie' of Africa. These were put in fresh water from the spring, and, as the moment of the arrival of the horses came nearer, the smell of the maize, swollen and full and about to ferment, filled the stables and its outhouses like the scent of a meal being prepared for celebration in our own large kitchens. It was for me a most exciting smell, and when the new batch of horses were being led to their looseboxes in the stable and this smell assailed them, their nostrils would begin to quiver and a shiver of delight go through their burnished bodies, and at times I thought even their manes quivered with anticipation and delight. Once they were in, and each horse was fastened to the long wooden crib which connected the string of looseboxes, I would put myself into a corner against the wall nearest to the entrance and watch Bird of the Wind take bunches of the newly threshed corn and cut them into short lengths on a sickle firmly fixed in the wall of the crib. As the pile of straw lengths rose higher he would shove it from one end of the crib to the other. This added to the excitement of the horses, who began to get restless and make noises to one another, almost as if to say: 'How much longer is this going to take? And in any case, what the hell are they giving us for dinner tonight?'

This feeling of anticipation and excitement would communicate itself to me, and there were moments when I was so identified with the horses that I became critical of Bird of the Wind and thought that he was deliberately slowing the process down and teasing the horses unnecessarily. But when the crib was at last full of straw he went out and brought in buckets of the swollen corn, and instantly that smell of clean straw, of freshly groomed and brushed horses and the dry bedding spread on the cobbles underneath their feet, joined together and became a kind of incense, the thought of which excites me still. The wet and swollen maize was then thickly spread from one end of the crib to the other, and in the process Bird of the Wind deftly mixed together the cut straw and the maize. By the time he had finished, the horses had their heads so eagerly and busily in the crib that he could no longer make his way upright to the door but had almost to crawl on his hands and knees below their arched necks to get out of the stable.

The sound of the horses munching was sheer music both to Bird of the Wind and to me. He would look, with the twilight clearly on his face at the door, like someone whose special mission had just been fulfilled. And although they were horses, and I knew that he was just a person whom time had brought into our lives with one of its unpredictable gusts, his whole attitude and expression reminded me of a New Testament story told to us by my mother, where our Lord gathered his disciples around him and said: 'Feed ye, my sheep.'

In addition to the feeling of wellbeing and enjoyment which

the occasion gave me, I felt also that it was a very authoritative way of eating, and for a long time at dinner at night I tried to see if I could not chew my own food in so loud and authoritative a manner. I was secretly disappointed that my own chewing sounded extremely feeble, and that even a burst of the loudest chewing I could accomplish did not seem to have any effect at all on my brother and sister sitting beside me. When on one occasion, in despair, I asked them if they had noticed anything special about my chewing, I was reduced to silence because the retort was a crushing: 'If we heard anything of the sort we would report you to Miss F for bad manners at table.' Miss F was a governess specially imported from Holland to prepare my sisters for life and in general to impose a Dutch idea of good manners on us. Neither of us found anything to favour in the other, and her power of curbing my natural ways was already so great that I was not going to allow her to spoil what was an exercise in pure music to me.

Even after being in the stables for the whole ritual I would often, after prayers when the house was being prepared for sleep and the last reminiscences of the day were being mulled over in the drawing-room, slip out and go to the stables and take up my position in the corner. By this time the horses seemed to have accepted me as one of their company and always emitted a sound of some kind and occasionally even an heraldic nicker of welcome, and I would sit there for as long as I could, listening to the munching as if there was nothing more wonderful than munching that way, on and on into the night.

So in this and many other ways I grew closer to Bird of the Wind's community of horses, as I came to think of it, and not the horses the rest of my family knew – more or less only when they met them for a specific function, in carts and carriages or as mounts to ride around the farm on duty, hurry into town on an urgent mission to fetch the doctor or bring out overdue mail, ride to dances and drive the older people to and fro to call on neighbours and, above all, to go once every three months to those imperative holy weekends of the year when the celebration of Holy Communion was obligatory. I knew the horses like that too, but I had a profound satisfaction that they, through Bird of the Wind, were always at home to us in a way they were not to any other two people in the world.

Good as all these things were, and good as they still feel in recall, there was one question that puzzled and bewildered me: why did Bird of the Wind's encounters with the horses always have to start with their sniffing Bird of the Wind all over? What was it that made the best of all our horses – assigned for duty only to pull the Spider (our equivalent of a coach of state, and always named after a legendary Dutch aristocrat) – not only sniff so pointedly at Windvoel but, as he inspected their bridles to see that their harness and headstalls were properly in place before the start of the final journey down the hills and through the pass into town, try to put their noses into the bulging side pockets of his coat? I was certain they were not looking for the sugar we might have kept there, as we sometimes did for our favourite horses. Windvoel would never have given them sugar and became very angry when he saw other people doing so.

What puzzled me even more was what followed the sniffing. From where I sat or stood I would notice Windvoel looking around him to make certain that we were busy getting into the Spider in an orderly manner and that he was unobserved, and then his hand would vanish in his pocket and within seconds the horses withdrew their heads and seemed unusually contented, looking straight ahead and chewing over their bits. What is more, on the last lap of the journey down into our little town, past the church and along the main street where the farmers had opened up their church houses and were either talking in groups in the streets or sitting in the shade on their verandahs watching what passed for great traffic in the village, Windvoel on the box seemed to change personality and become a person of great importance and would start to sing quietly, between half-open lips, little songs in praise of himself.

Over the years, particularly when I came to ride my own horse beside the Spider and next to his coachman's box, I heard enough to get the drift of these refrains. Invariably they were to this effect:

Who is he who sits so high?
Who is he who tells the horses the way?
Who is he whose feather in his hat travels in the dust of the
*   street beside him?*
Who is he who fills the eyes of everyone on the road?
Why, Windvoel, you child of a Bushman, it is you.

And the refrain had a rhythm to it which was syncopated to the rhythm of the horses' feet.

I would notice that at this stage of the journey all fatigue had left them; they were picking up their legs high and bringing them down with a will, so that the sound echoed from one side of the street to the other and an intense feeling of occasion possessed us all, so much so that we could have been the forerunners of a royal procession straight from the land of Windvoel's wildest dreams, following up in the most stately fashion behind.

I did not know the answer to my question until just before the arrival of Diamond in my life, but the quiet speculation which went on in my mind constantly could easily have turned to some sort of nasty suspicion and caused me to speak to my parents or even to my grandfather about it if it had been connected with anybody else but Bird of the Wind. It was almost as if I was on the fringe of some kind of sacred mystery, something that I could not understand without speaking the language of the horse as Bird of the Wind did, and as the horses themselves understood Bird of the Wind.

But there was one aspect in particular that troubled me and brought me near to doubt. I began to notice that, every time we returned from town, for several days our special horses seemed curiously unsettled, restless and almost erratic and jerky where they had been steady, calm and rhythmical, and that, whenever Bird of the Wind appeared near them on the veld, they would detach themselves from the other horses and gallop towards him and submit him to another round of sniffing.

The mystery all this constituted became of such intense import to me that I might have shared it with those closest to me, but I had a feeling that that might be an abuse of privilege and that if I did so the mystery would end and the atmosphere of magic that surrounded the world I shared with Bird of the Wind would vanish for ever.

The answer I was seeking came at the height of the lambing season before Diamond – already my life was approaching its divide into the world 'before Diamond' and the world 'after Diamond'. Everything that happened in that last lambing season, and indeed on the farm and in town, seemed taut with a tension of unconscious, and therefore profound, transition. I found myself looking at things all around me and for the first time having a feeling that I was about to say goodbye – not to anything specific but a goodbye in general, a goodbye to everything – and on this cold, clear winter's afternoon I was sent to accompany Bird of the Wind to look for lambs which had presumably been lost, because in counting the breeding flock that afternoon it was found to be seven short of the number that had left in the morning. We began our search in the hills immediately behind the homestead where there was shelter against the keen winter air and in particular where there was a long pool of water still half full from the rains of a plentiful summer. There were rushes, bushes and grass around it, birds with their nests like golden tassels tied to the tops of a kind of bamboo reed, and it was one of the favourite places for turning out ewes coming down to lamb. Bird of the Wind said that he would search the whole of this area because this was probably where most of the gathering would have to be done, and he sent me on a long, roundabout route to look through the hills rising in a rough kind of semicircle above the pool and the shallow depression of grass beyond it.

My search, which I conducted on foot, first imitating the bleating of a ewe that had lost a lamb then standing still and waiting for the reply, took a long time, and when I had come to the last tip of this crescent of hills and emerged between two ironstone boulders, red in the level light of the sun, with two of the tallest wind aloes standing like Byzantine candles beside me, I did a last imitation of a mother's despairing bleat, of which I was rather proud, stood still and, listening for a while, looked around me. At that moment my eyes caught the light of the sun, yellow in the pool, and beyond the pool something else which had not been there before. It was a very still moment. There would be, I was certain, a cold breath of air which the dying sun always expels in its last moment on the dark blue horizon, but just now there was not enough movement to stir a leaf. It was silent and it was still, and not a movement of air or sound could have gone undetected. Indeed it was as if the stillness were a pool without a ripple upon it but so intense that it was on the verge of some kind of substance, transparent with calm and as yellow as the pool and the westering light. And then, hard by the pool at the heart of this golden stillness, there was a movement behind a clump of bamboo reeds, strangely without the birds that should have been perched there, saluting the sinking sun with song and ready for the nest at so advanced an hour.

This movement had colour to it but barely any substance. It was not the colour of any air or of anything substantial, and I could only think it had to be some kind of smoke that I had never seen before. I lost all interest in ewes and missing lambs just then, and began to stalk this something rising so slowly like the intention of the sky to form a cloud rather than the achieved cloud itself. I found myself full of a kind of awe which only an excitement I had never experienced before kept at bay, and I went on stalking, as Bird of the Wind had taught me to stalk. He had taught me well, so well that his teaching was his undoing, because I came to cover behind a clump of bamboo reeds without having been noticed, slowly rose inside it and looked over it, and there, stretched out on his tummy, was Bird of the Wind. I could see his face, strangely resolved and ecstatic, and his mouth inhaling from something invisible, and then his whole head and face withdrawing as he turned on his back and slowly blew a strange-smelling smoke into the sky.

For a moment I panicked. I wanted to creep away and pretend that I had seen nothing of whatever it was that was happening, something I now was certain could only be utterly forbidden. But I just could not and had a sense only to withdraw slowly until I was about a dozen or more paces away and then call out 'Windvoel!'; and as he came upright in his place, I walked to meet him and said, 'Windvoel, what on earth are you doing?'

For a moment, as he looked as if he were searching desperately for a plausible lie, his expression became that of the Windvoel of what Klara had called 'a cunning without malice'. But this went, as the most innocent and resolved look came over his face, and he said, almost as if in a whisper: 'Little old one, this is where I breathe fire and smoke.'

And then it all came out, and as it came out I had a sense of foreboding and of guilt and of doing something that my elders and his betters would have condemned if they knew. But the moment the spirit of condemnation fled I began to take great pleasure in the revelation that followed, and I could not do anything but marvel at the beauty of the invention.

At places on the edge of the pool the sandstone layers hidden deep in the earth protruded and formed overhangs that were like the mouths of smallish caves, with the openings hidden by the grass and rushes that grew around them. In between and on the left facing due east was the biggest of these openings, and there, in the darkest corner underneath the ledge, where it would have been normally almost too dark to see but where now with the level sun from the west there was enough reflected light, I saw what looked like a miniature oven, beautifully made out of the dark black clay of the pool, 'pot clay' as we called it, because we could make pots, urns and indeed, as we children did, fashion toy cattle and animals for our play. The shape was very like the inside of the great big oven we used for doing all our baking at the homestead. The only difference was that at one end it had what looked like the mouthpiece of a bamboo flute, and at the far end it had some kind of hard-baked clay container which seemed to be oozing this blue smoke which had drawn me to the place. Beside it stood a rather battered enamel cup which Bird of the Wind always carried tied by a thong to his waist. The mug was half full of water, and on the other side of the oven there was a small pile of dark brown leaves of a plant that I instantly knew, because it was the equivalent in our world of what forbidden fruit had been in Paradise. It was what the Bushmen called 'dagga' and the Zulus ''nsangu'. Although rare in its wild state, it was known all over Africa and in many parts of the world, including Mexico, which gave it the popular name it possesses to this day – marijuana.

It was a plant so coveted in the ancient world that societies who took to it and used it regularly to raise their spirits and imagination to a Dionysian or Bacchic height, were inspired to form strange brotherhoods of its initiates, the most famous of which perhaps were the Hashish-Hassan of the Middle East – their name for the plant being 'hashish'. They went on to exploit for illicit purposes the strange fervour it aroused in their spirit and hired themselves out as professional murderers, so that the word 'assassin', still used in precisely this way, is a derivative of 'Hashish-Hassan'.

However, there was no trace of any criminal or abnormal intent on Bird of the Wind's face when he spoke to me, only a strange look of something pure and innocent and childlike, mysteriously recovered of some kind of secret joy hidden in the midst of a harsh, bleak and unforgiving upbringing. It was a look that came from behind life, of a childhood of great suffering and deprivation and a life that was not natural to him, and that the look was not of my imagining then, or a projection of hindsight earned in the long years since we stood there, wrapt in the yellow stillness of a declining evening with the great uplands of the interior of Africa flung wide open around us like the doors of a vast temple, is as objective and inspiring a fact as the crest of Everest.

He even found words instinctively to confirm this, saying in effect: 'Little old one, this place is where I come when I feel weak and want the weakness to go.'

'And this,' I added, 'is what the horses are really searching for when they come up sniffing all over you, and this is where they get the power to go through the streets of our town raising their heads so high and almost dancing along the road.'

He smiled an unforgettable smile at me, and his whole face creased into more wrinkles than I had ever thought could come into one face. With a giggle that I had never heard before, he exclaimed happily: 'Little old one, you too are a rogue like all of us!' And for rogue he used that untranslatable word '*skelm*', which meant a person not only full of cunning and ingenuity without malice but one with a secret so dear that he holds to it as if his life and growth depend on it.

For a moment it was almost as if Bird of the Wind and I had participated in a kind of communion. He went down on his hands and knees, put his mouth to the mouthpiece again and tugged at it until the densest mist of blue I had yet seen came from the far end of the oven. His cheeks bulging with smoke, he withdrew from the mouthpiece, picked up the mug, swallowed some water and then spat it out with some of the blue smoke not absorbed accompanying it like a wisp of final mist. Then he stood up, looked around him as if in guilt, and exclaimed: 'We must hurry! We still have some lambs to find. But don't worry, I know where they are.'

I did not need convincing. Somehow I realised that he had known all along where they were. But I did worry. I worried deeply for him, because I knew that if his secret were ever discovered he would be subjected to the heaviest of penalties under our law, penalties from which no love of our family would have been able to protect him. So in great fear I said to him, 'Windvoel, for Heitse Eibib's sake' – I used the name of the Hottentot god as being dearest to him – 'you must never let anybody find you doing this. You must never let anybody know what you are doing to the horses. You know what it will mean if they find out.'

He was unshaken by my concern and just said with a smile of utter conviction: 'But, little old one, the horses won't tell.'

And then there was not only sincerity and cunning but also 'cunning without malice' in the answer because he knew, putting it that way, that it would not occur to me to tell. And until this moment I have not told, and perhaps would not have told even now if it had not summed up so much of the inner eventfulness on the way to Diamond and beyond.

But the feeling of 'all being well in the kingdom of the horses' which my life with Diamond and Bird of the Wind kept alive in me, and which even in the hindsight of many years seems to have dominated the main shape of my life, was suddenly shattered. In the world of the human beings that surrounded me everything changed, and changed, I felt, for the worse.

I was barely seven, and all the wonder, the magic and the miracle packed into those seven years made it into a great era, compared to which many of the decades that followed seemed at times to be mere spans. Then my father died, and the family gradually left the farm; and before long I went away to school.

Although our life became very different, my own contact with the world of Bird of the Wind and our great farm continued. My elder brother had come rushing back from Cornell University in America when my father died, to help my mother with the farm. He decided to make his base there, but he had come home with a strange epileptic-like disease, which he kept hidden from the rest of the family and of which only he and I and my mother knew. I was often sent to keep him company in case he had one of his horrendous spasms. Everyone commiserated with me for having to leave my friends and the pleasures of the vacation they were about to enjoy, and I set off at first in a mood of rebellion, but once on the farm, alone with this strange and at times almost demented brother, but with a vast library to draw on and the company of black companions and, above all, Bird of the Wind, I became singularly content, and when the time came to go back to the city to school, I felt like someone returning to prison.

And yet, with my father's going and his whole world now out of reach, there was nonetheless a great feeling of deprivation and the sense of a black hole in the midst of all my contentment. I do not know how long it lasted in days and months, because calendars do not measure the length of either joy or misery; indeed they tell one nothing whatsoever to enlighten this inner relativity of time. But I do know the day came when I was out of it. It came when I had gone to the milking kraals. That was something that gave me great satisfaction: watching the cows being milked at night and in the morning by their own 'Sutho herdsmen. They were the best milkers I have ever seen in the world, and the force of the milk going into their gleaming metal pails was almost like the sound of a small storm of hail until the bucket began to fill up, and then it was like the rush of a minor cataract, until finally I could see this wonderful white substance rise and the foam raised by the force of the injection of the milk from the udder stood high in the pail.

It was my task to carry the pails from the milkers, empty them into large gleaming cans, and return with them empty to the milkers. I had just emptied such a pail, and the sun was already sinking behind the hills, when Bird of the Wind appeared.

I saw at once that he was in the grip of excitement. He urged me to come with him as soon as possible. The moment the last cow was milked and the impatient calves, who had been kept apart during the milking, were once more restored to their mothers – sucking the milk that had been left for them by the milkers with their eyes shut, so that nothing could intrude into the place within where they savoured this wonderful gift, and acknowledging it outwardly only with a flickering of their tails – I left, and could hardly keep up with Bird of the Wind.

He walked fast and far into the hills to where the horses had been turned out for their season of freedom in the veld, towards a circle of dense broom bushes. There, on the side of the bushes, stood one of the best of our mares, suckling a new-born foal. The foal obviously had already drained the mare but was allowed, with the patience and obvious happiness of the mare, to go on sucking. Indeed, the foal was already so well fed that the moment Bird of the Wind spoke in his horse patois to the mare, the foal withdrew and swung round so fast that it nearly fell over, and had great trouble in steadying its untried and ungainly legs. To me it was always one of the wonders of foals that they seemed to be born with all the length of leg they would need as grown-up horses, but with a very little body that was all head, mane and tail above.

But once this little foal was steadied he looked at us, wondering whether he should go on looking or go for shelter on the far side of his mother; then he put his head slightly down and, although all aquiver with the tensions between curiosity and fear, went on bravely staring at us and, wonder of wonders, seemed to steady his look ultimately on me. The strangest of sensations went through me. It was as if I had known the foal before, as if I had known him well, that we had already been companions for long, long unremembered years, and were just about to rediscover something great that should never have been lost. Again I do not know how long this inspection between the foal and myself lasted. I was aware of a change in Bird of the Wind's patois. He said less and less, and ultimately was silent and joined in the staring. But in the end he could not resist, and the sound of triumph that would normally have been a yell of great excitement broke out of him and he said:

'You see, little old one, I knew it. I have been full of this coming for days. He knows you as you also know him. He is yours and you are his.'

The sound was enough to upset the delicate balance of considerations in the young foal's senses, and he whirled about so suddenly that again he nearly keeled over. He steadied himself and went behind his mother, only to reappear a little later in front of her, underneath her large neck and head, looking silently in our direction, and finally settling on me.

I could say much more about the encounter – it was full of the most exciting little incidents to me – but all that matters is that from that moment this black hole, this profound sense of deprivation, went, and something else moved into the vacancy; and at the centre of it was this little foal staring at me steadily with the yellow light of a fresh morning on his head, still with the sheen of the new-born like silk upon him, and already a dark brown mane and a black tail and a body of a burnished tan, and in the centre of his dark head, between wide eyes widely set, a white diamond which Bird of the Wind said was there to show us that it was a mark of something very special and rare that he had within. So there for us was Diamond.

For me and Bird of the Wind things were never the same again after the coming of Diamond. In one way nothing was changed. All that was good and rare between us was still there, but somehow within themselves had acquired something new, and the something new demanded that for some weeks, every morning when the milking came to an end, Bird of the Wind would join me, and he and I would go to visit Diamond and his mother.

The first night after our meeting I had been unreasonably afraid for Diamond. All the large carnivorous animals in our

area had been killed, the last of the leopards not long after I
had been born, and the last of the lions in my mother's girlhood.
But we still had masses of jackal, and in the hills a lot of little
families of lynx, one of the bravest and most beautiful of the
cat family in Africa. I did not really see those as a danger, but
I was worried about the great striped hyenas, the wolves as we
called them, who were great villains of Hottentot myth and
legend. One could never be sure about them, and that night as
I listened to the night plover piping up the stars on board the
ship of the night, and then the jackals with that strange melancholy yanking noise of theirs, I felt terribly uneasy that the
silent wolves with their powerful jaws could go for Diamond
and his mother. Although I had never heard of anything like
that happening in my lifetime, nonetheless the fear was there,
and it was with some relief that we found Diamond and his
mother safe and I could give the mother the crusts of bread
which Bird of the Wind had brought along with us, and begin
to make friends with her.

Within days I could see them looking eagerly towards us as we
came, and at last even walking forward slowly and confidently to
meet us, with Diamond frisking ever more energetically round
his mother and making little forays in our direction, and then
whirling about as if he had been too forward and sheltering
behind his mother for a moment of quiet meditation over what
he had dared to do without permission.

The best of these moments for me were the increasing number
of times when Diamond, comparatively near now, braced himself as against a wind, lifted his head and looked at me steadily
with those wide, large dark eyes of his, purple with the reflection of the great amount of blue above and about us. I would
look back, and the feeling would come of amazement that something so young could look also so old, like such an utterly new
version of all the life that had ever been, a life of which we were
not even conscious, but was present in this form of young being
facing me.

It was surprisingly like the look I had seen on the face of Bird
of the Wind when I first met him. He never looked anything
but a child of all the first and the oldest things in life, a poignant

paradox of utter innocence and unappeased hunger. The result had been that I never thought of Bird of the Wind as a creature of time. He seemed in a sense a timeless phenomenon, totally inexperienced and yet full of a knowledge of how and what to experience. But now I noticed that something else had come to him. The man-child that he appeared to be seemed to be joined by a child-man, and he looked suddenly as if he were about to be fulfilled and to become – I realised with a sudden fear – what the world would call truly old, old in the way which clearly meant that whatever he was, was not forever.

And this 'not forever' was more stark and underscored when, instinctively, as it assailed me, I would look from him to Diamond. What was it that made me think such strange things and made the three of us almost so out of contact with all that was going on around us? What was it in Diamond which made all that was so old suddenly so young and new, and yet when added to Bird of the Wind, with all that living old-youngness, made him look so old and transitory and myself suddenly not only myself but a new kind of observer, watching myself with strangely withdrawn and objective eyes? This, of course, was not a thought that went on nagging at me, but it made a difference to the whole climate of my thinking, rather like a first stirring of the wind of morning from a new direction, with an indication of rain to come.

From the beginning it was accepted that Diamond was my horse. I say 'my' with diffidence, because I never felt a particular 'my' about it. I just had a feeling that we belonged and were committed to the same pattern in time and in being. It was significant that, although it was quite a habit on special occasions to give members of my family some domestic animal for themselves, Diamond was never formally allotted to me; he was just always recognised as mine.

Bird of the Wind had indicated from the very first day how he regarded this relationship as something pre-ordained and an indisputable fact of life, but he also showed it in a different and more subtle way one morning on our way to visit Diamond and his mother. We had to pass through the community of horses running free on the veld, where Bird of the Wind had to pass a particularly intense sniffing examination. When it was over, and Diamond took his first faltering steps towards us and even kicked with both his hind legs for joy, I suddenly felt a great fear and turned to Bird of the Wind and exclaimed: 'You will never . . . !' I did not finish the sentence, because it was not necessary. Bird of the Wind knew the question and the answer, and said with one of the most moving, long-distance looks in his ancient eyes I had ever seen: 'No, I will not, by Heitse. He is not one of those. He will never need it.'

It was amazing how full of grace the day suddenly seemed, and how beautiful and how wonderful that Bird of the Wind and I had crossed a great hurdle without ever having had to name it.

Six months after Diamond's coming, my mother, who felt that this special relationship with a sick and unpredictable elder brother was wrong for me, decided that, although I was still nearly eighteen months younger than the normal age, I should go at the end of the winter to boarding school. Diamond's upbringing from there onwards fell entirely to Bird of the Wind. He was initiated into being exclusively a horse for a rider, a saddle horse and not, as most of our horses were, dual purpose horses who had to draw carts as well. He was never to draw a cart in all his life, and I do not think that anybody ever rode him except Bird of the Wind and myself. Whenever I came back from school and went on to the farm, as soon as I had done all my human greetings I went with Bird of the Wind to greet Diamond.

The stories of what had happened to Diamond and Bird of the Wind together were many and would fill a book in themselves. I can only dwell on them in general and pause, as it were, at the milestones on his journey into horsehood.

According to Bird of the Wind, he needed hardly any training. He seemed to know from the beginning what to do, and in a sense to find some sort of satisfaction in the relationship with his rider. At first I did not particularly want to ride him. I was never very keen on riding. Although I had a lot of it to do, I never felt any particular joy in the act of riding, as most of my family did. It seemed rather a rough thing to do to someone like Diamond, and I would often watch him and speculate on how I would set about it and what I could do to make it less burdensome. And he would look at me almost as if he knew what was going on in my mind, with some process of questioning not so much of the mind as of that incredible spirit which horses seem to possess to a greater degree than other animals.

But when the moment came to ride him I knew that it was right for us to move together over the earth and through life in that way as well. I mention this matter of spirit because Bird of the Wind believed that horses have second sight, some more than others. He believed that even in the dark at night, if one leant forward in the saddle and looked along the mane of the horse and between his ears in the direction in which he was heading, one would see things that other people could not see. He thought that Diamond had this gift in the greatest measure of all the horses he had known, and he told me many strange incidents that had happened to them when he and Diamond had been riding on errands in the dark; and how once, lost in the dark of a great summer storm, he had dismounted and just walked beside Diamond, and Diamond picked the way without losing direction until, two hours later, they were fumbling at the stable door.

One experience with Diamond has always stayed with me and been a mark on the map of my life which I think I have instinctively used as a kind of direction-finder. It happened late one night, when Bird of the Wind and I had been to our little town to fetch some cattle medicine that was urgently needed and, of course, the mail. We were both tired, but happy to be heading for home, and I remember that at just about eleven o'clock, when we were coming up towards the summit of the ring of hills that stretched for some seven miles across our land – an area where the night always seemed much darker because the range of hills cut out nearly half the light of such a weight of stars that the sky sagged with them – we put our horses into a long swinging walk. There was no moon, and the nearer we came to the summit, which was called the Mountain of the Wolves, the darker it became, and as it did so it sounded to me as if the noises of the night were quickening and somewhat uneasy. The jackals and the wolves in particular had almost a note of hysteria in their melancholy noises that spoke perpetually of want of appeasement and rejection, to which the night plovers joined in with those strange piping voices of theirs which spoke to me always more of the sea than of so great a land. And then, when we were just abreast of the very tip of the mountain and I remember that I had just taken a measure of the night behind us and seen the Southern Cross almost over Diamond's tail, standing on the top of the Mountain of Mercy, it happened.

I had hardly settled in my saddle again to enjoy the rhythm of Diamond's supple walk when the sky all over and from end to end of what I could see was suddenly brilliantly lit. It was a light that seemed even brighter than sunlight. It was not lightning, because there was not a cloud in the sky, and in any case it happened faster than any of the lightning I had seen in Africa. It had no edge to it, as lightning has, and no point to it, as the day has in that great wheel of the day over Africa. It just appeared suddenly as light and nothing but light and with nothing whatsoever to indicate where it came from.

Bird of the Wind's horse snorted and reared, and even he had some trouble in quietening it, not least because, as he afterwards told me, he himself was 'not in his body'. Diamond just seemed to stop without a jerk in his walk and began to quiver as if he were suddenly made all over of electricity. I sat deeper in my saddle and cannot remember even now what happened to me except that I was part of this quivering, quicksilver kind of shivering that had gone all through Diamond. What was even more alarming was that the flash went as quickly as it came, almost as if it 'was and wasn't', undivided, and so fast that it left no scar in time. It was direct and clear and just of itself and with no follow-through as one finds in lightning, and when it had gone I could hardly believe that it had been everywhere around us and in the heavens as far as I could see. Yet in the return of darkness there seemed to be, in the centre of the sky, a black streak, clear-cut against the light of the stars, from the highest point of the sky right down to the earth, and then there came a sort of rumble that was in a hurry too and also had that 'there and not-there' quality about it. Yet the streak remained, and I do not know to this day whether it was something left on the retina of my eye that I projected from within onto the night, or whether it was, as it seemed then, the track left by a light in its descent from heaven to the earth.

I do not know how long we sat there before we spoke again and resumed our journey home. By then the night had gone as silent as we had. The hyenas, the jackals, the night plovers and the owls, who occasionally had joined in to raise a philosophical question with the silence and the dark, were silent and I think, like ourselves, speechless. Ultimately Bird of the Wind was the first to break the silence and just exclaimed: 'Heitse Eibib has got him! He'll never again appear among the stars!' What it meant I do not know, except that it seemed both an expression of some profound foreboding in his primordial heart, and exultation of a victory for his god-hero in the everlasting battle against the forces of darkness, but I do know that we suddenly felt the need to get home as fast as we could – to find that no one believed our story and that the general comment was that, as usual, the two of us were making very much of something very ordinary.

But a week or two later, when our next batch of newspapers arrived, we read that a group of American astronomers, who were working nearby planning to build a giant telescope because the air there was the driest and the clearest in their experience and perfect for observing the stars of the southern hemisphere, had recorded the falling of a meteorite between the Mountain of the Wolves and their site on the River of Mud – which put the point where the meteor struck the earth very near to where we had been at that moment.

When I told Bird of the Wind this he seemed to take it as some kind of a privilege, and the news made his reaction suddenly very positive where it had been negative before, and bore the conviction that Heitse Eibib had done it to show to his chosen children how well he commanded the light. I myself have always believed that the two of us are perhaps the only people in the history of observation of the heavens on whom the stars themselves, those stars shooting in and out of heaven like spies and snipers of the night, had scored what we in our war of the world called a 'near miss'. All I can say is that in the special nature of the bond between the two of us and Diamond, our brief lives had already been marked and were still to be marked by a great many coincidences and extraordinary ordinary happenings, so that we seemed to be destined in the course of the traffic and the travel of the universe to continue to receive messages from strange addresses.

Indeed, I had already experienced something even stranger which bore resemblances to what had just happened, except that it had occurred not in the dark but on the bluest of mornings under a cloudless sky. I have written about it elsewhere and need only refer to the incident in the most factual terms. It happened one morning when I was on my way across the river with my dog and gun to bring back some fowl for our old cook. I was walking along in the happiest of moods looking at the distant hills when suddenly there was a tremendous flash of lightning, the kind of lightning which must have launched the expression 'a bolt from the blue' on to the English language, and I turned instantly about and ran home in as great a fear as I have ever experienced. What is strange is that I did not immediately connect it with the experience the three of us had just gone through, despite their similarities, but the fact remained that light from the heavens transcending night and day had entered my imagination and influenced, in a way I cannot adequately describe, all the years of my thinking and doing to this day without yielding in any essential of their mystery.

But perhaps the happiest and not least significant of my moments with Diamond were connected with sheep. We had some thousands of sheep divided into flocks and located in different areas of the farm, where every night they were brought back for their safety into the kraals with very high stone walls to protect them, with their shepherds and their dogs housed nearby in their little mud and wattle houses. The sheep were counted out in the morning and counted in at night to make certain that none had been left out in the course of their grazing during the day. If there were any missing at evening we went out to look for them immediately, because they would not have survived the dark. The way the search was carried out depended on where the flock had been grazing. If near at hand, it was done on foot, as Bird of the Wind and I did it on the day when he went to his little shrine to breathe fire and smoke, but very often it had to be done further out and on horseback. I had a feeling that Diamond enjoyed this part of the work more than any other, because I was conscious of a certain participation of emotion whenever we stopped and I imitated the bleating of a ewe that had lost a lamb and we waited patiently for the air of the evening to bring us an answering bleat. When we failed to get a reply and I made him walk on, he would always step forward with a peculiar sort of shake of his head which I came to call the 'Never mind' shake, or the 'Better luck next time' shake, and when we did get an answering bleat, which was drowned in the immense golden pool of silence at that hour almost as soon as it was uttered, I felt he was as excited as I was. He would start out at once in the direction of the sound without any guidance from me, and when I dismounted and came back into the saddle with as many lambs as I could manage, I was barely in the saddle before he turned and did what all horses and animals and ultimately the whole of the human spirit loves to do above all else, headed for home.

I remember in particular one very cold winter's evening. For some strange reason that I can no longer remember we had our lambing season in the winter, and in those uplands, even after the sunniest of days, as the sun drew level with the earth the cold took over with an almost frightening speed and there would be frost before we got home. These extremes of cold at nightfall and heat by day gave us many problems, because once the lambing flock had settled down to grazing in the warmth of the day, and the lambs had been fed and usually settled down in the warmest of shelters behind a boulder or group of bushes and fallen asleep, the flock would gently graze on, and by the time the shepherds began to gather them for the walk to their kraals they would be so far from where they started that in the change of mood and bustle of being gathered together the ewes would lose their lambs and we would have more lambs to look after than ever. On this particular day, knowing how cold it was going to be, I had put on my saddle one of several thick old army greatcoats left over from the Boer War and used by us all as a common pool of clothing for work in the twilight hours of winter. On this occasion I found four lambs and came back with two in one pocket and one in the other. I would have liked to put the other in there as well, but unfortunately I had forgotten to remove a copy of the latest G. A. Henty book which I had put there the day before and so had to carry the lamb in front on my saddle. I had no problems with the lamb on my saddle but the three, comfortable and warm in the pockets of the greatcoat, took this as a perfect occasion to rehearse their bleating and, far from being disconcerted by it, Diamond seemed to take it as the lambs' equivalent of a thanksgiving for being rescued from the cold and perils of the night. He may well have been right, because we got rather a special reception from the old shepherd who loved his flock and stood waiting for us, leaning on his stick like some figure from an island in *The Odyssey*.

Sometimes, too, I would have to take a whole flock on my own out for grazing and I would take my bread and a flask of water and a little bag full of dried apples for Diamond and a book and lead my flock some two miles from home and let them choose grazing of their own. I would dismount and loosen the girth of the saddle and the bit and bridle from Diamond and just let him graze with the sheep around me while I settled down to being both an ardent reader of stories of impossible adventure in improbable lands and, at the turn of every page, a shepherd looking over the top of my book at my charges feeding happily all around me. I found this sound of animals, unafraid, grazing all around me almost as satisfying as the munching of horses in the stable.

This sort of experience, and there were many, many more, seemed to me far more satisfying than anything I had found in playing with groups of my peers in the streets and surroundings of our very special little town while they in turn, whenever I came into the town for mail and supplies, would gather round and commiserate with me having to be alone on the farm. I might have been alone, but these days passed without my experiencing anything remotely like loneliness. I had not only human companionship of the most original and imaginative kind but I also had, even more special, an intimacy with the life of man's remotest beginnings through the animals, the plants, the skies, the winds, the clouds, the seasons which even in their most severe or most generous moments, whenever and whatever they happened to be, gathered me from all ends of my being and perception into the totality of the universe, as if into the heart of a family singularly my own.

When, in the way of things, all this came to an end I lost something which I was never to find in the same degree anywhere in the world which I was to travel more widely than most people, and certainly not in the great cities that my life compelled me to inhabit for many years. I was in my last year at school and looking forward immensely to the long vacation which would take me back to my home, to Bird of the Wind and to Diamond, when the news came that my brother was leaving the farm, selling all the animals and letting it to a stranger. He was not, he said, well enough to continue running it. What was even worse was the news that my mother had decided to sell our great and much loved home in the little town nearby and move away to the capital, to be near universities and colleges and 'the centre of civilised things'.

When the end of the year came, all these things had to be accomplished; and I meanwhile had decided that I had had enough of learning from institutions. I found my whole nature rebelling against going to university, which was the family tradition and something my mother dearly wished me to do and all the rest took for granted I would do. I decided, against all the pressures, to go out into the world on my own, taking with me, in some keep of my spirit, all these things of which I have spoken and of which I remember far, far more than I have been able to put on record here.

All these things are just special little samples of something much greater, but they convey what I know has been true – that I would not have been able to follow the compass of my own being as nature had predisposed me if it had not been also for the earth of my native country, the land, that vast, vast land and immense sea of sky and all its manifestations of nature and life upon it, particularly the life of such phenomenal companions as Bird of the Wind, Diamond and the experience of that awe-ful twosome: the light greater than the light of day, and the other light, greater than the light of the sun which came out of the darkest hour of the night, a visual realisation, perhaps, as I came to wonder, of the Chinese midnight when noon is born.

My last term at school began in the last week of October after my last vacation on the farm, which summed up in the most singular way all that the farm out of its own nature had given me in life. September is the spring, and when the rains come early, as they had done that year, the earth and the sky, both night and day, seemed to be atremble with birth and new life, and, as the pattern of my life seemed to have arranged especially for me, my contribution to life on the farm was confined to setting out early in the morning with Diamond and the flock of spring lambs and their mothers.

It was always a joyful dispensation of work, because the lambs were as strong and even stronger than their mothers. They could be taken quite fast into the ridges between the hills where there was no view of homestead or man, but where the wolves, the jackals, the lynxes, the owls and a rich variety of hawks and falcons had their homes and we all were accordingly as close to a natural version of original Africa as one could get. Also I had some reading with me in those days that was very special to me. A future brother-in-law had just come back from Oxford and lent me a very early copy of T. S. Eliot's *The Waste Land*, which joined my little collection of literature that had the most profound impact on me. The April which Eliot wrote about, 'the cruellest month . . . mixing memory and desire', as he put it, matched the role of our September in the procession of the seasons. Somehow it was one of the most unproblematical and most immediate poems I had ever read. I read nothing else for nearly three weeks. I would go from beginning to end and start at the beginning again, and as a result I had a period of feeling totally fulfilled, with no need to look before and after, because the 'now' of those days seemed timeless.

One particular day had gone so well that I had to wrench myself out of my reading and set about the business of gathering my scattered flock. I had left it a little bit late, because the sun was already drawing near to the top of the hill that we called Blue Cliffs, so named because the summit was a bare reef of cliffs composed of a blueish compound stone. At the base it was covered with wild olives and lush bushes all glowing in the sun, and I knew that several small caves within the cliffs where families of red lynxes lived, members of one of the most starlike breeds of cat, would be shining like lamps just then. All in all this sort of blue summit seemed a proper foundation on which the temple of the deepening blue above it could rest securely. But now, looking at the space of light left between it and the sun, I knew the time had already gone when Diamond and I should have been taking our flock home.

And yet when the gathering was done and I came through a small cleft in the long ridge between Blue Cliffs and the Mountain of the Wolves and saw the great level plain leading up to the homestead, I could not help pausing for a moment. In one of the clearest lights on earth, I could see the dust in four different places where other flocks were being taken to their kraals near permanent water points scattered over the farm. But, what was most exciting, I saw our own herds of springbok and blessbok moving gracefully in between. I always marvelled how at such distances and on such days the light made their bodies strangely insubstantial and almost transparent, so that they looked not so much flesh and blood, which we all share, as a flicker of flame and light thrown on to a screen of distance as if through a slide of some cosmic magic lantern.

And then there was something else which tended to sanctify the moment. There was the equivalent out of our earth as of Byzantine incense. As I felt the cool of evening moving around me where I sat above the bustle and the smell of dust and sheep, it brought that scent I have mentioned before, of the wild freesias that covered these ridges for miles on end. It is of course a scent which everyone finds appealing, but no one can know what it is really like until it has come to him on the air of evening or morning in the heart of Africa, where it is poignant and charged, as it were, with the quintessential quality of my native continent, which in nourishing so starlike a flower with so delicate and tentative a scent proves that in the sum of itself and all its incalculable passage of years and future to come, it would never allow its giant strength to be used like a giant.

Meanwhile the lambs themselves were infected by this exhilarating feeling of return to the kraals of their birth and became more and more excited. They started running out from the main body of the flock and going wild in all sorts of unpredictable circles when they were clear of their elders. In their rounds and the climax of their dashes forward they jumped like gazelles, and when not jumping began to bleat. All their mothers, as sheep do, hastened to conform, and some four hundred sheep of all ages joined into a bleating which was not at all like normal bleating. It is a sound that is always full of nostalgia and reflects a certain kind of melancholy and frustration at being compelled to live life, which is so wonderful, as a sheep. But on this occasion the sound had an air of emancipation and fulfilment, which became an increasingly loud form of sheep's 'Hallelujah'.

Diamond and I, in the midst of it all, felt as if we were moving in a deep sea of sound, and with the level sunlight surrounding us all in a yellow ring of light, the new wool on the lambs, and even the mature wool on the backs of their mothers, seemed to be aglow. The flock arrived at the gates of the kraal where my mother and our head shepherd were waiting to count them, and where all flocks would normally have hesitated and waited for the goat which usually led them in, since sheep were far too timid to commit themselves to any enclosed spaces, even one which had been their home, as the kraal had been for many nights before. As a rule, indeed, the bell which the goat wore around his neck to signal with a lovely ringing sound that his was the leading role in this last act of the day would dominate all other sounds of a great homecoming. But now it was inaudible, and the goat himself, normally so full of himself, as all males of his species are, was comic in his surprise at being hustled through the gate by the urgent throng behind and around him, and clearly put out by what he regarded as a gross breach of good manners.

In this and every other way it was an exceptional and beautiful homecoming, and it seemed to me as if it had been recognised by circumstances themselves, because it ended up as one of those very rare occasions when a flock in the pride of its lambs was counted in at nightfall as it had been counted out at dawn.

All that was left to do then was for me to walk Diamond from the kraals to the stables. It was a good thing I did not know then that I was doing it for the last time, because it would have been different and certainly not so rich with a feeling of fulfilment. There was nothing more that I wanted consciously of life at that moment, because if there was I would have thought of it and it too would have marred the moment. It was just good to walk away from those ironstone kraals with a feeling of work well done, and on over the footpath which had been made by the soles of feet and hooves of animals I had never known; and yet, as the path turned to avoid an awkward rock in the ground here or a steep rise there, and then picked its way with all the assurance coming from the experience of the feet of the generations of vanished people who had made it, I had no sense of guiding myself but rather of following in a direction and manner communicated to me in the most moving of ways by this idiom of a track trodden in the scarlet earth. And that feeling of company that came from it all, too, was good.

Through the trees I could already see the light of the lamps in the main rooms of the house and barns like combs of amber honey, transparent in the darkening air. And, nearer still, there came from the kitchen the smell of dinner being prepared and a whiff of cinnamon, nutmeg, tamarind and saffron, like an incantation from the great epic of the history that had brought us all there.

I did not put Diamond into his stable at once. I unsaddled him and unbridled him and put on his own soft, well-worn halter and then walked up and down with him between the stables and the dam some two hundred yards beyond, built when my grandfather was a boy to hold just enough rainwater for his family until they could find permanent sources nearby. As the rains had been early, the dam was full, and although it was nearly dark, and one could see it darkening before one's eyes, it was so still with water and shining like a mirror that we saw all over it, more like reflections than they themselves, wild duck and wild geese, herons and cranes, all staring at their image with every neck and head now tiara'd and necklaced with the emerging stars. The moment was so overwhelmingly lyrical that some bullfrogs joined in the scene. All over there came the same brek-a-keks-kek which the frogs of the marshes and bogs between the world of men and Hades raised when Dionysus went on his fateful journey to Hades to summon back a great spirit of the past who could speak to the Athenians who had lost their way, and remind them of what sort of people they were. And what sort of people were we? What indeed was I, and I to Diamond, and both to such a fall of night as this?

Every time we walked to the stables and back again, the number of bats zooming through the air increased and the greater noises of the night began to be heard, dominated by the hyenas and the jackals and the plover of the night with the forever bleeding bleat of a sheep, uneasy even in its kraal, joining in the abiding harmony of sounds of the night. And nearer home too there were the birds not saluting the evening any more with song but every now and then gurgling like little fountains in their throats with the purest of sound, as they nestled deeper on to the eggs in their nests. We walked back and forth like this until I was certain that Diamond had cooled down, and then I took him to the great trough which held water for the horses and allowed him to drink. The trough itself seemed to be so full of stars that one wondered how it could hold any water, but Diamond knew better. Fastidious and delicate in his tastes, like all horses, he sniffed at the water compulsively and then concentrated on one spot and blew several times across its surface before he put his lips to it. But once his lips were there he drank long and deep, as if it were not water or even champagne but the draught of some African bacchae, and only then I put him in his stable, currycombed and brushed him, made certain that his long tail and thick hair were no longer entangled and dusty but smooth, unentangled and long, so that he could lay himself on bed and pillow, if there were such things for horses, and not disgrace it or the linen of his clean straw. I tied the end of his halter to the metal ring in the wood at the bottom of his place in the long crib, where Bird of the Wind had already made a meal of meals for him, and then, because I was leaving in the morning, I sat at the end of the crib beside him, as I had done so often before, and listened to him and the other horses munching.

Finally, what was perhaps best of all at the end of the day, as I came out of the stable to walk home and looked towards the northwest, I saw, below the horizon, the sky being swept with great flashes of lightning, rather like giant searchlights, and the clear indication that there was rain on the way – and for me there never had been, or could be, such a moment of conviction that all is well.

5
Horse-Man

The fact that I had to leave Bird of the Wind and Diamond without knowing that I was leaving them for the last time is still painful to me. I do not know what difference knowledge of the final parting would have brought to my farewell, but it rankles deeply that I did not know it at the time, for something in the nature of such a goodbye would, I feel, have drawn on some source buried deep in the instinctive knowledge of life we bring to the world at birth, and would have been imparted to them and consoled them, as I wanted to be consoled and comforted myself. I can only think that, whenever I remember that going and have this feeling as of a physical pain over the matter, it is a measure not only of how much they meant to me but of how unconsciously I must have gone on missing them over the years that followed, when to all appearances they may have seemed forgotten. But as it happened, I can only speculate that, whatever ritualistic farewell I might have summoned, had I known I would never see them again, I would have found the experience of parting almost impossible to bear.

However, as I expected to see them again and again in the years ahead, and to have news of them from neighbours and friends as I went along, I did not view the lengthening stride of our separation with apprehension. The longing to go back of course remained there, and yet making a living of my own – in a way which the world, set in its conventions and traditions of what young men should do in a pioneer environment, found eccentric and wayward, if not dotty and utterly irresponsible – committed me to a search wherein I had no model to guide me and indeed demanded all I had of imagination and concentration. So there were many valid reasons why I could not break away to see them, and I did not know properly how long and how awful my separation from that part of myself had been until, unexpectedly and in the most casual of ways, I heard of their deaths, strangely synchronised almost to the day, and in the same form, one stricken, rainless year. Instantly a process of grief and self-recrimination, utterly personal and private, began in me which continued, known or unknown, and erupted suddenly to reveal a power it had held in store all along, when I became aware of this whole dimension of mortal sickness not only in flesh and blood but in the general trend and character of our time.

And yet there was, as Manley Hopkins might have put it, a dear goodness in the deep of these things. It is good, for instance, that I find them living on in a far greater degree in my imagination than I have been able to indicate here in this pattern of a story. And as I came to this re-tracking over the dead days of the years I spent with them, I realised what an enormous contribution Diamond had made to my being and thinking and still continues to do, no more so than in the story of the champion jockey and his horse, and the recovery of both the horse from severe injury and the jockey from terminal cancer. Had it not been for Diamond, I could not have held with such conviction that the jockey would not have been able to recover from the terminal cancer if he had not had this singular bond and faith in horses. And yet there were times when I doubted my conclusion, and thought it was too subjective to have objective validity.

Yet I could not get away from these four manifestations of cancer which presented a certain mathematical wholeness to me. In the beginning, when men first started to wonder about these things, that mathematical kind of thinking was a deeply religious occupation. All the great mathematical axioms – which drew me first to mathematics at school – were religious statements, as well as scientific assumptions on which one day great towers would be built to pierce the skies, great bridges thrown across the widest and most dangerous rivers, and great ships made of matter heavier than water to round stormy capes and outride hurricanes, typhoons and the fiercest gales.

This was my point of departure, and was a part of something that had no substance or magnitude but possessed only position. Once one had position, the retreat of chaos began and meaning was born. The sense of meaning that I was finding on this trail in and out of time, and with a seemingly absurd and random chronology of its own, made no sense of the chronology of watches that tick and clocks that sound the alarm. But then, the valid role of the exercise of reason, which is so legitimate a part of the elements which constitute our greatest awareness, has become inflated until it is a form of tyranny and superstition in this time wherein we live, and has grown so totally out of proportion that sooner or later fate, as our ancestors called it, will discipline it, and confine it to its ration with the three other instinctive faculties that constitute the full range of consciousness.

My son's experience with terminal cancer had started with a dream. I decided to go to one of my closest friends, who was not only a great physician and psychological healer but had devoted most of his life to a study of dreams. This was Fredy Meier, who held Jung's old Chair of Psychology at the Federal University of Switzerland for so long, and I remembered his story of the Swiss farmer who had overcome cancer purely through faith in the healing powers of a distinguished surgeon.

'Is it too fanciful,' I asked him, 'to think that this horseman was able to heal a terminal cancer within himself through his profound bond with a horse? Could he have been in touch, somehow, with all that the horse has at its disposal of ancient energies of healing, and with which modern man on the whole has totally lost touch?'

To my amazement he responded without hesitation and with an authority so spontaneous and conclusive that it needed no emphasis. He took from his mouth the pipe that was casting its shadow on his shoulder in the slanted light, and uttered a quiet: 'Of course. Have you forgotten the Centaur, the horse-man Chiron? He was the great healer of antiquity. He healed gods and heroes and trained Asclepius after all. His pattern is still there for those who look for it.'

He made it sound so decisive a statement of the obvious truth that I was totally reassured and excited. The hair at the back of my neck went atingle, and I was back with a strain of music that, on a day of deep personal mourning, defied the laws of acoustics in St Paul's and came so clearly to me that it became visual, and I followed a boy in naked feet mounting a horse, bareback and without a proper bridle, and riding over an immense green sea to where the blue of the sky and the blue of the distance met at the horizon and became a line of black, and boy and horse, as if taking the last fence in a point-to-point, rose united in sheer grace into the air, went over and above the last horizon and then down and out of sight, and the music ended and now returned as something that also preceded and followed Diamond.

And I knew that, however forgotten Diamond and Bird of the Wind had been on the surface of my mind, their relationship had been centaur-like, and without them I would not have been aware now of things that were already strange familiars among my instincts, and that the dimension wherein these instincts arise within the human spirit was still as active and powerful as ever, and that they were still participating in life and had entered their proxy in man and horse, to ride to victory in a Grand National of life.

And from there, inevitably, I was off the radar screen of our day and back with the Ancient Greece I first knew as a boy. It started at a very early age, in the climate of things told and discussed naturally in our home and in the books already made available for first reading in our nursery. Two of my earliest presents were a simplified account for children of the myths and legends of Greece and, as birthday and Christmas gifts from my parents, illustrated versions of *The Iliad* and *The Odyssey*, so that, one way or another, from the simplest visual forms right up to Burckhardt's magisterial account of the spirit of Greece, at all times these things were available to one's imagination, which grew deeper, higher and wider with their nourishment.

I did not then think of them as 'stories', which the world today so dangerously regards as having only a non-true kind of truth, a form of playing with the truth and not, as I believe, a fundamental truth and reality in their own right. They walked my world, these gods and heroes, these forms of life wherein animal and man, beast and god and all the natural elements of the world and time combined and played a part in the history of the human spirit, in strange and vast personified forms. They were a fact of one's life, as they were a fact for the Greeks. They walked the streets of Athens with both the most enlightened and the least cultivated of men. They were present everywhere, and there was no event in the great evolution of the classical world of which they were not the inspiration, and man their chosen instrument. The traffic between this dimension of the myth and legend and the mind of man was two-way traffic, and so great and abundant and rich and powerful that the way of the imagination was almost overcrowded and, not surprisingly, often snarled up by gods, or inspired or inflamed heroes, hastening to do something about the symbols and the improbable purposes and impossible journeys and tasks which this two-way correspondence imposed upon them all, keeping the heavens as busy as the world below.

And I believe that what made this world so accessible to me and my friends was a feeling of it being so young and so fresh. I still remember how in glancing through one of my father's favourites, Schwab's great book on the myths and epics of Greece, I saw that an Egyptian priest, representative of the oldest civilisation then on hand, told Solon, the sage of Athens: 'You Greeks are always children. There is no such thing as an old Greek.'

Even Aristotle, whose imagination was illuminated with reason and committed to clarity of thought and shape, would say: 'The friend of wisdom is also a friend of the myth.' He did not hesitate to make a personal confession which even then might have been thought far from rational: 'The lonelier I am, the more of a recluse I become, the greater is my love for myths.'

I found this love already there in my spirit when I first became aware of an identity of my own as a child, and it is obvious that that love has followed me around and has not diminished but grown greater over the years. And what has been a constant is that from the beginning, as I visualised these myths and legends and the world in which they manifested themselves, the world had for me a light of its own that I found in nothing else that I ever read of history or literature. Everywhere else there is night and day, and the elements as we know them, especially the light of the sun and all the shadows it casts and the colours it provokes. It is, I believe, a light we can still experience to this day. The moment my imagination entered this world of Greece, this other light was there. It was there as the unique colour of the temperament of some of the great painters, as with Rembrandt, for instance. No matter what he is painting, from portraits to great scenes of history and the life of his time and of legend and myth, and even in the greatest of all, his self-portraits, this special colour of his own temperament is basic and presides as if drenched into the canvas. All the immense variety of colours and combinations of colours that are used by the spirit of genius take their tone from it in this manner. This light was always there, not all-pervasive but, as it were, a light that was not only in the outer dimensions of this world but also a twin emanation coming from the earth, the plants, the sacred rivers and the fountains and sanctified woods and valleys and the mountain tops to meet one another and form a harmonious but utterly inexpressible and imponderable green-gold composition.

But the moment I followed these myths on into their Latin versions and their Roman patterns and names, the light was not there. I had a suspicion then, as I have it now, that it was lost on the way from Troy to Rome, because in the transport the living myth, and fact of life it was, disappeared and 'mythology' took its place. The further the gods withdrew themselves from the streets and from such visions of materialisation of the pattern of the myth which gleamed in Greece as the Parthenon – in the Athens which Shelley spoke of as 'a crest of columns gleaming in the mind of man' – and all the temples to Dionysus and Apollo began to crumble where they stood, firmly fixed in Dionysian clay or Apollonian summits, and Apollo's greatest injunction to man to 'know thyself' was more and more forgotten, the further man removed his spirit from those, and the more exalted he made the gods, so that ultimately they were transferred to the stars, the more the human spirit and imagination was deprived, and the measure in which the world of today remains deprived is the distance between him and the living myth. Already the planets to which they were removed have been closely scanned and may be soon visited by tourists and found vacant, and the first spy of a new kind of consciousness in man is now itself vanishing into a darkness which for the moment appears unilluminated and impenetrable.

Yet the world of the myth is still alive and real. I know, because I walked it again with Diamond. I have been led back again and again to the great mountain in the Caucasus where all that is titanic is made flesh and blood in the shape of man, beautifully proportioned with a burnished skin, burning like a torch in the blue-black of that mythological heaven. I imagine that everyone who has read this far will know that this torch of suffering flesh and blood chained to a rock on the lip of a purple cliff dropping down into the black, fathomless depth of the world, is Prometheus. They will know the stories, or at least one of the stories, about Prometheus, and the essential in all these stories, however much they may differ on technicalities of method and doing, that it was Prometheus who stole fire from the gods and gave it to man; that it was he who committed what Milton called the act of 'Man's first disobedience'. At the beginning there was an act of culpable disobedience seen from the point of view of the gods, but an act which raised the question which has not been answered except darkly and in part: what would have happened to the gods themselves if someone strong and brave enough to go against their will had not appeared on the scene and given fire to man? There are even versions which hold that Prometheus himself created man and that no man existed before Prometheus.

Taken literally, this question is, of course, unanswerable and, seen in terms of cosmogonic meaning, academic, because all valid speculation on this first confrontation with Prometheus, on fire himself with a fire he wanted for man, point to the conclusion that if there were some sort of man around at that precise moment he would not have been man in the sense that gave any meaning to his role in the unfolding drama of creation, because he would have been just another version of the abundant nature over which the gods exercised their power and led their strange lives. The whole of creation would have stood still, with the gods free to indulge themselves endlessly and, one feels, would have vanished unfulfilled and as an amply discredited and rejected essay among many other failed ones in the history of creation. Prometheus, it seemed to me, appeared at the moment when the gods themselves had come to the end of a phase of themselves, and if they were to live on beyond time which begot them and serve a timeless end they needed renewal, and renewal demanded something like man, and man armed with fire which ultimately is the fire of consciousness. From that moment neither heaven nor earth nor whatever enfolds them of stars and suns and comets would be the same again, because the fire, the light, the warmth that Prometheus brought to the scene of creation would never again be put out but would grow great, because if it did not, the gods and all else would have failed creation and been expelled from the scheme of meaning and timeless life. Indeed the gods themselves had to learn again obedience to the great law of their own creation. They themselves would have to die in order to be born again and renewed in a more meaningful and conscious shape than they had been before. Their path, like my own fumbling little way, led to this highest of mountain tops in the Caucasus where Prometheus was bound and Hercules took Chiron one day and unbound the titan so that the great healer could take his place.

Again and again in my imagination I saw the way to this mountain as a path of the greenest grass and, though well trodden, not made by the feet of ordinary men. One followed it through valleys where the mountains on either side were covered with ilexes, pines and wild olives and spaces in between thick with myrrh and asphodel and occasionally a laurel which always trembled in that special light as if Daphne, after which it was named, was near. Indeed the woods and the hills, one felt, were full of life and a keen air of expectancy lay over the track and the distances, as if any moment Narcissus hastening to his pool, or Artemis in pursuit and protection of her own, all sorts of fawns and even a titan or two might be moving there. The country was full of bird song and vibrating with processes of growth of plants and renewal of all forms of life with an urgency and abundance as if the earth had never been so charged with fecundity.

But as the track wound higher and the air became cooler one's imagination rounded a bend and there was a sheer barrier of mountains that took up half of heaven, and among the mountains a deep cleft, and at the side of the cleft a peak of rock higher than all the rest; and as one got nearer there was a living creature shaped in every detail as a man, but in its proportions more than a man and, with the sun of this world which was always gold falling full on it, at a distance seemed like a great torch of flame held up in the sky. But as my mind drew nearer I was horrified to see the head hung in agony and a great stream of blood coming out of its side and, hovering over it constantly, a kind of eagle greater even than the 'lamb snatchers' of the mountains of the night I knew in my life at home, and every now and then the eagle would swoop and, to my horror, fasten its talons on the flesh of flanks with its skin like foil of gold, and plunge its beak into the wound and then launch itself over the abyss in the mountain tops and soar away to begin a round upwards on currents of Zeus's own air of thunder and lightning to resume his watch over that figure, bound to the mountain top, waiting for the next pang of its insatiable appetite to send it swooping down again.

It was Prometheus, of course, and the vision of Prometheus I describe was as childlike and as simple as this but so real that when I first grasped it it made me sad and cry for days and haunted me as it has haunted so many generations throughout the desperate millennia behind us. He stole fire and gave it to man, and for this sin – or 'first disobedience' – he was chained forever to that rock to endure the endless repetition of that daily visitation from dawn to sunset by an eagle whose appetite never grew less. Only at nightfall was the wound healed and the liver, the essence of life, fully restored, only to feed the eagle again in his agony when the blessed night was over.

And from the beginning one had no sense of time as to when Prometheus was chained by the smith of the gods to those rocks, when he had given fire to the flesh and blood he loved more than his gods and overlords. One cannot say when it began and how long it had gone on before one went through this childlike personification, because within the meaning of the myth, within the heart of the reality, there is no time, and one came to realise that from every generation to generation, from every cradle to every grave it presupposes, there is Prometheus again, stealing from the gods and suffering in the way of which these visual presentations are intimations of an inscrutable and inexhaustible symbol. And always the eagle is there, the eagle which perhaps is an image of the fire, in so far as fire is a symbol of consciousness, raised to its greatest height and its most extended field of vision, indeed achieving the ultimate power of vision at the expense of inflicting the Promethean elements to which it and man owe all, with a suffering that is daily enacted on that purple rock on the lip of a fathomless abyss.

Were it to be left in the human spirit at that expression of itself, it would be intolerable; the human spirit could not endure the affliction it would be, because it would be a pointless repetition of an exercise in power without meaning, when all the detail that surrounds the mythology of Prometheus indicates that he had not come for that, but as a strange plenipotentiary and intermediary of what the gods themselves were there to fulfil and yet had not been able to achieve and could do so only through the creation of man who would serve them and himself to carry on the act of creation to a definite and happier ending. And so there was a discovery one day when I came to read the labours of Hercules.

For some years I was not drawn to Hercules. Strangely enough I knew a giant of a man who was called Hercules. It was a common name that our Huguenot countrymen brought with them from France. This man of great strength made me fear that Hercules was far too physical and wanting in spirit and rather a cosmic bully, and had my eye not fallen on a page one day where I read that Hercules was a friend of Chiron, I would not have known how different the story was and how that strength was also used to such divine and tender ends. It came to me so clearly that I saw him in my own version on that track of grass following Chiron who, I hasten to add, I already loved because I knew him as the great healer who had herbs and medicines that healed all wounds and diseases. I knew him as a tutor of heroes, as a great archer and a musician who it was rumoured came near to rousing Apollo's envy. This Chiron was Hercules' closest friend, but one day, in a battle with centaurs who had had too much to drink, Hercules, shooting an arrow at a creature who endangered him, found to his horror that the arrow glanced away and went on to penetrate Chiron's knee. As the poison on Hercules' arrows was divine, the wounds it inflicted on Chiron even Chiron's own herbs and Hercules' powers could not heal or take the agony away, so that Chiron, who too was immortal, would have this suffering imposed on him for ever.

In this condition they approached Prometheus' summit of suffering, and although one observed it so long before the event, it was the same suffering whose meaning only became apparent in the Job-like comparisons I made with the dear threesome inflicted with cancer in the course of my own life, where I hinted that what they suffered was part of what the creator himself suffered, and the creator in Prometheus was a suffering creator. From that I paid special attention to one of the greatest sayings that has come to us from this classic sense of wholeness in archaic Greece, that 'only the wounded physician heals', and learned to cherish it ever since.

Happily it was an element in that great universe of mythology in which they were all involved like suns and stars and moons, with prescribed roles and courses of light in darkness. Hercules was born to see that it was not all left at Promethean suffering with consciousness confined to an eagle role, feeding on what gave birth to consciousness in a conscious abuse of the power consciousness confers. So Hercules – and it happened so quickly in my vision – Hercules had hardly appeared with Chiron when he had an arrow in his bow, shot the eagle and unbound Prometheus. Then, sadly, he allowed Chiron to take Prometheus' place, although in doing so Chiron had to surrender his immortality, so that death would one day relieve him of his unbearable suffering.

Just as Prometheus – whose name continues to recall the

vision I had as a child of a titan made beautiful in manly proportions, with a burnished skin, burning like a torch held
against the fall of night in a blue-black heaven – opened up
for gods and all life on earth a great new phase of renewal of
themselves, this awesome moment of exchange of two great
hostages of fate, the divine horse-man and the immortal titan,
introduces a new drama of creation, the drama which begins for
me, as I look back, the age of modern man.

For what happened to Prometheus after this exchange? The
myth, that was soon to abandon the streets of Athens and move
first to the top of Parnassus and from there go on its journey
to Rome, where the gods were to be removed to the stars, does
not tell. It may not tell because from that Promethean moment
the spirit of man began to lose touch with its immemorial past
and all the great forces and energies and inspirations assembled
there and, among many other things, raised him from clay and
gave him the power of fire which is not only a momentous outer
event and source of physical and material power but, far more,
inwardly is the great image of this new and strangely resourceful
and wayward thing men came to call consciousness.

Always I ask myself the question: where did Prometheus go?
And always I feel that he, relieved of his special form of suffering and immortal chains, is moving onwards in the spirit of
man, and where he and the spirit of man will go cannot be
known until the purpose for which the first fire was lit is one
day understood.

As for Chiron, the great teacher of heroes, the tutor of Jason
and Achilles who taught them the art of war and the language
of music, who became a great healer and could cure all forms
of physical suffering and sicknesses except his own, he, it would
seem, has taken on the Promethean role. In him consciousness
is not bound and, though unfettered from the rock, is still linked
more firmly than it could have been through chain to all the
memory of creation and the purpose for which creation came
out of chaos. He is the living keeper of life's continuity with its
origin and its destination. That is why he comes to us as an
image of the horse joined to the man – the instinct and the
intuition, the feeling and the heart of the animal in man – whom

Prometheus, according to the mythological exegesis, taught all the arts and the crafts and the skill and gave him the inspirations of art and science as well as the conscious power to be where he is today. Again, how the mythological Chiron has evolved, like Prometheus, is unknown. There seems to be a law in all this that these things can only be known when they have been lived. All that we can know is that part of their invisibility, to put it metaphorically, is lost in the heat and the battle and the fogs of the war for greater awareness and meaning, in which flesh and blood are still engaged. They are invisible because, paradoxically, they are too committed to be seen and one looks in vain behind to see anything except these vast and gigantic silhouettes like stormclouds in the last light of day, or extracted in isolated visions almost as pieces in some cosmic museum, like Prometheus holding himself as a burning torch in heaven or Chiron suffering in agony because of that great decree that only wounded physicians can heal.

But this I know, they are there and they were there in the great Grand National of which I have spoken as a contemporary image of the triumph of what the spirit of man can achieve when he is still in contact with what Chiron represented and so promoted in the Promethean cause of life.

With this conclusion one has a feeling of coming near to rounding the circle one has tried to make of the square of oneself. The world of Greek mythology, its heroes and its legends, were so much part of my daily food, and I took them in with such excitement and such an acceptance of their validity, that I even organised the boys I knew in the heart of Africa into 'Greeks and Trojans', enjoying the patronage and enduring the enmities of the men who fought on the great plain of Troy beween the beach and their black ships and the walls of stone of one of the proudest cities in the early days of man. This division into two opposites proved so valid in the context of Africa that it was totally accepted and became an incentive enough to make us fight in play harder than in our previous battles of 'French and English'.

As I grew older and read more and more not only of Greek but of world mythology, I found that the Greek was by far the richest, the most precise and all-embracing mythology available. As a result, going back to it now on this trail where Diamond had led me, I was amazed how, wherever I touched it, it brought new interpretations of meaning to me and so much unimagined illumination that the light in which it happened for me as a child shone more intensely than ever, and the daily scene appeared more and more like camouflage and superficial disguise of a more highly orchestrated and complex form of the mythological pattern at the beginning.

An illustration of how enlivened the scene in my imagination became at moments was when it found itself again in the company of centaurs and horses and what lessons and warnings and navigational directions of immediate and contemporary import were there concealed in other myths, legends and stories. For instance, the centaurs were not all Chirons. In their masses their spirit swelled to a dangerous collectivity, highly suggestible and inflammable. Indeed, over and over again in their myths and legendary characters, they made clear the peril of numbers to the human spirit. There is a great story of the marriage of Hippodamia in the land of Thessaly, when the centaurs, invited to the wedding en masse, got drunk and ran amok and started a war which ended in their expulsion from the land of their birth. Yet when extracted from the collective crowd and given the opportunity to serve the horse and the man and the spirit of the archer and musician in themselves, like Chiron they became essential instruments for the renewal of man and his societies. It would seem, indeed, that before the centaur in man could fulfil himself and establish how individual all points of departure were in the story of man, the horse had to find himself as something more than horse. This too is a special feature of Greek mythology: the horse has a crucial role in this unfolding of the drama of the universe and the painful evolution from a world of gods and titans towards one lone, individual, immortal half-horse, half-man, charged to save the gods themselves from their increasingly arrested selves by renouncing his own immortality to enable a renewal of life to take place both in heaven and on earth. At so many points when the progress of differentiated life on earth seemed arrested and in danger of faltering, the danger was overcome with the help of the horse – once even with the dreadful and spurious wooden horse of Troy – and life moved on again.

And there were great mix-ups, for instance, of which the chimera was the most striking image, a creature with the head of a lion, the body of a goat and the tail of a dragon and a mouth vomiting fire. It is not necessary to analyse what this mixed metaphor in flesh and blood tells one except that it is a horrendous mistake and an offence to the laws and order of beauty, harmony and ultimate proportion. It had to be removed, and one of the loveliest myths is that of Bellerephon mounted on Pegasus setting out on his quest to find this dangerously confused and mixed-up monster and remove it from the path into the future.

And in Pegasus the individual role of the horse in the mind of man is made manifest because Pegasus was winged, and where he went creation followed, so that just by striking a rock with his hoof on Mount Helicon he made the sacred spring, called Hippocrene, gush forth. The one clear interest in a horse shown by a divine feminine spirit of which I, with my limited knowledge, am aware and find singularly poignant is when the wide-eyed Athena of the broad and calm brow gave Pegasus a halter with buckles of gold, which perhaps is not surprising because she, of all the Olympian lot, came the nearest to being a rounded spirit.

For the rest, the association of the horse with the feminine is not only rarer but tends to be more negative. Selene, of the moon, had her own mane-swept horses, although I do not think they were ever named and they are just there to show how her heart, that gave light in the dark hours of the spirit, had intimation of the potential of spirit in the horse. This example did not take the feminine far, because as far as she was concerned the horse, which did proxy for Poseidon, sovereign of the white horses of the sea, was never a totally resolved image and tended to dominate the scene in a role which, however essential and fateful seen from the purely feminine point of view, was ambivalent to the point of treachery, and always stained with the recurring tragedy of Persephone.

Yet in the world of the masculine there continued to be so many horses that, by the time mythology became legend, and poets like Homer began to sing of the heroic and mythological past, horses, like other heroes, were acknowledged and received their praise as if they too were divine. I know of no other history or mythology in which so many horses appear by name and were known to have gone into battle with their gods and heroes. For instance, one of the most awesome moments in the battle for Troy was when Patroclus was arming himself for his last battle, and sent for two horses called Xanthus and Balius – and the poet is compelled, because it is held to be so important and just, to remind the audience listening to his song that one of them was born of Pegasus the Great. Accordingly his story adds lustre to the epic tale and, with the lustre, a new dimension to the killing of Patroclus, which was to have such a fateful effect on the last battles to be fought before the doomed city of Troy, because the account of Achilles' own reaction to the death of his friend naturally dominates the impact which Homer's epic has on his readers. And yet these two horses not only add to an understanding of Achilles' sorrow but, in a sense, illuminate it and give it a validity it could not otherwise have had, because the horses themselves go into mourning in a horse's way, refusing to be comforted by their grooms and owners but kicking and rearing and plunging and battering their heads in agony against walls and doorways, as if to say: 'This is too much. We cannot bear it', and their demonstrations of grief speak for all the armies standing in front of their black ships, and for the countless generations who have taken the tale into themselves.

I have often thought that it would be interesting to make a great roll call of all the names of those horses, reverberating still in the minds of men as when they were alive, and follow all that is told of their role, their pedigree and their origin, but alas it would sidetrack me so much as to prevent me from getting on with my own business, which is just to say enough to show what company Diamond enjoyed in my spirit, and why, when Blady came into my life, I had to follow this strange zigzag of association, with its own enigmatic laws of chronology, from the time when Bird of the Wind breathed fire and smoke in the valley and Diamond, newborn and glistening like silk, stood trembling on his legs for the first time in a world painted gold by the African sun. And all along Blady has been in a sense striking fire out of the flint of the cobbles in the stable of my mind wherein she has been kept, nickering with impatience to come out and join in this procession of private and personal meaning. Even now I have to mention her because I am coming near the area where she enters the world of outer events – and yet I cannot lead her forth at once. I have to talk first of all about the girl.

And this, in a curious way, is one of the elements that, although it is present in the mythology and legends that played so great a part in my imagination, is never given the role which creation meant it to play but perhaps did not allow it to play because it was intended to save the spirit of man from coming to the end of itself in a partial expression of his mission on earth, as the gods had done on Parnassus until Prometheus and Chiron came to give them a new goal. No, the history of the gods and the spirits of which I read, although less so than in other histories and mythologies, was largely a masculine-dominated history, and the role of the horse was on the whole prescribed by man and not woman. The horse moved in an area that was almost exclusively male, and in spite of powerful goddesses and wide-eyed feminine spirits like Athena, the tone was set by men and the power ultimately lay in men.

The result of this masculine one-sidedness showed itself in the tragedies that afflicted the lives of so many of the greatest heroes and finest women in the stories of Hellas. Of course the one-sidedness is redeemed, in a sense, by the fact that *The Iliad*, that moment of mad collective confrontation of two opposites in the spirit of the day, led to the great journey of individuation we call *The Odyssey*, of which the ultimate lesson of war was the need of man to rediscover the constant feminine in himself. And even that was not all, for having rejoined the island feminine again Odysseus had to do yet another journey to a great continent of reality that would end in sacrifices to all the gods of the Greek world, not just a favoured one and his or her allies, but all the warring gods in heaven, and so find a way of wisdom and greater discrimination beyond.

However, in the meantime the underground stresses caused by this elevation of the masculine, however necessary, and the general lack of recognition of the importance of the feminine, caused the great war of the Amazons which came near to man's undoing – and that pattern too, as I came by it on my trail with Diamond, was strangely contemporary, for I recognised all over the place, particularly in the places of European man, a kind of gang warfare raging between the angry and rejected feminine and the men of power and establishment. I could name many of them and give chapter and verse of their work and their histories, and show how the rejection has been so deep that they denied even their own feminine nature, just as the Amazons did, and pursued an ersatz masculinity instead. Happily there has been as yet no repeat of an all-out war, because there are too many other signs of a healing totality, a foursome at work in the spirit of man. I refer to the feminine in the man and the masculine in the woman, no longer denied either by the man or the woman but two twosomes making a fourfold spirit with a fourfold vision of life. And that, too, I am certain is where Prometheus and Chiron are busier than ever before, and the rounding of the square of ourselves is to happen.

In this regard I often ask myself, what is one to make of the fact that in recent days a new planet has been discovered, close to the sun, and that something in the astronomers compelled them to call it 'Chiron', so that in outer space, home of the banished gods, there is this bridge of being? The healer and the servant of music and harmony and order has joined the company.

But here in my own small way I was coming to a track where the horse, all unseen, was entering the life of the world of today in the service uniquely of the feminine.

6
The Horse Woman

Hoping that Blady by now will know that it hurts me almost more than it hurts her to obey the laws of reality in the telling of what led me to her and, even if she does not appreciate it, understands the wisdom contained in the old English saying that 'the longest way round is the shortest way there', I turn to the girl.

She is as real and as much a fact of the living truth as everyone else in this account, and yet I hesitate to refer to her by her own name. It is not because, happily, she is still alive, but somehow, like myself, Bird of the Wind and Diamond, the story which circumstances made of our lives is not a subjective one, although it could not have been experienced more subjectively. It is infinitely objective, I feel, and it really is true, known or unknown, for all human beings, so to give it the specific name under which it went in this brief and butterfly pattern of my life seems not only inaccurate and somewhat egotistical but takes away the freedom it has to be incorporated and identified in the lives of others. Like that last camp at the end of years of desert journeying that I mentioned where, for once, I could not put a name to it and it has been left on my records as 'the camp that could not be named', I feel that perhaps she should be the woman, the essential feminine that could not be named, or whose name, as a famous ballad sung by my Cape-coloured countrymen says of an unknown but fateful vehicle coming over the horizon towards an outpost of their life: 'It has no name yet; its name has yet to come.'

So I shall start by saying that I knew of her long before I met her. I knew of her family long before I knew she existed. I knew a boy whose family left South Africa in disgust after the

Anglo-Boer War and went to settle in the Argentine, of all places, to escape British rule in Africa. They settled in Patagonia on the Strait of Magellan and continued there, as they had done in the heart of Africa, to farm with sheep, sheep imported from the heart of Africa. And I remember at school how, with my love of the sea and history, I rejoiced in thinking of the African bleating mingling with the great choirs of wind soaring to their crescendos round Cape Horn and the hooves of breakers pounding the southernmost tip of the far-flung Americas. Far as they were from their home, the families concerned were so dedicated to the earth of Africa that those who could afford it sent their children there to be educated.

I often talked to this boy, and he would tell me of sheep-farming the African way in Patagonia and gossip about their neighbours and, in particular, a Scottish border family of an ancient clan which I knew by reputation, as it were, from several historical novels. He had the greatest admiration for the translated border Scot who was head of the Patagonian clan, and spoke not only of his sheep but of the way he had become a renowned breeder of special Argentinian horses.

Somehow, although of no particular relevance to my life, the story vanished only from the surface of my mind and lodged somewhere else, alert and vivid, waiting for another call onto the stage of my self.

It came in 1939 when fate was at its busiest and most profoundly committed to perhaps the greatest mythological war in the history of man. I know that those who read history only as a process of dramatic and manifest outer eventfulness will find this an unreal and ridiculously fanciful way of speaking about a war that caused so much destruction and the loss of so many millions of lives. But one day I am certain that this war too will be clearly seen as a mythological unfolding of inevitable horror and awfulness of the kind which is the only means left to fate when human beings refuse to enlarge their awareness and insist on living a partial self at the expense of a lifegiving whole. It will be seen, moreover, almost as an act of impending despair from creation itself that men, on whom it had conferred the Promethean gift of fire, this divine gift of consciousness, were failing consciousness itself and turning it into a source of corruption. In a sense the whole of the apocalyptic view of the history of murder and killing behind us speaks of corruption of power, but never has consciousness been so dangerously corrupted by the power the Promethean gift has given it over the natural world, over lesser forms of life, as it were, than it is today, and never has the whole, as we have seen in this pattern of cancer, been invaded all over our beloved earth in so total and lethal a manner. In so far as a war which ended with the explosion, so symbolically, of two nuclear bombs can be seen as serving a positive end, it is as a warning that life had to move on and could not stand still, as the gods themselves had once stood still in one favoured and comfortable expression of themselves. Never has the necessity for a way of wholeness, stretching beyond all the divisive opposites of life for a way transcending good and evil and the redemption of the abuse of the divine power Prometheus had given to the mankind he loved, been so great and urgent as it was through the terrible war that broke out then and distorted the pattern not only of my own life but of all the actors who were preparing themselves for the coming of Blady.

It was one of those strange coincidences that, preparing myself to go to war in that lucid and ample summer of 1939, I was asked if I would help to publicise a book my friends and family thought of the utmost importance, which had appeared almost on the day when Hitler invaded Poland, and was called *Mythology of the Soul*. I have not read the book since that September, but I thought it a breakthrough in a dimension of awareness to which intuition had brought me from the time of my birth, and to which Diamond and Bird of the Wind also belonged. It was a book written by Godwin Baynes, who was a friend and colleague of Jung, had gone with Jung on his fateful journey to Africa in 1926 — the year in which I myself walked those African uplands for the first time — and thereafter settled in England and tried to make people aware of the role of what came to be called the 'collective unconscious'. The concept of the collective unconscious was providing more and more grim evidence of its own nature and reality, but nobody was

147

interested in these things or, for that matter, in any books at all except perhaps those of a light weight that could be slipped into military greatcoats and not be in the way when the real shooting took place.

How I got the book noticed is another story and not relevant here, but the point is that I achieved it and, as a result, had a brief contact with the author, who was already a close friend of my parents-in-law. He telephoned to me one day and asked me if I knew anybody at the Foreign Office who could help him to obtain for a girl, who was a close friend, the necessary papers to enable her to go to Spain.

I did not meet her at the time, but all I heard suggested an exceptional nature to me. She was in the far north of Scotland when war was declared. She came from the Argentine but was of Scottish descent and, while all the men and women around her were united in a common desire to do something for the war which had broken out, she had just one clear instinct: she thought of the great shadow of death, almost like an eclipse of the sun that would last for many years, creeping over the light of day and mind, and her duty was imperative. There was a man in Spain she had promised to marry and, before anything else could happen, she must marry him. It was the classical imperative of the feminine throughout the ages in times of killing and death to re-create, and that was where she was going to begin. She was going to Spain.

I was able to help her, and she vanished from my sight and preoccupations and might have been forgotten, but there came a moment after the war when I myself had to go to Spain and my family suggested that I go and see her. They went on to explain that, although the laws of the dictatorship in Spain had made it impossible for the man to obtain a divorce from his first wife, they had set up an establishment and had children of their own, with a home in a great city and a farm in the hills above Barcelona, where one of their great delights was training and breeding horses. She herself was an accomplished rider and took great part in eventing, and she had a small collection of silver trophies that showed how successful she had been at this sport.

Once we met I took to her and her husband greatly, and from

then on saw them regularly. The more I knew of her, the more I was convinced she was a member of this family of whom I first had rumour at school. Her love for horses, like mine, was there from birth, and even more highly orchestrated and consciously cultivated than mine, because her father had wanted a boy and when his wife had presented him with a daughter, consciously and unconsciously, he had brought her up as a boy. She had no Bird of the Wind to keep her company, but she had *vaqueros* and horsemen for friends. She learnt her riding from them, and all the arts and sports which their harsh lives allowed them.

She was to tell me that she never knew better horses than the horses bred for daily use in the Argentine. They were not wild and unpredictable, but they were never tame. They had a resilience, an innate sense of adventure and a spirit that could not be broken. As her drawings so clearly showed, they were heraldic in spirit and naturally legendary in performance, and one of the legends of the horse already made contemporary was due to a friend of hers called Tschiffely, who took three Argentine broncos and rode them day after day, and sometimes all through the night, in an unbroken chain of effort and diversity of circumstance, from Buenos Aires to Washington. She had a large photograph of Tschiffely riding to the cheers of a vast crowd towards Capitol Hill in Washington.

It was not surprising, therefore, when I talked to her of the race against cancer won in Great Britain by a condemned jockey and a condemned horse, that she was pleased by the story but was not at all transported as others were. She welcomed it with a 'But of course . . .' as if in the world where she went with horses it was a matter of normality.

Before she was ten she could throw a ranchers' knife so accurately across a room that it split a fly on the wall. She walked, not like a man, but rather like a young boy, and there was always something boyish in her manner, something slightly urgent in her step, as if it were perpetually on its way to fetch a horse from the Patagonian prairies.

Even in those years when it was not yet as fashionable as it is now, she cut her hair rather like a somewhat effeminate boy, and she had the openness, the freshness, the directness and the innocence of a boy before he is highly educated and compelled to settle for less within himself.

She had piles of drawing-books which she showed me, full of drawings, paintings in watercolours, technicoloured in crayons, of horses of all manners and kinds and patterns and positions and movements. And what was interesting to me was the fact that in not one of these books was there a drawing of a horse as we see them in the world. They were all of horses as they walk only in the light between dreaming and waking or, as I would have thought of it, that light which presided over my portion of the great memory of the world of gods and titans of Greece.

Yet later, as I went with her and her husband to some of her sporting events, not only in Spain but in France and Switzerland, she was dressed as impeccably as any other feminine rider in the field, and no one would have known that the horse she was riding and the race she was trying to win was not of the then and there, but of her own special within and forever.

There came a time when, because of the work I had to do in the deserts and bush of Africa, I did not see them for some years, until one day I found a long letter of reproach waiting for me on my return, and the invitation implicit in every sentence of the letter coincided with a wish which had become increasingly urgent within myself.

I had a great longing to go back to the Mediterranean again. I had spent two long winters on an island in the Mediterranean. I had written my first book on this island, and the longer I lived there the more I felt that there was somewhere a Mediterranean person in my line of life between the past and the present. It may have been something that I owed to my love of Greece and its mythological manifestation. I do not know, but I remember feeling with a great and acute nostalgia, like a physical pain, that after so much war and fragmentation between exploration in desert and forest, and working in London, I should go back to my island again.

So I thought I could combine these things, sent a cable proposing some dates, and when an answer came back that I should meet them on a certain day at Nîmes and drive back to Spain with them, I arranged my journey so that I could begin it with some days on the island. And from that moment, I think an old pulse began to quicken again.

When the day came to arrange my journey to the island, I very nearly walked out of my travel agent's office, and thought I would change my mind. I knew that the Germans had occupied the island throughout the war and done some damage to it, and in general I had become afraid of going back on my physical tracks. I had discovered that one could not go back in time, as it were, in a wilful way as if there were always a straight line of approach between oneself and any places that one remembered. I had found that lethal to my memories, because when I had tried it, although the physical change in the places of return was not change in any particular, something had gone from the scene. The life that had been within it had been withdrawn, and one was presented with a kind of mummy, an embalmed and well-preserved something which once was as vibrant with life as it was in the memory but now found itself denied by the reality of the present. There was perhaps only one way of a true return, and that was a return that happened out of an immense circle of one's life: a final round-up of all that one has experienced, bringing one back to the point of departure, so that it presented itself in a way so fresh and meaningful that it was as if one was seeing it for the first time.

The changes in the Mediterranean world since I first knew it at the end of the 1920s have been as immense as they are horrendous. I have already hinted at how far the world of Greece today was removed from the world of Greece I had entered through my reading and yet was being evoked continually so that it was more alive in my imagination than ever. Greece had become scorched earth and the physical scene such a terrifying metaphor of the deprivation of life brought about by the withdrawal of the gods and the heroes from the scene, that I could not leave it soon enough, and I never wanted to see it again.

But this island of my first book had been different. It was still an island in the Homeric mode. There was a small harbour for fishermen, and perhaps a score of fishermen's houses, all arranged in a square with a church presiding over it. The foot-paths that led from the village to the extremes of the island were all made of earth, and there were perhaps half a dozen farms with modest little Mediterranean houses, surrounded by figs and olives and, of course, sizeable vineyards. Pine trees and the odd ilex or two covered the rest of the island from end to end, from the surf of the sea and its stretch of curved beaches to the hilltops and the cliffs on the stormy side of the island. In between, the trees were dense with undergrowth, with the smell of herbs of all kinds dominating and purveying the scent as of preparation somewhere for a banquet of ambrose and nectar. There was everywhere asphodel and myrrh, and a miraculous bush called *arbouse*, which grew the flower, the bud, the unripened fruit and the mature red-gold berry all at one and the same time, and seemed to be forever in a state of production, decay and reproduction.

On the stormy side of the island there were some caves, and in one cave, which was still known as the Cave of Pirates, when the mistral was too much I slept with the fishermen and ate bouillabaisse laced with absinthe for breakfast in the cold dawn of their winter.

Happily, the island was privately owned, and the owner mar-ried into an English family I knew well. They loved the island and would not in any way allow it to be developed, but merely looked after it without violating its natural classical shape. I had a room of my own in a little hotel called L'Hôtel les Pal-miers, wherein I could begin my writing work at last. I had eight months there finishing my first book and found that the island, through the nature of its earth, evoked so much of the climate of man's Mediterranean beginnings that it felt as if designed to fit my own need of rebeginning.

I do not think I have ever had happier or more meaningful months, writing from dawn to noon, and then walking all over the island in the afternoons, making friends with the fishermen and the few people around, and in the evenings reading in French as I had never read before, because the whole new flavour of life and civilisation was like having the savour of a precious salt that had been lost, back on my tongue.

Sometimes, because I needed the money, I would work for some days with the fishermen, and even some nights, which I preferred, because fishing the way they did in a moonless dark brought strange excitement to my senses. They fished, I am certain, in the way that fishermen in classical Greece fished. I say this with certainty because they fished with tridents shaped exactly like the tridents I knew from visual representations of Poseidon. Every boat that went out at night had its expert 'tridenteer' – that is the nearest I could get to a name for him in English, rather than something like 'harpooner', which would diminish the image of a fisherman silhouetted against the starlight with the glow of the lamp focused on the sea beyond the prow, like a black silhouette from a Greek memorial vase. He would stand there as the boat moved silently and all was so still that one could almost hear the sound of the stars mingling with the lap, lap, lap of the crystal waters of the sea. Sometimes there would be a swirl on the waters, and giant eels would lash at the surface like the ends of waggoners' whips, but they would always be ignored, because what he was waiting for was the most cherished fish in the islands: the beautiful, the swift and the bejewelled *loup de mer*. And when at last he speared one of those 'wolves of the sea' with his trident, and leaned far backwards as he heaved it from the water and for a moment held the body in the glow of the lamp before it was lifted into the dark starlight, there was not a cheer so much as a musical vibration in the throats of the crew.

There were many moments such as these which maintained my connection with mythological beginnings, as for instance the wine harvest in the autumn, with all the women of the island washing their legs scrupulously and then treading the grapes with their bare feet until their white legs were purple with the juice of Bacchus; then the tide of history seemed to be rising in the great mould wherein they trod.

There were the things we talked about, too. I can remember a conversation that occupied nearly a week of the long intervals between dark and dawn at sea, when I thought that the crew were going to fight one another, and was certain they would not speak to each other again, because the arguments raised had been so long and violent and rough. Yet the subject would sound almost derisory when one thinks of the great world issues passionately debated by the Foreign Secretary one finds in every family, café or club in the world, because it happened to be the season of mushrooms, and the islanders cared passionately about which mushrooms were the best, where they grew, how they had to be picked and, above all, when picked, how they were to be cooked, and that really was the rub. That was fighting talk and, trivial as it may sound, was a warning sign to me of how near to nature we were.

I was somewhat appalled, then, at how I had agonised over returning to the island and how nearly I had not gone, for I realised that it had not suffered all the horror of change else-where and still possessed something recognisably of its begin-nings. It gave me too, short as it was, a respite from myself, from a self that was rarely still but inclined always to travel, as if it were dangerous to sit still and to become a husbandman, rather than be a hunter and a searcher. In that sitting still I thought a great deal about my increasing preoccupation with cancer and its roots in my little story of the headache which inspired the first major enlargement of the theme in *In a Province*, and was now leading me back not only into my own child-hood years but to the moment when the world itself was young, and listening to myths and legends as we had done as children, to fairy tales we believed in more than grown-up truth. How far this concern had already come into my life was exceptionally clear to me because, just before I left, a dear friend telephoned to say goodbye, her voice still ringing with distress as she said: 'Where is it going to end? I have five close friends dying of cancer at this moment.'

I thought then more intensely than ever back over the pattern of the horse and the horse-man in this regard, and of the reunion I was about to have with this horse woman with whom I had had so unlikely a meeting, as it were, on the road of life and become such close friends. I found myself encouraged by the way in which the horse, which in the beginning had had so little to do with the feminine, had now moved over as if its allegiances had been changed and today belonged more to the world of women. Men of course still played a great role in the life of the horse, but they did so more and more professionally, like the rider who recovered so miraculously from his cancer. As far as the male was concerned, the horse was part of a masculine élitism and entertainment, but in the world of the feminine he was sought out for his own sake and for the pleasure and the lift of imagination he gave, particularly to young girls, so that by the time they were adolescent and about to move on into life, they had reached that new moment of birth into themselves helped by schooling and graduating from ponies up to horses. Boys more and more had their minds full of internal combustion engines, and aeroplanes and rockets and cold, bleak, icy speculation about robot-like people among the stars.

I am not suggesting in all of this the kind of criticism it would imply, but trying to draw attention to the neglect of a certain pattern which is always deep in the human spirit and has access to energies of growth and renewal that only it, and no other pattern, possesses, and pleading that this pattern should receive contemporary recognition. It is in this sense that I welcomed the increasing partnership between woman and horse.

For me the only mystery about this partnership was that it had taken so many millennia, if not billions of years, to re-emerge, because it was undoubtedly there in a mythological beginning. Athena had hardly sprung from the head of Zeus when she set about the creation of the horse. On one of the most beautiful reproductions of the frieze on a burial urn I have seen, one of the oldest in existence, the moon is shown as a goddess in a chariot-like vehicle driving two spirited horses. It was an illustration which clung to me all the way on my steep progression up and out of the world of my native Africa, because when the moon was full for us in Africa, black, coloured and white and all the shades in between would look at it and see a cart and two horses in it, and the vision made us strangely happy and our eyes oddly filled.

But greatest of all was the story of Demeter, the mother of all growing things, who could fulfil the whole of herself even in a single tare of corn. Poseidon, the King of the Sea and all its white and black horses, almost as powerful as Zeus himself, wooed her, and she tried to evade him by turning herself into a mare and joining the vast herds that were everywhere in the beginning. The great god, if he were ever to mate her, had to do so on her terms, and turn himself into a stallion. It was out of this mating that sprang first the horse of the great black mare Arion and subsequently Pegasus himself. In one of the oldest stories of this myth of the power and the glory invested in the imagery of the horse, there is a description of the great wind blowing through the mane of Arion, and the storyteller calls them 'the dark locks of the god'.

In these moments of retrospection and introspection there was no doubt in my mind that an ancient, neglected and most powerful source of energies was becoming reaccessible to mankind through the woman, and because the island gave me the time to think these sorts of imponderable thoughts it was ultimately a happy return, so happy that when I was asked by the BBC later to do a programme on Shakespeare's *The Tempest* for television, I could say immediately: 'On one condition – that we do the programme on my island.'

I said this because, from *A Midsummer Night's Dream* to *The Tempest*, Shakespeare's entire work seemed to me, for all its diversity of dramatic form, united and but one work, one long journey in search of the soul which, however subjectively and profoundly of Shakespeare the man, was also of immense objective importance to life and the universe. This journey is travelled in many ways in the world without and, above all, in the world within, and always appears to be in search of something specific but unknown. For an extravert it is called exploration of the geographical and physical unknown of life, and it is only through some act of grace, or by chance, that at the end he finds the physical has really been camouflage for a hunger of the spirit, for nourishment to face and fulfil the future. For Shakespeare it was a journey in his imagination, pursued in the extravert aspects of himself through his comedies, though always with an undertone of another and deeper meaning, until with *Hamlet* the focus is withdrawn from the world of the senses and he plunges deep into his own nature and the spirit of man to explore the dark, the hidden, some would say the tragic, and the flawed aspects of human nature. He does so under the label of the writing of great tragedies, but they are tragedies only in the Greek – the Aeschylean, Euripidean and Sophoclean – sense, because without them there is not the happy ending that awaits creation, that moment when the man who only knows darkly will know in full and know as all along creation has known him.

In *The Tempest* the ending, which makes Dante's *Commedia* and Shakespeare's journey divine, is told, and told as it could only be told, on an island. And what has become a journey of a great and abundant summer of Elizabethan imagination ends in the fulfilment of all four seasons of life.

And I thought of Edward and his island. All that I had said about his affliction being some sort of dark privilege came back to me; and this, inevitably, like all the other winding trails of the imagination, led back to Chiron, because his story is of the suffering which made St Paul talk of 'the priesthood of suffering'. This, at its height, was the suffering on the cross; and all pointed to cosmogonic values, to ultimates, where to suffer freely, not on behalf of the immediate flesh and blood but on behalf of the Creator, or better still 'that which is without name', bestows a meaning that makes questions of happiness and unhappiness, comedy and tragedy, almost irrelevant.

For me Chiron was the earliest and most complete personification of perhaps the greatest element in life, which contains great goodness and great suffering simultaneously, so that in their totality they make more than their sum. They make the two and two of the four of which I have spoken at some length, mysteriously into a five.

For me this potential of fulfilment, which brings to creation something which was not there before, was realised and made accessible in the minds of human beings, so that the gods and all living things were emancipated from outworn aspects of creation in an overwhelming movement of metamorphosis, of which death was as natural and creative a part as birth; where birth, as it were, seen from without, was an exit, and death, seen from the Chiron end, an entrance into a universe of new meaning.

I remember walking back from Le Cap des Deux Frères and being overtaken by the dark. It was an evening after days of mistral which, at the time of writing *In a Province*, I had already instinctively described as 'a long-maned wind, coming down to the sea from the highest mountain in Europe, streaming aflame and neighing for home'. It was an evening bespoke for thoughts about the ancient Mediterranean gods. The clean wind had blown the sky clear of all impurities, and the stars came out, precise and bright. With it all came a picture of Chiron as he was depicted on an old Greek vase of the kind that Keats addressed as 'Thou still, unravish'd bride of quietness! Thou foster-child of silence and slow time'. On this urn Chiron is shown coming back from the hunt with what the poet describes as the spoils of his chase. Before him goes his dog, and on his shoulders he is carrying an uprooted tree. As an image, it is complete. It says visually all that there is to be known about Chiron.

The immortal dog which precedes him is a personification of the intuitive elements of life which came into being with life and gave it a sense of its origin, its direction and its destination, which would never leave it. Always in the earliest beginnings in Greece, in processions leading to such mysteries as those of Epidaurus and Eleusis – and of which those who had participated in them were forbidden to speak to others, not only because that would have been a form of blasphemy but, more, because ultimately no words could speak for the experience – a dog was shown in the forefront of all the many illustrations of Asclepius, the great healer, in front even of the Hippocratic staff and the serpent which entwined it. Asclepius, of course, was one of Chiron's greatest pupils. Chiron protected him, taught him and sent him on his way to heal and to make whole and to start this great movement in the Western spirit which seems for the moment baffled, uncertain and almost powerless as it faces the sickness of our time.

The spoils of the chase are important too, because they are an image of the way in which the hunter represents the element in the human spirit that seeks nourishment for the soul as well as the body.

But then there was the uprooted tree, found by most people who are interested in these things so enigmatic, if not incongruous, and yet perhaps the most important, least ambiguous part of the total picture. I have already devoted a whole chapter to 'the great uprooter' and the sickness of our time which uproots so many lives around us, and it is clear that Chiron already, by carrying this uprooted tree on his shoulder, has accepted that, in helping Hercules to unbind Prometheus and set Prometheus free, he must surrender his immortality and join the human race as they pass through the wings to birth, and death.

It was for me a most moving image, and walking by the foreshore it seemed to me good enough to carry me on to the end of my own road, and beyond. Then, as if to confirm all, I remembered how in all this Chiron was wrapped in a robe of stars, as this island, with the wind barely a sound among the pines and ilexes, the sea lapping like lakewater around me, the smell of myrrh and asphodel and *arbouse* on the mistral air and all that it evoked of our Mediterranean past and present, was wrapped from end to end in stars as well. A feeling of reassurance and belonging, in a measure I had not experienced except in the heart of the Kalahari on nights of stars such as these, when the new, young feeling of release from death and killing and a recovery of innocence was at its most intense, walked almost like a beloved presence hand in hand with me. But something else had also come, to raise it to another dimension, out of time and out of my experience, which sprang from the image of the uprooted tree carried on the shoulder of this great immortal, because it seemed to tell me and all people who would listen and hear, that the images which come so naturally out of our dreams were still as valid, as urgent and regenerative as they had been in our Promethean beginnings, and as relevant today as they were to the imagination which first spoke for Chiron and drew on the same unfailing source as the dream from which my son's version of it had come, uprooter and all.

When I left the island, I travelled in a roundabout way through the pass at the back of the mountains behind Toulon and Hyères and through the great Forêt du Dom, where I remember eating at an inn whose proprietor served me with wild boar and wild turnips and a varnished sort of wine that all seemed strangely and deeply Mediterranean, and finally, as arranged, I came to Nîmes.

There I met my friends. We had a joyful reunion, but we all, in our different ways, were anxious now to take to the road, knowing that the real meeting could not take place until we were back in their home in Spain. Soon we were on what was left of the old Roman road. The time of the day and the nature of the road were perfectly designed to give us, all three, the space of mind we needed to finish the processes of thought and imagination which had brought us there, and to be free to be together without any unfinished business of fantasy or imagination to intrude. Indeed, for me, the nature of the country and the hour of the day still encouraged the mythological and legendary tendencies that had come so alive in the island and were not quite spent. The road crossed the Camargue, the heat making the heavens melt into a burning glass and distort the vision of the world, so that olives looked like giant oaks seen in the blur. One had to endure one's vision of the world as something seen in a fever of hallucination until an everyday platitude of that world brought us all out of our several preoccupations. We saw, not far away, our first farmer tilling the ground with his plough, and the plough drawn by a horse.

Suddenly, there was a loud shout from the girl – which caused me great alarm, but it was only a command that had to be obeyed – for her husband to stop. He looked up at her in amazement, both surprised and somewhat irritated that a woman should exercise so great a power of command over him, and asked: 'What's the matter?'

She replied almost curtly, as if angry at his lack of comprehension: 'That horse! It's got no business to be pulling a plough!'

'Why not?' he asked.

'Can't you see?' She almost shouted at him. 'It's a born jumper!'

'That's interesting,' he said, 'but there's nothing we can do about it. It's not our business.'

She jumped out of the car with that boyish immediacy I have mentioned, calling over her shoulder: 'I shall make it my business!'

With that she stepped off the road and went with her long, boyish stride through the grass and down a row of vines to the far end, where the man had just turned his plough and horse and had stopped, watching her in that still, uncommitted, concentrated way that people of the earth have for strangers. Soon she and the man were in a deep and quiet conversation and we both knew that he had come under the spell of her charm and attraction, which were great and gave great pleasure to all who knew her. But before long there came a movement when the peaceful conversation was shattered and the man began to wave his hands and to make remarks which were emphasised by a sort of pecking movement of his head and chin into space, which I knew of old and which endeared the people of Provence to me. It was a movement which for them was meant to put a greater emphasis on their words than even their expressive shoulders and hands could do. Had I not known the men of my island I would have been alarmed, as my companion was, because to him and to most people, at a distance it looked dangerously like signs of a quarrel. I hastened to reassure him, but he insisted: 'I think we had better join them. Let's go along.'

My instinct was to desist, but I noticed how great his anxiety was. I got out of the car and followed reluctantly. We were not halfway there when the man unhitched the horse and, leading it beside him, came following the woman towards us. We saw as she came nearer to us that she was excited, her face somewhat flushed and her Patagonian eyes wide and shining, more from within than lit from without. She said: 'I have bought the horse.'

There followed protests from her husband to the effect that she could not do that, she was depriving the man of his living, that in any case she did not need another horse, and that it was the height of stupidity just to buy a horse like that without knowing all about it. How many horses had they not bought already, with the knowledge of generations of their pedigree, only to find that they had not bought the horse of their expectations? His reasoning was lucid, long, comprehensive and, by our understanding of logic, irrefutable, and could not have established more conclusively that she was doing something extremely foolish, if not utterly idiotic.

But she stood her ground. She explained that she was paying the man enough to buy himself half a dozen horses, and that she was certain this was a horse of horses, and nothing would stop her from taking it home.

At that point it was warfare between the two of them, almost naked and unashamed, there under the hot Camargue sun, and the sense of war fever was heightened by all the mirages and hallucinations of shapes and shadows, as if we were in a gigantic hall of magic mirrors in a cosmic fair, to heighten the drama of it all. It ended, as all wars of this kind have to end, in a truce which implied only a cessation of immediate hostilities and not the end of what could be a long campaign. The former owner of the horse – because that was what he had become, and in so becoming was diminished in his role as an actor – was brought in only to advise as to where they could find somebody who owned a truck and a horsebox so that she could instantly take the horse to Spain. I was asked if I would stay there with the horse, and they went off to the nearest town, some ten kilo-metres away.

So I sat under an olive tree with the halter in my hand, and the peasant sitting nearby, making conversation with great dif-ficulty, because the man was still suffering from shock at what had happened to him. From time to time I could hear phrases coming from his lips, like 'Good blood of the wood!', followed by a shake of the head, and 'My God, what a lady!' One remark was uttered as a sort of question to me: 'They say they are Spanish, but how can it be? They are clearly not Catholics because what that lady is doing is not Catholic.' In the sense that it was not perhaps a civilised and Christian way of setting about life, but a pagan deed prompted by pagan instincts and a pagan god, he was right.

There followed a long period of silence in which all three of us, the horse, the peasant and I, followed our own thoughts. He broke his silence with an occasional mutter, not of rebellion so much as exasperation, until at last he jumped up and burst out: 'And that is the end of the haricot beans!' He brushed imaginary dust from his hands and said to me: 'To tell you the truth, Monsieur, I am not sorry to see this horse go. She is not a bad horse, but she is neither one thing nor the other. Look at this,' and he waved his hand at the vineyard behind us. 'This is not real work, but it is as much as can be expected of her. She cannot manage a real plough, and now I shall have the money to buy a proper farm horse.'

As he spoke I noticed that the horse was looking from him to me and had already established a difference between the two of us. She was restless from the flies that had gathered about us, shifting from foot to foot, swishing her tail, and shaking her long, unkempt mane. But, with it all, there was a remarkable, still, focused, calm, almost philosophical expression on her face. She made me think of Diamond, although she was not like Diamond. She was bigger, more physical, stronger but beautifully proportioned, and perhaps lacked Diamond's intelligence. That 'tiny, little Chinese-y mind', to borrow Charlie's expression, might just have been the tiniest little bit smaller than Diamond's, but there was the feeling of an immense heart and spirit, and with it a kind of positive acceptance and an implication that every moment of her existence would be the total moment, a moment treated as if it were to be both the first and the last moment. It seemed ridiculous to think of a horse in that way, but I was not thinking it; the horse made that impact on me.

I thought it best to introduce a new subject of conversation and asked the farmer about the Camargue, which stretched way back eastwards behind us, not earth so much now as a sheet of flame. Were there still cowboys, and wild horses? I knew there were still flamingoes of a rare kind. Had he ever seen them? Were there still bullfights at Nîmes and Arles, and did they still use lassos and bolos? And what about the mistral, one of the great winds, so real that it could not just be expressed in terms of the compass and other statistics but had to have this special, lovely name? Did it still blow here as it blew in my young day, and as it had blown throughout the history of Mediterranean man? Yes, of course, he knew about the mistral and what a pest of a wind it was. He would say yes to all these things, except that he had never been to a bullfight, and had never been to see the flamingoes, because people like him, unlike people who just passed through, had to work hard for a living and had no time to stand about and look at things.

I began to think less of my own thoughts and observe the horse, and the more I observed the more I realised how both the peasant and I were fidgets, with all sorts of trivialities of a passing nature buzzing in and out of our minds like flies, whereas the horse was utterly absorbed and content, resolved in a belief of waiting without even thinking of an end or purpose to waiting. I noticed particularly her head and eyes, and though I could not visualise what the woman had seen in her of a jumper, I had no doubt of the spirit and the will to do whatever had to be done immediately and to the full. I began to have a feeling that the horse felt itself known in me, and that I had to respond to her as I had not done since I left my boyhood home. It was a good feeling then to be back in emotions that one had thought lost for so many years. The more resolved the horse and I became, the more the peasant fidgeted and the more impatient his glances measuring the height of the sun.

Just before my friends got back I asked him what he called the horse. He said, as if it were another reason for not setting more store by the horse: 'It has a name of which none of us know the meaning. Even the lady did not believe it could be the name when I told her. That, Monsieur, that creature calls itself "Blady".'

When they appeared, a long train of dust showed that they had wasted no time. When she jumped out of the car and handed him an envelope full of money, he could hardly wait to count it before he was off, at a pace he would maintain all day, to a distant clump of buildings. Everything he had said implied that what had happened was all the horse's fault. And yet, to do him justice, there was something about the affair which made him, and indeed all of us, behave somewhat out of character, an exasperated feeling of not really knowing what we were doing, all heightened by the special effects of a day of extraordinary heat and sensations. It was the hour which I, as an African, always experience in the way the Africans themselves do when they call it the dead hour of the day, when the ghosts are beginning to walk. Indeed, I was convinced I was on an earth where the ghosts walked not at midnight but at noon.

I watched the figure of this overwhelmed little man of the earth, settling down to his day-in and day-out, year-in and year-out pace, which would last almost from the cradle to the grave. The farm buildings to which he was walking had already lost contact with the earth, the buildings had been rendered insubstantial and become part of the burning glass of the day, and the roofs of the house and the barns looked detached and rather like the hulks of ships caught in the doldrums of another Sargasso Sea. The tops of the poplars, which in my part of Provence were called *trembliers*, had lost their tremble, and it looked as if they were the masts of ships gone dead and invisible in the fiery surface of the sea of heat. The man stopped walking just before he too could be claimed by the mirage-making element of the day, stood still for a moment, and then turned round and looked at us. For a moment I was hoping I had misjudged him, that he was coming back to say goodbye to his exceptional horse that had earned him suddenly such undreamed of wealth, but I remembered the few words of conversation we had had, and his expression, and realised that his was probably a far more human thought, so natural in a person like himself for whom life had never been anything but a battle for survival against great odds on a ruin of land in an unpredictable climate. I felt sure he was wondering if he had charged enough for the horse, or whether he should not go back and ask for more. But the sense of the formidable feminine spirit which had compelled him to sell the horse, I believe, made the proposition for him so unpredictable that he abandoned it after a while. In a way, seen from his point of view, it was perhaps a pity, because I am certain that, had he come back and asked for more, he would have got more. As I turned from him to the woman and watched her carefully brushing the hair from the horse's forehead and keeping the flies away from Blady's wide, dark eyes shining steadily back at her with a look of acceptance as if to confirm a sense of total arrival, I knew that there was something invested in Blady and the future which was already there; something far more precious than all the gold in the world.

Perhaps it was conclusive that Blady walked into her horsebox unled and unprompted, almost as if she owned it, and by midnight she was in the stable which, after what her life must have been, could only have felt to her like the horse's equivalent of a castle in Spain.

I did not, on that occasion, see much more of Blady. Already by evening of the next day she was on her way to the farm where the couple's other horses were kept. But from then on I was to meet Blady over a number of annual visits to Spain, and she was included in all the news I had from there.

I have never known enough about horses, and in any case was not greatly interested in seeing them jumping over hurdles and other obstacles at point-to-point. I never took greatly, even when I had a farm in Great Britain, to joining in hunting in colourful packs. Besides, I was not very good at it – although falling off, even quite a lot, would not have mattered had I liked the sport.

But even I was impressed the first time I watched Blady, some two years later, by the ease and grace with which she went through her exercises. I expect that in her memory of her apprenticeship to the plough and the regulation of her life to the petty pace and exactions of peasantry, leaving the earth with such a lack of effort and gliding over fences with so little movement, almost like a bird on outstretched wings, must have been all poetry and music and ultimate freedom to her.

The woman, of course, was entranced, and in her letters could not find words to express what Blady had brought to her imagination and expectations and, indeed, how eventful her whole being seemed to have become. Her husband admitted, after all the effort that love of the woman had compelled him to bring to the matter, that Blady had done much better than one had ever had any right to expect, but he feared she could not do better than she was doing at the moment. Blady, he whispered ominously to me, with a mixture of fear for the woman and satisfaction within himself, good as her performance was, would not be good enough, because her ability to jump was not matched by her speed. Blady was a little too slow ever to achieve anything great. He was too fond of his wife to express the doubt to her himself, because the prospect would be, in her state of expectation, too devastating, but it was there, and he suspected that one who knew as much about horses as she did would have noticed it. In fact, it was not just a subjective impression of his own, it had some objective validity. In practice runs with a young and rather arrogant German businessman and neighbour, who also trained and rode horses, Blady on several occasions had been brought to exercise with his best horses. Blady had done well but had never yet come first. Somehow he suspected that unless Blady was first in everything, the consequences would not be just another of those disappointments to which lovers of horses are accustomed, but far more serious.

I listened to all this and took it seriously, but not as seriously as he did, because it seemed to me that already to have Blady in their stables had brought something special to them and made the whole sport more interesting than it had ever been before.

Blady, in any case, was a joy just to have about. She was good to look at, beautifully proportioned, a black and tan mare with a long black tail and black mane, a lovely head, a wide brow, eyes well apart, beautifully shaped nose, and nostrils always delicately aquiver and perceptive of the subtlest change of sensations. She had a graceful neck, perhaps a wee bit longer than usual, which made her, when running to the full stretch of her abilities, seem streamlined and organic, a part of the current of speed in which she was self-contained. I had good reason, therefore, for realising how important the future of Blady was in the deep of that exceptional relationship of my two friends.

I happily joined in, and I am glad that I have in my possession some photographs of myself and Blady. I do not say that because Blady was a kind of Diamond to me, or even a substitute for the vacancy left by Diamond, but she was important as no other horse had been to me since Diamond, with an importance that was a kind of visitation from somewhere else in my life. It was almost as if the pattern of my life had brought me to be present that day in the hot plains of Provence, in an almost troubadour moment in the heat and resolution of the day, to be ready to bear crucial witness. But witness to what, and where, and when? Certainly to the strangest of all encounters between a woman and a horse and three of the most unalike men of such different and remote origins that anyone betting at the course of chance would have got the most favourable odds laid against their meeting.

I can only say that in these snapshots I have got, Blady and I seem to be very good friends. None of them show me in the saddle, because I would never ride Blady, although I was invited to. I had a feeling that Blady belonged so singularly to the woman that nobody else should ever ride her if it could be avoided. But I am often there standing with her on some chosen place, surveying the horizons of her Catalan world. There are many where I am walking her barefoot in some surf of the Homeric Mediterranean sea.

There is one special one where I am standing by her head, and there is an endless succession of white sea horses pounding the yellow sands. As their arched necks and heads straighten and they withdraw into the deep, the white surf spreads itself out like the hem of a dress of someone curtseying in the presence of royalty, almost touching the feet of Blady and wetting my own, before retreating to leave the yellow sands shining like a mirror; and in the centre of the mirror are clearly outlined Blady's shadow and mine.

In my part of Africa my indigenous countrymen, when they want to convey to another person that they recognise him fully, will say: 'Indeed, you throw a shadow', implying that he is not one of those thousands of see-through strangers but real, because only real things throw shadows. So it is a happy, primitive thought and satisfaction that I have a record to prove that Blady and I too were real and once, together, threw a distinctive shadow on a shining Mediterranean foreshore.

I think it must have been some four years after we met Blady, when she was just coming into her prime, that I got a cable from my friends, pleading that I come to a horse event that would be the climax of the great fiesta in that region of Spain.

Hard on the cable I got a note from the husband, begging me to come, and he said as a joke what he feared in earnest: 'She is expecting the event to be a form of translation of Blady. Taking "translation" to mean what I, as a Latin scholar, once defined in a classical tag, "To translate is to betray", I fear for us all that Blady's translation too, one way or another, will betray.'

I was aware of the implication of unease in the relationship of man and woman in the atmosphere of the home which I loved, the moment I entered it, yet strangely enough there was something real that it conveyed, and although it was a source of discomfort to anyone who cared about the relationship as much as I did, it did not arouse any fear in me for the future. Of course, problems in human relationships are always far more than they appear and have roots that go far beyond the often trivial disagreements and domestic events in which they reveal themselves; the roots always go back to the deepest areas not just into which the roots penetrate but where the seeds themselves are buried in order to conceive. To me it seemed to be focused entirely in the ancient world of horses, and somehow it was in that world of horses that the transformation and resolution vital for the future would come. I think I could not have felt this if it had not been for Diamond, if it had not been for all I have told of horses up to now and especially, perhaps, that jockey whose horse rode him out of the deadly world of cancer into triumph in one of the greatest races on earth.

It seemed to me somewhat confirmed when one night, after a late Spanish dinner, my senses already full of sleep, we were drinking our coffee and she was going through volumes of all that she had ever drawn of horses. Just when we were about to call an end to the day, an exclamation of great satisfaction came from her, and the words: 'Ah, that's where you've been hiding!' She called me over and I looked on the book with its thick, wide pages of a slightly off-white, superlative drawing-paper, and there on the page was a drawing of a horse.

I knew immediately why she had been looking for that horse, because it was clearly an anticipation of Blady. I uttered a rather feeble: 'Gosh, that looks like a younger and another Blady almost – am I wrong?'

'Not at all,' she said, pleased. 'I'm so glad you spotted the similarity without any prodding from me.'

'It's a real horse, then? You had a horse like that once, didn't you?' And I added, without knowing I was going to do so: 'It's a "Once upon a time . . ." horse, isn't it?'

She instantly entered another dimension of time and said in a rather withdrawn kind of voice: 'It is based on a horse I had once. I loved to ride him on a shining foreshore on the edge of the Magellan Strait.'

'He looks good enough to have taken you right round Cape Horn.'

She smiled before she answered: 'Yes, even the original horse could have done that, but this is a drawing of what I knew the original could become and was meant to be. It was a very special horse to me, and it was my last really personal horse before I left Patagonia for good. But it was still a very complex horse, because it had been badly treated before it came to me. Only I seemed to be able to manage it, and there were moments when even I thought he was too difficult, and that I was too young to make him what he should be.

'I had a feeling that perhaps only a man could do it, a man who was incredibly wise and knew the horses as they knew themselves. I felt it so much that I remember in one of those family discussions, half in play, which disguised something that was wholly in earnest, we discussed my future and speculated on the sort of man I would have to marry. I brushed aside all prescriptions and descriptions of the man they proposed for me, and I said that whoever it was, when he came into my life I would not go any further with him until I had taken him to this horse and he had proved himself in the way he managed it.'

She stopped and said no more, not for lack of more to say but because there was far more of an immediate wordless concern, as when the spirit falls off the tightrope of itself in the circus of life and in the deepest of all deeps falls in love.

The sound of her shutting the book firmly and decisively cancelled the image, of which she said, as she stood up, in an almost too matter-of-fact way: 'Isn't it just like Blady?'

Alone in my room, I thought of that final remark again and

again, and my imagination was seized with the feeling that
Blady, and the whole pattern of all our lives centred in Blady,
was summed up in that expression. When finally I went to sleep,
it seemed only a few minutes before I had to get up and get
ready, because the horseboxes and the horses were already at
the gates, and our journey to the fiesta in a province of Iberian
Spain was about to begin.

7
Fiesta

It does not matter whether it is a dinner or a dance, a conversation in the street or at a table in a restaurant or on a road where people meet, they never seem to do anything in Spain without noise. Not a nasty sort of noise, but a noise that is loud and has authority, to indicate that something of meaning is happening. It is often a problem for me, staying at the houses of friends in Spain, because silence, even in the small hours of the morning, is very hard to find, in the sense of silence without a background of human voices.

On this particular morning it was louder than on most occasions, because all knew we were setting out to a fiesta at which there were going to be many events, dominated by the fact that the mistress of the house was riding a horse against famous horses from all over the world. The courtyard at the back of the house seemed full of people, horseboxes already loaded, and she was there by the special horsebox wherein Blady was standing, still and shining and intent with the expectancy of waiting.

Our lady was obviously impatient to be gone, but joined in the last exchanges meticulously and, when she left, was given a farewell not without a tear or two, as if she were going like a Columbus of a new world on a first voyage of discovery. She left first because she was going by a longer but easier route to the regional capital. Her husband and I were going in a Land-Rover with a smaller horsebox and her number two horse, Epinard. We were taking a road that went through the hills and in one place followed a long, winding pass, rather steep in places – a pass which Epinard had travelled many a time. Blady had never done that journey, and her mistress explained that she wanted not to expose Blady to any more than she already carried within her. I have never been certain of the explanation but I feel sure there was an element in it of something which mattered more to our lady than what was about to happen, and which she wanted as much as possible to be between her and Blady alone.

We left next, with almost as abundant a ritual of farewell in a great chorus of Spanish voices, in the Latin language which is perhaps my favourite. He was driving, I sat beside him, and behind us was their senior groom – who in the way of the best Spanish households was on familiar terms with his employer – watching every bend in the road as if it might be rounded to bring us face-to-face with a peril to his horse, and freely giving advice on driving, without offence and frequently in a manner that made us laugh.

But as we were about to enter the pass, the morning became more overcast and we soon came into a drizzle. It had not rained for months and the dust on the road became slippery. We went more and more slowly down the pass, although never, it seemed, slowly enough for the groom.

I have always loved rain, and I have loved the hills, the mountains, the plateaux and the earth of Spain, because it seems to me as if there is something of Africa in its nature, and the Mediterranean world stretches out a warm, experienced hand, almost to touch the land of Africa at the straits of Hercules. As a result, a feeling of welcome and belonging seemed to surround me, and as we came out of the drizzle into the steepest part of the pass and could see, through the distant cliffs, the wide Mediterranean scene flung wide open before us, I was keen all over with delight.

We had not gone down far and were rounding a bend when we saw, fifty yards ahead, another vehicle and a horsebox with two men on the road beside it. The horsebox was dangerously tilted on its side and the men were obviously wondering how just the two of them were going to put it right. One could tell from the change of their attitudes when they saw us coming that they were relieved, and they hurried to welcome us. But even before we stopped, our groom delivered himself, in his most dismissive tone, of a remark: 'The driver must be French or I am not Spanish.'

My host and the elder of the two men, to my amazement, immediately recognised each other, and were greeting each other warmly and elaborately before they went into explanations. Yes, it was true, they had skidded. They had driven with the utmost care. They were certain it was a fault of design in the horsebox and not in themselves. He had warned his son, the elder man said, that he should not buy these latest horseboxes from America. The Americans might be very good engineers, but who really knew what horses meant better than the Spanish . . . and so on and on, until my host realised they were talking Spanish so fast that I could not follow them, and that in any case I had not been introduced. So at a polite moment in the flow of explanations he took me by the arm and brought me forward, saying: 'Señor Goyoago, a friend of ours from England would be glad to know you and to help.'

The five of us immediately looked for some form of leverage, and were just about to see what we could do when we heard a cry from below. We saw two people, who turned out to be father and son, coming up from a vineyard far below, waving to us as if they were used to walking steep mountain sides like level roads.

The seven of us then did not take very long to get the horsebox back onto the road. The horse, considering the way it had been left tilted sideways against the side of his box for so long, was calm enough to suggest a formidable competitive temperament. He allowed himself to be brought out and walked up and down the road, and then was re-embarked, and to the sound of great and loud expressions of thanks and farewells, went slowly down the road to the same destination as ourselves.

We stood there for a while with the men from the vineyards, watching them vanish down into the pass towards the great gate in the hills at the end. My friend, who was one of the most sensitive and imaginative men I have known, felt deeply indebted to the men from the vineyard, knowing that without their help we could not have done the work so well and so quickly, if at all. He talked to them at great length, thanking them for what they had done, telling them about the importance of the horse and answering various sorts of questions about the fiesta, which was news to them and material of great drama.

In the process of making them feel how important was the service they had rendered us, he asked them: 'Do you know who that gentleman was?' The answer was that they both had been troubled because they felt they had seen him somewhere before; there was something strangely familiar about his face.

'But surely you recognised the horse?' my friend suggested.

'Ah, señor,' they replied, almost together, with a laugh, 'all horses in Spain are great horses, so many that you cannot immediately recognise them all. That one, we are certain, is one of the greatest.'

'Well,' my friend said, full of the climax of the little drama, 'that gentleman is the father of Francesco Goyoago, and that horse is Goyoago's horse – the most famous horse in Spain, if not in all the world.'

Their faces were almost comical with the conflict of their doubts about something almost too good to be true. The younger of the two exclaimed: 'That was Paco's horse?!'

The fact that he could immediately drop into the common form of endearment under which all Francescos go in Spain was proof enough that he was referring to the Spaniard who for some years now had been the champion rider of the world.

'Yes, indeed,' my friend confirmed. 'And since you have performed for him, and all of us, such illustrious service today, you must please allow us to treat you to a celebration worthy of the occasion,' and he held out his hand which gripped quite a sizeable amount of paper money.

At that, both the men became very serious and even their bodies stood almost to attention with pride and doubt as to how they were going to handle this offer of a reward. But my friend had done his part so well that there was no outrage of pride or sensitivities except an odd exchange of roles as if they were, in that part of the road which ran through the vineyards, the hosts, and we and the Goyoagos and their horse had been their guests. The old father said: 'We thank you, señor, but on this piece of earth you must pardon us. We would like to do the giving.' My friend was about to press, but the old man raised his hand before he could speak, and said with a charming smile: 'And you know, señor, there is no point in giving us money in this valley. We would only spend it.'

We got into our truck as if we were leaving a court and place of grace, and had to ride on to the heat and the dust of the vulgar world of competitive men.

We were just pulling out into the road when the younger of the two men appeared at the driver's window and said breathlessly: 'We shall ask the saints and patrons of this valley to bless your horse and make it win, even against Goyoago.' Neither of us had the heart to tell him that, unless the heavens fell in, the horse that was going to run was not Epinard, fetching enough as he looked in his box, but a horse on what we hoped was proving to be a safer and better course.

My friend too must have thought something of the sort, because as he thanked the young man and before his hand came back to the wheel, he crossed himself, a gesture which was spontaneous and suggested a deep kind of anxiety, but above all to me as a symbol looked curiously young in all those hills covered in heather and pine and Mediterranean scrub, and ancient herbs spreading the scent evoked by the slight fall of rain everywhere around us.

I have already mentioned the Afro-Iberian quality of the earth, and this symbol brought to my mind, with great force and clarity, the way that an old African would have acted in begging life for grace in granting such a wish. It would have been so important that the individual would have felt too feeble to know what to do himself and would have gone and asked the best of his doctors, the kind that were also prophets and healers. I suddenly thought of such a healer in the heart of Africa who lived just below the lip of a sacred hill. On impulse I turned to my friend and said: 'I will get in touch immediately with a prophet I know in Africa, and ask him also to add his blessing.'

I was tempted to say more about the prophet but I thought it would be too much for one of so rational a disposition, already somewhat in revolt against the whole trend of such a non-rational series of events as he was involved in, against will and reason. What, for instance, would he have thought of a prophet who claimed that in his sacred cave on the hills he communicated regularly with his serpent, who was a direct descendant of the first serpent that was created? On certain nights of the moon, on the summit of the mountain, there appeared a crooning crested cobra to deliver itself of the most oracular instructions. It was this crooning crested serpent who crooned him from his sleep one night right up to the summit of the hill, and made him watch the stars when five great stars were to be seen falling out of their courses, reversing the natural course of heaven, beginning to travel ominously from west to east; it turned out to be the night that the First World War was declared, and five great nations – France, Germany, Austria, Russia and Britain – began the most intensive slaughter the world had ever seen. Consequently, his authority was great, and his powers of reading the future validated in African terms; and for a few moments, although my body was travelling in Spain, he occupied my thoughts on this other more complex journey on which I was bound.

As a result, I heard my friend thanking me from far away, as if he were welcoming me into a game he was playing, while he admitted, in a spirit of jest, a kind of foreboding: 'You know, Paco is the best rider in the world. There has been no one like him before in Spain, and I doubt there will be again. He has no weakness that I know of in his art of riding, no weaknesses of character or technique. He is at one with his horse, and the whole of Spain loves them both. So that even if Blady survived all the formidable heats that will have to be run over the week, which I doubt, I do not think she could seriously be matched against that combination of horse and man.'

I felt rather unhappy at what I had to admit was the probable truth of his remarks, but he himself felt that obviously there was a factor omitted which tended to diminish the negation implied. After a while he said: 'But you have to admit that it is very interesting that she refused to take the same road as we did. Had she done so, she would have travelled in front and might have skidded where the Goyoago horsebox skidded. You have to give it to her, she has uncanny intuitions.'

Of course it is a valid 'might have been', but even if she had skidded at that place, I felt Blady would have taken it at least as well as, if not better than, the Goyoago horse. With that we drove on, I felt with some accord of spirit, but yet as if there were, on the far horizon of my awareness, a dim sliver of wondering whether that which enclosed us all in the totality of this pattern of men and women and horses had done with that slight incident as my friend seemed to have done with it.

We completed the rest of our journey saying very little as we took to the plain beyond the pass. Although the earth retained the quality of fundamentalism and implication of having been in at the beginning of things, the size of the vineyards increased; there were more olive trees, and there were bigger farms gleaming with walls so white that looking at them in the heat of the day made one's eyes smart. Over the plain and the lift of hills on the eastern horizon, the sky had an African immensity about it and a sweep of blue so dynamic that it was a visual movement of such force that the solemn farm buildings looked a crushable lot. I had no words to match the emotions it raised, and just nudged my friend and exclaimed: 'Look! Great stuff!'

At one place there was a wide and deep spread of oranges in blossom, and their scent, standing in the air like heavy water, made one's senses feel as if they were about to drown under that perfume. As we approached through the hills, the road began to rise to 'my Castellona', as my memory came to call it. At a distance the capital had a clear centre which had a castle-like form and proved to have been the heart of what local legend told was the first Phoenician-Iberian settlement. Of course there were traces of all sorts of Mediterranean cultures, with the Roman era dominant, but there was evidence of the Moorish epoch in buildings and streets, a flash of garden here and a fountain there, but most of all in the genes of its inhabitants. We encountered faces that might have come out of *A Thousand and One Nights*, as well as of the dunes of the Sahara and the Atlas Mountains, striking, vivid faces, eyes full of Moorish lamplight, and noses of the men who brought mathematics, gardens, tapestries and carpets and all manner of things harsh and ruthless as the Bedouin blood of their origin demanded, but also refinements and a central Asian, knightly and heraldic state of mind, in the mould of the myth grown around Saladin.

This impression was all the stronger in the fiesta dress which was imposed on the town, because the nearer we came to it the more we began to get whiffs of something special in preparation. Already there was a flutter of banners and emblems, a flag or two over the rooftops, and lots of houses were already breaking into flower.

The flowers seem in my memory all to have been red, the kind of red I have never seen anywhere else as in Spain, not even in Russia – a nation that seems to believe almost that it invented red, and the word they use for it is so possessive that it is equated with the word for beautiful. They were flowers of many varieties, but I remember above all the geraniums and the red carnations with their special scent that seems to smell almost more like spice than pollen, carrying with it something of the east and of Aztec Mexico as well as of Inca Peru. Indeed, in some odd places there were red dahlias too, a flower that has always said to me: 'I am not of today and I am not of Europe. Look at me. I am Inca.' And of course there were sunflowers to keep track of the sun so well that they were there to greet it at dawn after its long journey through the dark.

So although the festival did not have its opening for another full day and night, it was already present in the visual scene. Our eyes, our noses and even the dust in the streets were fully aware of its coming. As we entered the narrow, winding streets leading to the heart of the ancient little city, I noticed that on either side shops and houses were festooned with firecrackers. We were followed on either side by long lines of firecrackers, linked to fuses of perhaps half a mile or more before they emerged in the centre of the town, leading to a cluster of lethal-looking fireworks that looked to me far more like scarlet mortars of death than instruments only of bangs. Their fuses at every point on the perimeter of the ancient city were there to be lit on the night which was to be the climax of the celebration, after the Goyoagos and – how could one forget it? – our Blady and her lady had run their final race. But another fuse was already lit and the fire running, in the sense of history and the

179

spirit of men gathering there from all over Spain to set off the explosion which was feebly called fiesta.

So we arrived at our sprawling hotel, which too must have had a long history, with its foundations of great antiquity. Inside, the reception hall and desk, the lobbies and lounges, were on a modest scale, the corridors narrow and winding endlessly east and west, but the ceilings were lofty and the diningroom was enormous. All this was taken in at a glance as our baggage, and our lady's and the groom's, were quickly unloaded. Epinard, who was now clearly of a mind that travelling could be overrated, was led from his box, and there already, looking over a stable half-door, was Blady, and beside her, fastidious as if not only the horse had been well-groomed but she had come to her fresh from her bath, was her lady. It was, I must admit, a good picture to meet one at the end of such a day. Our groom was immediately enlivened by it, and Epinard even ventured an effort to nicker his satisfaction, but Blady just pricked her ears and, unbelievable as it may seem, seemed to incline her head gracefully from a great distance and height, as if already she had absorbed it all and was in the company of her lady as usual, not only there but also somewhere else.

One of the great joys of Spain to me when I first travelled it was that one could go anywhere and find hotels where it appeared to me horses were marginally even more welcome than humans – perhaps because visits from horses were already becoming more infrequent.

Inside our hotel, as we headed for our rooms along the winding corridor, shaded more against the sun than walled against the cold, we met a man walking with a singular face and stride. I do not think the face itself could have been far out of the ordinary of the generic frame of the human race, and perhaps it was just something belonging to the expression and carriage of the man; but as he walked towards and past us his stride was too measured and, as it were, carefully rehearsed. He went by as if he had not seen us, and I felt he was something extraordinary. We rounded a bend and saw three more men talking by a door, obviously knowing one another and having just arrived. Although their features were of a totally different cast, they also gave me the same strange feeling as the man in the corridor had done. Hardly shown through the door to a rather small room, but with a window over the garden and beautifully quiet, both my friends asked, almost in a whisper: 'Did you notice those four men?'

I said I could not help noticing them, their impact was so intense.

'Well,' they whispered in awe, 'they are the four most famous bullfighters in Spain!' Our lady continued: 'We have both seen many bullfighters in Spain and they all have the same, utterly singular look as those four men. No two of them are physically alike, and yet they are all alike.'

I found her remark deeply satisfying, and remembered a Japanese way of describing the singular or unique, above all when referring to Fuji, their sacred mountain. They call this phenomenon a 'not-two', and indeed, there was in a diluted form a 'not-twoness', a Mediterranean 'not-twoness' all over the place, which I took to heart and which settled me first in some rare ante-room of sleep before I fell into what, for men's spirits in an age so full of unease, was a true slumber.

But perhaps the ante-room was even better than the slumber because of the sounds that came to it, those human noises full of anticipation and excitement, no longer disordered and feverish and full of busyness but pleasantly aware that duty and labour were suspended and a moment of irresponsibility was upon them. It was rather like the noise and the kind of voices I heard on the last night when my whole boarding school in Africa was breaking up for a long vacation.

As the voices ceased there was a faint rustle of leaves, then a nightjar seemed to do his best to spoil the rehearsal of prelude to the harmony of a cloudless night, and only ceased his clatter when an owl decided to interfere. It must have been an owl of the most magisterial proportions with great authority, because he immediately asked, as it were, for papers of identity to be presented by all the creatures of the night, calling out three times: 'Who, who, who? Who is there?'

That one call brought a powerful sense of reassurance to the night. All the irrelevant noises seemed to vanish then, and only real sounds of the night moved into their place and kept in their place, because whenever they seemed to be in danger of scattering, that voice came back and asked, again and again: 'Who, who, who? Who is there?' – until I almost came to the point of starting a philosophical dialogue with myself and turning it into a 'Who, who, who? Who is there?' not just in the night, but in me.

I was so refreshed by morning that I dressed early, and as I was shaving I became aware of strange kinds of swishing sounds coming from the corridor. The sounds were fairly irregular and of a kind that I had never heard before but felt appropriate and singularly domestic. I could not place it until I opened the door of my room and, as I looked up and down the corridor, to the left and right of me there were silks of the most unusual and beautiful colours spread out on the carpets of the corridor and, leaning over them, almost in the attitude of Muslims in prayer, with expressions of singular reverence were the four bullfighters I had briefly seen the day before.

They took no notice of the opening of my door and me standing beside it, and I soon realised that they were not at prayer but bent over the biggest domestic irons I had ever seen, and obviously pressing the cloaks they were going to wear in battle with the bulls that day. The impression of men engaged in something special, if not sacred and close to prayer, remained. The air of a singular dedication and commitment one had felt about them the evening before was present in a heightened form. Certainly, in spite of being occupied with a visible and important worldly duty, they were also engaged in a profound concentration of spirit within.

I went quietly, almost on tiptoe, and with the most fastidious and meticulous of steps and movements on the little there was of free way in the passage, but they did not once look up or stop their ironing, and when I looked back at the point where the turn in the passage was to take me out of sight, they were still there, and from that distance looked like four monks attached to a sacred élite, preparing for some enactment of an ancient mystery uniquely in its keeping.

Below in the dining-room, as I opened the door, I was met

with the sound of light-spirited and uninhibited conversation and much coming and going between tables as people recognised one another from previous fiestas and rose up to welcome and greet one another with great enthusiasm, if not rapture. At our table my friends had not yet eaten, because they were standing with a circle of friends and acquaintances around them, and the atmosphere of reunion and escape from the anonymous world of everyday life in cities, or on painfully exacting farms, as well as the sense of participation in the climax of their own interest in horses, made everyone happy and excited.

I did not get a chance to take in all this for long, because I was immediately seen and summoned to our table and introduced to an almost plump and rather tall man, dark with distinct traces of Moorish features, except that his mouth was partially hidden by a thick and long moustache. I do not remember his exact title, which is a pity, but it was old and illustrious and perhaps the equivalent of a baron. He was the president of the association which lay down the rules and governed this particular sport in Spain. There were so many people to meet and indeed things waiting to be eaten that the introduction did not last long and I did not see more of the Baron then, but I do remember the moment because I think he gave me the clue to something important about the spirit in which the fiesta was to be held, and the spirit in which men met and did these things with horses, particularly in Spain.

When we sat down, our groom appeared between our lady and her husband, not to eat, because all the grooms preferred to eat at the same table so that they could discuss their work and collect gossip for their owners without inhibition. He came just to say that Blady and Epinard had slept well and seemed as fresh and bright as if they had not travelled at all. Then he asked his employers: 'Was that man speaking to you really the Baron?' The question was almost as aggressive as it was curious. 'Yes. Why? Have you not met him before?' And they mentioned some other famous fiesta. The groom was not interested in that part of the answer. He had something more important on his mind which he revealed with indignation: 'Then he is a disgrace to his title, and his office, and should not be wearing the kind of moustache that makes him look like a retired corporal of the Foreign Legion.'

He turned his back on the table to convey his outrage, and hasten this piece of intelligence to the other grooms.

And so the process of identification, re-orientation and differentiation of our community of observers, spectators, owners of horses, grooms and bullfighters and, not least of all, horses in their stables, had begun. It was almost as if all the horses taking part in the competitions that were the core of the fiesta were there together at that time and that place, with one exception: the great Paco, his father, his horse and groom and American vehicle were housed in some privileged elsewhere, not because of a sense of dissociation from our assembly but because, once identified at any fixed place, Paco and his horse tended to be mobbed, and that, according to our groom, could not be tolerated because it was bad for horses. He seemed to think that for horses to be mobbed was the worst of all forms of blasphemy, but did not seem to mind what it did to their riders.

As we prepared to leave our table the doors between the dining-room and the kitchen flew open. I caught just a glimpse of some golden bread crusts side by side in their great pans as they were pulled out of an oven, attached to an immense kitchen range, so large and hot that my imagination, stained as it was with the Huguenot history of Roman Catholic persecution, thought it might have been designed by the Inquisition itself, because it had a grill big enough to roast saints upon, perhaps even the one who said: 'You've done me enough on this side. Perhaps it's time to turn me over?' It was of course a bizarre and ridiculous image, and was instantly redeemed by seeing an immaculate cook taking out the loaves and wrapping them in damp bread sheets, which were instantly so hot that they began to steam. They were joined by masses of croissants, and the croissants of Castellona, perhaps because it was a fiesta and a special spirit ordered these things – possibly even some Moorish sultan's baker with a Sufi soul which demanded their moon-shape – tasted better even than the croissants of Aix-en-Provence, so that we were commanded by my host that we must, in honour of the occasion, of the cook, and of all the croissant lovers of the world, show solidarity and sit down and eat a croissant with a fresh cup of coffee as well. I do not think I could have done it if that wonderful smell of fresh bread had not come to dominate the air in the room. I do not know of any smell at the beginning of the day which is so life-giving, so full of reassurance, making the beginning of the most ordinary day an extraordinary day, and a feast day, above all days, almost portentous with fate.

We had barely finished this addition to our meal, so good that had I been pressed I could have managed more, when a girl burst into the room. Burst was the only word for it, because she was so impetuous that the doors, which were together one minute, at once without pause seemed to fly open, and she seemed to come through them like someone through a paper hoop in the circus. She must have known where we sat, because she made straight for our table, and was fully as alive as her entrance had suggested. She embraced and re-embraced our lady and then quickly, tightly, but once only, her husband, and then again our lady, and started speaking Spanish so fast that although she had the clearest of voices I could not follow except that it seemed to be about a new horse she had bought, and our lady please had to stop eating and come at once because she wanted her to be the first to see and approve.

It was only then that she seemed to notice me, and for a moment her face calmed and she looked at me steadily. I found myself looking back at one of the most beautiful sixteen-year-old faces I had ever seen. She then looked at our lady and fastidiously went through the ritual of being introduced, but the moment it was over she had our lady out of her seat and into the courtyard, on their way to the far end of the garden and the stables.

'Well,' my friend said, not without amusement, 'you have met her at last. I knew that you would meet, and the manner in which you would meet. She is like quicksilver, Mercury on wings, and mad about horses.'

There followed a short who's who account of the girl, her rich and aristocratic family, her difficulties with her parents, her complex character, and her obsession with horses, particularly difficult horses.

'You never know,' he said, 'what sort of horses she would have bought if left to herself, but fortunately her father is a connoisseur of horses, and he made sure she bought horses of the best pedigrees.' He paused, and his rational predisposition nagged at him again, and he said: 'I could wish that our own choice of horses showed a little more respect for breeding.'

I knew to what he was referring and came near to protesting and to saying that to the eyes of an observer like myself, recorded or not recorded, if there was one thing Blady seemed not to lack, that was breeding. But I held my peace and, as I held it, the two women came back from the horses, the young one calm and reassured, with her arm round the older one's waist which she unclasped as they came near to our table. She walked on and out of the room. We stood up as our lady came to our table, and it was unnecessary for him to ask the question which was plain in the look on his face, when she said, with a lift in her voice: 'I think she has really got herself her best ever horse. I am so glad for her, because she needed one.'

It must have been a long subject of discussion between them over the years, because there was just a tinge of doubt in his 'I'm glad, but you know I feel she needs more than a horse. She could do – indeed, all the family could do – with a first-rate psychiatrist.'

'I do not know about the family, but I do not think that there is anything that her love of horses and the years will not do for her.'

On this note we went ourselves to Blady and Epinard, and took them off to a long, slow, curved sandy reach of the sea nearby. There she took Blady briefly for a gallop along the sands, before walking her knee-high into the sea. It was a still day but a storm somewhere out in the Gulf of Lyons had sent a great swell into the bay. North and south, the sea came in with the manes of white horses streaming into a mist where their long, fine hair did not end so much as vanish into a vapour.

My friend remarked: 'You know, all our grooms and also my

wife believe that there is nothing better for horses, particularly jumpers, than to walk in sea water as lively as this.'

Thereafter I was allowed to lead Blady to cool down, and walk her up and down slowly in the shining sands among the marks of her galloping hooves, and on our turnabout we saw our lady mounted on Epinard, as good a sight as one could ever see.

I could not help noticing how fast were Epinard's bursts of speed and, remembering our host's reservation about Blady, yet I, who have no expert knowledge of these sophisticated aspects of the lives of horses and their men and women, thought that Epinard's powers of speed might not be matched by his powers of jumping, and either the capacity for jumping would be diminished or the achievement of jumping demand so much energy that the speed would slow down. I had a suspicion that Blady, largely due to lack of experience and through the exactions of her upbringing, had fallen so much in love with the proportion and measure essential for a hard life that she herself did not know the extremes of which she would be capable in a crisis. And all my instincts told me that the hour of crisis was about to break.

We went back to our hostelry, and prepared ourselves for an afternoon at the great bullfight which precedes all well-ordered fiestas in that part of Spain.

The girl who had rushed to our table at breakfast in the morning made four of our party, and we walked to the bullfight without saying much. I have mentioned how much of what happens in Spain is accompanied by rather loud voices and other noises, but on this occasion, although the nearer we came to the ring the more crowded the streets became, there was not much noise from the crowd. There was, however, what one can only describe in terms of a cliché: a great deal of electricity. It was something of which I had experienced aspects in different places and on different occasions, and they had all been important, portentous and, a number of times, horrendous occasions.

There had been times in Japanese hands when I was taken to see executions, and I was marched through crowds of Japanese given leave to witness the occasion. There was a peculiar murmur and a feeling that seemed part of a kind of unstilled air in the early afternoon hours over the purple lands and hills of Java, as if it were not only an earthquake tremor of apprehension in my own and the human spirit, but a ripple coming from the throb of the earth's own tom-tom far deep underground, from the lava and the earthquake propensities it had at heart. It was a kind of collective excitement which in recollection I found hard to understand, however much I expressed it and got to know it intellectually. I would ascribe this element in the afternoon only to the fact that we were all, whether we liked it or not, going to witness a killing; not just an ordinary killing but a killing that had to represent one of the greatest patterns of symbolism and mythological poetry in the ancient Mediterranean world. One did not take this reaction too far, because there was another element which made the crowd rather hushed, and tended to contain if not redeem the other. It was oddly enough the kind of spirit I had encountered as a child deep in the interior of Africa on a Sunday morning when, from all ends of our village and the scattered farms around it, people would set out in their best black, the women in long satins, and, apart from the crow of a cockerel which seems forever linked to my memory of Sundays, there were few sounds, so that as the people came down the straight of the street one heard nothing but the low murmur of special Sunday voices and, above all, the swish swish of the heavy satins brushing bodies and dust in the street. It was a sound both reverent and at the same time severe, austere and measured, and the crowds we passed reinforced this impression in their faces and moments of silence – and even a cockerel crowed to perfect this part of the impression.

All this was contained in an atmosphere of high expectancy, rather like the air a great thunderstorm pushes before it as it mounts, temple-like, towards its apex in the blue. I was, of course, open and impressionable before such an impact because I had never been to a bullfight before, though like everyone else in the western world I had read and talked and thought about them a great deal, and I had come to this bullfight reluctantly because, for all its significance in what it tells one about the human being's need for some abiding ritual in transforming the dark and monstrous patterns of forces he has still unresolved within himself, I had no taste for it and on my own I would not have gone. But I felt that all the things in my life which had brought me to that place, at that time, demanded that I should see it whole and not just savour the bits that I thought I would like of the experience.

Once in the ring itself, without the sort of shoving and jostling one is accustomed to in the theatre world of the west, let alone so-called sporting occasions, the compound of impressions that I have described was instantly dissolved in the glitter of dress and colours and sounds and excitements of all sorts that came from what was the largest theatre I have ever entered. I say 'theatre' because I knew instantly that it was theatre of the most ancient kind we had come to see, a vastly orchestrated form of a classical first night of a play by a great dramatist.

We found ourselves seated in the most prestigious place of all, over the ring. I was shown in first and sat on the far right, with our lady next to me, then her husband, and then our beautiful sixteen-year-old, who suddenly seemed shy, oddly vulnerable and somewhat apprehensive because she was immediately next to what was obviously going to be the highest place of all. Once settled down, they all three recognised and waved to friends and acquaintances they saw. I of course knew no one, but our lady whispered to me, for safety's sake in German, that I should just have a look at the man on my right whom she knew slightly, and who was very nice, and was the Duke of Malva.

It may seem unforgivable, when there are so many names not mentioned in this despatch from Blady's great campaign of honour, that I should put a name to this man but, although he was dressed in a grey flannel suit of a cloth and a cut that I envied and which might have been bespoke in Savile Row in London, he was history to me.

My emotions and ideas about his name had become so conditioned that they were almost a reflex. Indeed, in that regard, not even the best of Pavlov's dogs could have been more thoroughly conditioned – because it was perhaps the most hated Spanish name in Calvinist and Huguenot history. From the time I was born I had been brought up on stories and legends about this family's atrocities and cruel, Inquisitional Catholic persecution and wars in Holland. My own family, if I could trust our family mythology, had fought on many bloody occasions against them. All this had been so intense that, although I did not know it, there was somewhere a sort of Goyaesque painting of the man in the gallery of my imagination, so that when I did, as my hostess suggested, take in the man, he was so unlike the portrait, and it seemed such a bizarre caricature, that I began to giggle inside myself and came very near to doing the equivalent of what I had dreaded most as a boy in church: surrendering to the terrible impulse to laugh when the priest was making his loudest and most earnest of exhortations and summonses to the most exalted peaks of holiness. Fortunately, our lady leant forward to introduce us, and I was able to shake hands at last with history. The incident, slight as it was, made me feel naturalised and oddly at home, and I could sit back and look upon one of the oldest bullrings in the world.

It was, of course, a perfect ring, covered with the yellowest of sand, and everywhere one looked there were human faces staring at the gates where the uniformed servants of the theatre stood to open the doors and gateways, and guard the dark passages that led to the place where the men and the horses and, above all, the bull were being prepared for their entrance.

I thought of those passages between that place and us all sitting there in the early afternoon light of the Mediterranean sun, as a labyrinthine way, and the bull as the monster which Theseus had set out from Athens to Crete to kill, so that he could free Ariadne from the tyranny of the night of life. This connection with the myth was suddenly made, but of course it must have undergone a long preparation in my journey through the world of Greek mythology and legend, which started on that morning when I opened a gift from my father and found a book, especially composed for children, on the myths and legends of Greece.

In this way many of the reservations I had about participating in the bullfight were abolished, and it became part of a process of progression. That it was a ring in itself helped, because all rings possess instant qualities of whatever it was that originally made the circle magic. The greatest example of this was already in my mind because it came from Provence, whose earth was like Spanish earth and had that mysterious mix of Mediterranean Europe and Mediterranean Africa that made me feel so much at home in it. Provence, too, had its own way of acting out this drama of man's inborn role of providing male armour for feminine love, defending and rescuing the feminine from the monster in itself. I was soon to learn from a discussion which took place between the Duke of Malva and a fellow aristocrat – whose name I cannot remember, but who must have had an English governess because he spoke a rather 'prunes and prisms' English with a Spanish intonation – that there were at least two schools of thought in the Mediterranean Latin world of how the man and the bull theme had to be orchestrated. For one school it was obviously connected, as I had just made my own connection, with the labyrinth in Crete, with Ariadne of the golden thread and Theseus and the great rescue of the youth of Athens from being annually sacrificed to the monster. The other, and the more prominent perhaps, was the Mithraic school that went back to the Roman legions whose god was Mithras who had to sacrifice to the sun, to the god of reason, the bull that was really loved.

Although I did not know it then, the bullfight I was about to witness leant towards the feminine and her gift of the golden thread to man. This emphasis in Provence was even greater because from Provence there came the image of the vessel that was to be called 'the holy grail'. This word 'graille' was apparently the name given to an enormous circular dish around which a whole family could gather and eat together. In Spanish the word for not necessarily such a vessel but a round container became 'corral', and from Spain it went on to the Americas, and then from both Spain and Portugal it went to Africa and became the 'kraal'. Above all it became in legend that which transformed European culture, the vessel in which the blood of Christ was contained; and went on living mystically in the imagination of all western men in search of the vessel and the perfection of spirit and behaviour that went with its discovery.

Long as all this takes in the telling, these and similar sorts of associations crowded in on me. I even registered, and dismissed as quickly, a recollection of a corral in an American film that was called OK, and somehow this lifted the weight of the more solemn associations that were queueing up in my mind, and helped me to maintain the connection with the ring of the first circus I saw in the heart of Africa where my first white lady on a white horse stirred my imagination, and a clown came climbing out of an artificial moon at the top of the circular tent from what seemed heaven to me, but before he reached the earth missed a step and fell and rolled in the dust to make people laugh and feel superior and well within themselves.

Although I had never seen a bullfight before I knew that, whatever comfort I had in memories such as these, what was about to happen in the ancient circle below us was not going to be a matter for laughter and fun.

And then, despite the diversities of time and nature, all these occasions to which I have referred came together, as two ritualistically uniformed footmen of the ring in colours only found at a Mediterranean fête came to life almost opposite me as they opened one of the great wide gates in the wall of the ring. Out of the dark appeared two blue roan horses with long elegant legs and long-legged riders sitting high, wide and handsome with broad-brimmed hats which were impressive and decorative enough to make them look more like cardinals than horsemen of Iberia. The bright, bee murmur of the crowd was instantly stilled, and everyone, I believe, watched entranced as they moved towards the centre of the ring like animals that had learnt to suspend the laws of gravity and make a game of it, as if they were the horse's dream-equivalent of ballet dancers rather than four-footed things.

The Duke, capable of a detachment that I did not possess, whispered to me that they were Portuguese horses. The riders too were Portuguese, and he had to confess that the Portuguese had, perhaps, horses as good as those of the Spaniards and could ride them as well – and in some instances, like the present, even better. But it was just a pity, he said, that with such talent in the Portuguese bullring they did not kill the bulls. As he said it a nasty lash of history made my imagination wince and I thought: 'That is a bit more like a Malva.'

At this our lady nudged me and I turned my head and leant over and saw that her husband was nudging her too and had apparently initiated the process. 'He wants you to know,' she said, 'that they are horses trained in Portuguese bullrings, and he wanted me to tell you that the Portuguese in their bullfights do not kill the bull.'

I thought that they were telling me this because I might take a kindlier view of the complex of bullfighting from the Pyrenees to Patagonia, Angola, the Argentine and on to Mexico if I knew there was a gentler form. Whatever it was, I felt it was some kind of concession to me, but at the moment did not know what to think of it and asked:

'Which form of bullfighting do you enjoy more?'

'I am afraid,' she whispered, as her husband nodded agreement, 'we prefer this.'

I found myself nudged very tentatively by the Duke. 'They are right, of course,' he whispered.

'Why "of course"?' I asked.

'Well, for the Portuguese it is more of a game, a kind of entertainment, than it is for us.'

'But is that so wrong?'

Our lady who, when she was her full, intuitive self, could be very definite, answered with great force for a whisper: 'It is wrong to play with the bull and make him a mere object of entertainment and amusement.'

'Yes,' said the Duke, 'the Portuguese completely miss the point.'

I knew of course that the point of it all would be made at the tip of the bullfighter's sword in the vital area of the bull's neck at some undecided moment to come. Both my lady and her husband intervened: 'Yes. There would be no meaning in all this unless it ended in the killing of the bull. The monster has to be destroyed.'

She paused, not to let it sink in so much but as if she were trying to express something else that was missing in her words, and then in rather a faraway tone remarked: 'It is a paradox, of course, because the bull must not be deprived of his dignity. It is part of his destiny to be killed, or sacrificed if you like, and somehow, somewhere in all this, for all of us, there is something more than us that must be honoured.'

The blue roan horses were still dancing. I had never seen horses who made so much magic of their elastic limbs and eurythmic spirit and held the imagination of so many thousands of people so tightly in their grip. They ended in a way which I had not thought possible, with the riders removing their black hats and holding them out to the crowd before lowering them to their sides, and then with their eyes still fixed on the place of honour above the ring where we sat and, it seemed to me, without any guidance from the bridle reins resting lightly in their gloved hands, rode the horses backwards, or the horses took themselves backwards, gracefully bowing their heads, a certain toss in the rhythm of their going, until they were out of sight and a noise like thunder rose from the ring.

Up to this moment I believe my memory of the event is clear and accurate, but from then on until the bullfighter chosen for the great fight of the day appeared, I am not clear or certain. I remember the march in of the toreadors and being amazed at the amount of black that appeared in their dress and how suddenly there seemed to me a loss of colour, almost as if a sunset had vanished and the black of night was taking over. The procession seemed to me to be in earnest or, perhaps better still, deadly serious and made me fear for what it portended and how I would react.

I remember I was excited and uplifted when the bullfighter himself appeared, doffed his ritualistic hat and presented it to a lady in the place of honour. I wish I could remember how the hat was transferred from him to the lady, because it could resolve something which continues to be enigmatic in my impressions of the afternoon. The young lady of our party was seated just to the side of the seat of honour where the lady who was to receive the hat was installed. I have a distinct recollection that the bullfighter himself saw our young lady first and seemed startled by the beauty of her face. There was for me just a perceptible pause in the rhythm of his movements, a feeling as if the focus of his intention had changed and the direction of his movement deflected. I cannot be certain now whether he was on foot or on horseback, so that I must to some extent question the value of my own evidence, with so much of it unsettled in my imagination; but somehow, whatever happened that afternoon, I am convinced that in the face of our young lady the bullfighter saw something for which he had searched far and wide.

I find some confirmation of this in the fact that our young lady herself was suddenly startled and turned aside and clutched the arm of my friend and put her head on his shoulder as if put out, and in need of comfort. She did this not with exaggeration but naturally and briefly, and then forced herself to look up, flushed and bright-eyed, at the man who by then was delivering his hat into the lap of the lady of honour. The lady of honour was beautiful too, and beautifully dressed in an ancient, ritualistic lace and in black all over.

She took the hat in her hands and held it to her front, and a deep sigh of satisfaction rose like a wind from the ring. Yet I remember thinking it would have been perhaps greater art if the hat had found the virgin lap and fulfilled the baffled pilgrim soul of our lovely young companion. But much as one respects the complex capacities of chance and circumstance as craftsmen capable of the most fastidious precision, it would perhaps have been too much to ask of them a foreknowledge of the presence, on that shining, random afternoon, of a perfect candidate in the right position for their choosing.

Hence the predestined and fore-ordained plan, to entrust so pregnant a symbol to a mantilla'd lady, more mature and with a beauty which had achieved an inner as well as an outer form, remained inviolate.

One says the symbol of the hat is pregnant because, even in its uninventive form of the hat of the day, it represents all that is gathered in the mind and spirit of man of thoughts and attitudes and wonderings about the nature of time and life and the intimations of what kind of a search awaits him. For all of us at that moment, whether we knew it or not, the bestowal of the hat was a recognition of the Ariadne in all of us, even in the bull, and the feeling that the enactment evoked – especially for the fighter who in the end had to complete the reckoning with the outraged and powerful masculinity which has for so long dominated generations of civilisations – was the golden thread which would lead us all from the deeps and darkness of the minotaur at the heart of the labyrinth and out into the light of the day. This indeed was no longer a circus or a game but a labyrinthine reckoning.

It was significant that it was in one of those lulls that come in all storms, even in such an ordered storm of events that were following one another so rapidly, that the Mithraic and the Ariadne dialogue between the Duke, his aristocratic friend and my friends took place. But for all my interest I could not follow them for long, because suddenly the doors at another entrance were opened and, although these doors had uniformed footmen too, it happened so fast that I do not remember seeing any sign of movement from the attendants to tell us what was coming and that was, of course, the bull – moving so fast that the opening and coming seemed almost to be one and the same process.

The change of light and atmosphere and tier upon tier of human faces and strange horses all around him brought him to a standstill. His legs stiffened, the yellow dust spurted around him, and like an animal in a mist he shook his head from side to side and tested his horns and his muscles as if to see whether they were ready to thrust and to throw and to gore, rather as Olympic athletes do when they are trying out their muscles before the pistol shot launches them on their races. He did this and then looked around baffled, which was perhaps one of the most poignant moments of all, because one could not help wondering what horror had put him in such a rage to send him charging into a place, certain that he was called upon to fight and made him so determined to kill. And then he found this vacant tent of the blue of the sky above him, and thousands of human faces directed at him, knowing too well what they expected to be done to him.

Through other doors and openings in the balustrades around him other horses and men, above all the picadors whose task it was to dart him, were insinuated into the ring. Each dart had a pennant in proportion to its size and a bright colour of its own, perhaps not to decorate but to redeem the place of injury in some reminder that, ultimately, all was heraldic.

The course the bullfight followed has so often been seen and described that I have no intention of elaborating on it. Besides, I have not the power or the taste for it. I know Wordsworth told us that 'art takes its origin from emotion recollected in tranquillity'. That may well be how art worked for him, but for me personally it is not true for the whole of art in the hands of life, particularly in the hands of living gods, as that encounter with the bull appeared to me to be at that time and in that labyrinthine place. There are moments in life, no matter how great the tranquillity in which one tries to recall them, that just refuse to be part of the tranquillity. I have found, for instance, in the telling of objective stories of my experience in war, and even in times out of war, where I have a lengthening distance of years to advance the cause of the tranquillity of which Wordsworth spoke, that I was more tranquil in the midst of the events I was trying to describe than I am at the moment of recall, simply because at this moment of recall the context of spirit and the nature of the whole time which contained the instant happening are no longer there to help me and I have to face the moment alone – perhaps the kind of aloneness that the bullfighter chosen for the final reckoning would feel when that moment came in the ring. No, the Wordsworthian prescription certainly did not apply when I was forced to write about the ingredients of truth necessary for fiction, because when I forced myself to do so my hand shook and I was deeply afraid within.

All that I should say, perhaps, is that as I watched I had no taste for the various ways in which the outraged and inflamed bull was goaded and the padded horses hurled against the wall supporting the crowded circles of spectators and one horse so gored and bleeding that it had to be rushed through a side door in the ring.

The faster and more dangerous the confrontation with the bull became and the more blood there was on the sand and splashed on the walls, and the more violent the movement of picadors and their horses and wilder their charges to inflame the bull, the more I expected at any moment to see whatever shape the drama had, shattered, and chaos take over. But all was so perfectly contained that, although there was a great deal that was ugly and, out of context, would have been inconceivably repulsive, the whole never touched on what one could call un-beauty and even at moments rose to a great beauty as all conformed to the rhythm and measure that came from the lone fighter at the centre of the storm. He was strangely still; his movements hardly ever displaced him, and even when the danger of him being thrown and gored was at its greatest I do not remember him ever being forced into the slightest sidestep. He did it all by distracting the bull's aim with the colour and movement of his cape and just a slight movement of his hips and angle of his body so that the horns missed him by a fraction of the millimetre that was as good as a mile. At that still centre he seemed, if he had to move at all, to do as a ballet dancer might, so that, whatever else the spectacle might have been elsewhere in the ring, there at the centre, at the place where the point had to find the right position for the kill, he did not for a second falter or blur the overriding magnificence if not miraculousness of it all.

All in all it was done, it seemed, not for indulgence of a Roman sensationalism but as an image of how futile it is to deal with the forces that assail us in terms of mere action and re-action, and how, no matter how much more powerful than the original action the reaction becomes, the action beyond it is raised to greater powers and the whole design of conduct and spirit becomes almost a clash of great irresistibles and im-moveables until they stand locked and bankrupt and in need of something else to take them beyond.

That 'beyond' was in the bullfighter's keeping, and I do not recollect precisely when the moment came, but suddenly he and the bull were alone in the centre of the ring. He had clearly decided that he had, perhaps far more than the call of his duty and gifts demanded of his role in that particular theatre, given the bull an honourable opportunity to prove itself better than he was within himself, that he had done all that he personally could, short of destroying himself, to honour the power and

the dark glory of the monster. For a moment he turned his back
on the bull and raised his sword, I should imagine not so much
to the crowd as to the lady who had his hat – symbol of his
whole way of looking at life and the future – in her keeping.
He turned about – but not before I had recognised the face
of one of the bullfighters who shared our hostelry. Seated in
privilege as we were, I could see his singular face very clearly
and at once understood the pre-concentration of spirit which
had already begun in that winding medieval corridor of our
hostelry. But it had been raised now to something which I found
almost unearthly and which passed my own comprehension. It
was what the bullfighters call their 'moment of truth'. They
have called it this ever since bullfighting began, way back in a
very early Cretan moment of Mediterranean history. But one
recognised it even in our own day, which blurs so much of
reality with its superabundance of unnecessary things and trivialities. It was a moment in which there was to be nothing that
was false or spurious or contrived, not for the spectators, for
the bull or the man. It had come to what Euclid had called 'the
point of it all', or, with mathematical precision, 'that which has
no size or magnitude but position'. And that position was to be
found in a moment of the greatest possible tensions and, above
all, at speed somewhere small and narrow behind the head of
the bull as it charged. If he did not find that place the bull
would not be killed and the fighter could be dead.

I do not know how many thousands of us were there to
witness what followed almost with the speed of lightning but
with a grace and rhythm which lightning, however wonderful,
never achieves. But since it is true, as everybody knows, that the
numbers of people present at any particular event add to the
intensity of everyone observing the event and make it a highly
personal affair, I do not think I have ever had a moment of
brighter and more dazzling attention, without any form of
expectation. It was a moment when all the considerations which
govern in the here and the now seemed to have become irrelevant and suspended. The bullfighter, slim, broad-shouldered,
black below and green-gold above, suddenly stood on tiptoe,
elegant and alert and arched like a bow and, just as the bull

seemed on the verge of throwing him, his sword vanished into the neck of the bull and the bull fell, and died as it fell.

The bull lay still on his side, his head almost touching the silk of the matador's cape. The thrust had made the point of it all so well that the whole of the sword had gone into the neck of the bull and only the hilt showed above the skin. At that moment the matador was standing with his back to us, so that one could not see his face, but instantly it seemed he had withdrawn the sword, raised his right arm and extended it, sword and all, to the full. It was the antique world's greatest salute of honour with the most moving implication that neither the vanquished nor the victor had any share in whatever there was of praise or blame in the situation; that what had just been accomplished had been accomplished for the god of which they had been merely the instruments and the actors, the priest and the sacrifice, and had reached the point when the sacrament was fulfilled.

The matador held his salute longer, I was to be told, than usual as an acknowledgement of a confrontation that had been far more testing and evenly balanced than most, and then he turned about, the sword came to the ground and I noticed how in the turning the levelling sun threw their shadows well and distinct and elongated out into the centre of the ring. Once more he raised his sword, and I had no time to ask whether that upflung arm was meant as a salute to the bull or a gesture of triumph to the exalted humanity around the ring, but I imagined that it was both, and that through it all there was 'one and another' and that 'two-ness' of this ancient conclusion was there for all to see in the silhouettes on the sand.

In the end I think it was a feeling beyond the two-ness of reality, a feeling of the togetherness of the two and their shadows, and that the meaning of the moment of truth, as it was depicted there, was not to separate one or the other but to remember them as part of a whole of which the chatelaine of the spirit had the dark black hat in her lap.

It was significant that, even in the short time it took for this flash of thought, I had a feeling of being alone in the still place the ring had become. Indeed, just for a moment the silence could not have been greater, as if no one there believed what they had seen. And then there was a deep sound of relief – followed by uproar which I shall not attempt to describe because those who know the kind of Spain I have tried to describe can imagine the rest. I can only say, for myself, the feeling of being alone which had briefly intruded after the killing came back in force. There was no part of me that could join in that tumult of sound that went like a tidal wave through, over and above the bullring. I could only think of it as a tidal wave, like those upheavals of the sea which are caused by some eruption in a part of the Pacific where the sun goes down to send a great wave of water travelling east, north and west and then, many days later, somewhere on an innocent island of northern Japan where all is calm, order and beauty, appear and sweep away men, villages and all. This tidal wave which swept over us in terms of the history of man was caused by an eruption of the first archaic souls of men when they walked with gods on earth, and I could in no way contain it in any contemporary idiom of my own. I was just, it seemed, without defences, alone and moved in a way I had not been moved before. Almost by reflex and as if for comfort, I looked to my side and I thought I heard the Duke say: '*Deo solo invicto, Mitrae.*'

That told me where his spirit came in and no doubt where it would go out. Beside him the aristocrat with the rather spinsterish English voice appeared to me just to have crossed himself. To the side, my friend and host was looking at the sun and, as I knew him to be profoundly musical, I thought it was as if he were listening to some great Apollonian composition coming from beyond the sun, and of how Mithras loved the bull, yet had to sacrifice it to the sun who loved oxen and was jealous of the music the bull made in the minds of men and their ladies.

Our beautiful sixteen-year-old was openly crying, and our lady, with her chin on her hand, was looking deeply into the ring at the place where the bull was lying and where every now and then little dust mists rose from the sand to which he was about to return. She was, indeed, perhaps furthest away of all because, as I was to be told afterwards, she was thinking: 'They all end like this. I have been to so many bullfights. I cannot help it.

The bulls and the horses do things to me that no other animals or human beings do, and when I see them in these ancient theatres about to act out the antique drama, I have a feeling as the drama increases as if the secret of life itself is approaching and about to take one by the hand. And then comes the moment of truth, and perhaps one's hand is briefly touched, and almost as quickly let go, and the bull is dead and all is as before. Why must the questions of life be so posed that it is always a one, or another?' Forgetting that she had already answered her question rationally in advance, she went on to take into her heart, and add its reasons to the day, the great Provençal poet Mistral's poem on the bull, which concluded with the image: 'The awesome raven dips a trembling wing over the tragic scene, and leaves whoever can to divine its mystery.'

Knowing nothing of this, I only knew that I was looking through a very special mood, and beyond it saw the lady of the mantilla and the hat. She did not seem to be assailed by any philosophic doubts and, without knowing, was so much joined and part of the occasion that she was all in all glowing like a lamp.

And with that I just had a longing to be away on my own and, happily, found that all in our party had seen enough and wanted to go as well.

And so we left the ring hardly talking, and it seemed to me that, considering all the drama they had witnessed, the people who now spread out over the vacant spaces of the city had changed and what chatter and excitement there was came mostly from the young. The excited, expectant mood that prevailed before the bullfight had changed. Now the feeling all round and among my company too was one of fulfilment, as if all sorts of doubts and fears and restrictions had been removed and the calm of rare resolution moved into their place. As we walked with the vast crowd of people pouring into the square and filling the entrances to streets and alleyways that led in all directions into the city, it was as if a great tide had been reversed and the sea was pouring back the rivers and tributaries of people the streets and alleyways had become, to the source from which they had sprung.

I remember how low the sun of the transition season had sunk and how deep the shadows were and how beautiful the light. There came a moment when the bells rang from the chapel in the cathedral and from other churches nearby, calling out that the time for prayer at nightfall had come. They were not the great bells of the cathedrals and churches but, judging by their sound, the side bells or even perhaps handbells that spoke more intimately, as if assured that the men and women of Castellona were themselves in a state of intimacy and in the grip of something that would be better served by whispering than by shouting aloud.

Also I noticed how black the crowd looked, how many women and men were in black, how many black ties there were, so many that one might have thought it was all worn in anticipation of the fact that the celebration of a victory over the masculine beast in man would also presuppose a kind of funeral. I have already mentioned how red the red of Spain appeared to me. Here I felt that I had never seen a black anywhere else so true as the black of Spain, so great a midnight black, almost on the verge of a mad black.

As our hostelry was some distance from the bullring, it was nearly dark when we arrived and already the lights had gone up one by one all over the city, and wherever there were lights some sounds of lighter celebration went up. On the steps of our hostelry we met the Baron, needless to say also in black, standing singularly calm and dignified, and I doubt, if our groom had been there now, that he would have thought of him still as an ex-foreign legionnaire. The moustache which had provoked the groom's remark was neatly trimmed and finely pointed, and reminded me of the painted pictures I used to see in my childhood of a proudly tilted military face with lips covered with a moustache pointed like that, on containers of an ointment specially designed to improve the decor of the lip, called *pommade hongroise*.

He greeted us with somewhat less formality than on the first occasion and said he had just seen the bullfighter of the day off in his car. We all expressed our surprise that he had not stayed and perhaps rested, but the Baron said: 'I know him. He is one of the greatest. But after every fight I have ever witnessed he likes to be off as soon as he can because he has no wish to meet people and prefers to be alone.'

Our friend said: 'I wonder if that is the reason why he never appears in great cities? For instance, we have never seen him either in Barcelona or Madrid, although he is always in the news.'

The Baron shook his head, and the points of his moustache made indents in the half-light around us. 'I do not think he has any liking for cities. He is one of the older kind of matador. Nowadays more and more matadors go where the money is. He goes, I think, where the honour is, and of course – I know I cannot help being prejudiced – the bullfighter is never so evenly matched as at our little Castellona. The bulls are never better bred and so powerful. The contest, as you have just seen, could never be longer or more intense anywhere else. The attention of the people and their understanding of the subtleties and the meaning of the drama involved could not be greater. Hence, there is no place in Spain or perhaps the whole world where the honour to be gained could be greater.'

He stopped, not as someone who had finished with his thought but as if something he had forgotten had occurred to him, and after a while he said, referring to the matador again: 'People do not remember nowadays, or if they remember do not talk about it because they find it silly or are ashamed of it, but in my family it has always been taught that way back in the beginning the matador was a kind of priest and bullfighting a religious ceremony. One of my ancestors, the great old Marquis, used to say that the matador who did not go into the ring for the love of god had lost the battle before he started. He said that the true matador killed without being a killer in his heart, but . . .' There he begged our pardon for making a speech instead of answering a question from friends, and said he had better be on his way before he made another, because like everyone else from Castellona at the moment he could talk about bulls and bullfights and what had been enacted in the past at Castellona until cockcrow.

I went up and along the winding corridor. The door of the

room of the vanished matador was open. The bed had been stripped and a heap of untidy linen was on the floor and the window wide open as if to emphasise what the door already said: the matador had left in haste, and although I had obviously not known him and never heard of him before that day, I found myself full of regret that I could not see what the day had done to the expression on his face.

This may not be relevant to the story which has already pressed Blady, our lady, her husband, myself and her groom into its service, but the memory remains so vividly that against all reason I felt I had to include it in the reckoning to which, somewhere, it must belong. All this is confirmed by the quality of the memory. There is no doubt that memories can be lost almost as soon as they are made. There are other memories that can become processes of growth and accompany one for a while and then, like plants in a garden, begin to wilt and die and prove not to be perennial. But there are memories that continue to grow year after year until one day they burst out in blossom that glows almost as much by night as by day, and this memory of mine is here because after many a cycle of seasons, some bitter winters and many dry summers, it has grown, and all that there was about Blady was suddenly flamboyant and on fire.

8
The Race

I went down early to the dining-room to find it already half empty. The grooms had gone and only a few of the riders were left. Those who were still eating were eating in a hurry and there was not much conversation. For a moment I was rather taken aback that somewhere which had seemed so unique should now be filled with haste and take on the character of a place for travellers, always busy and always with trains to catch. Even at our table our lady was clearly keeping another kind of time within herself, and I had a feeling that the something between her and her husband, which I had first noticed on that day in the Camargue when Blady came into our lives, seemed to be somewhere in the air with more of a shadow than it had ever possessed. It was not that she was more anxious and committed to the events about to unfold than he was, it was simply that it still mattered to them in a different way, although nobody would be happier, I knew, than he if she and Blady did well. That 'did well' was significant, because it reflected how consciously he assumed that Blady could not do more. It was this assumption, perhaps, which set two people who could not have loved each other more somehow at opposing ends of the same stretch of their values.

It was perhaps to ease the tension that he said to me, with a smile: 'I hope you have kept in touch with your witchdoctor?'

Just for a second I was afraid that she might find the question too flippant, but she had switched away immediately from her own preoccupations and her face expressed renewed interest which encouraged me enough to laugh and answer: 'Yes, I have. I am quite surprised how I can go on doing it all the time, even when I do not know that I am doing it. It only needs something, even less than your question, to make the thought of him present itself: and even if it did not, I would go on thinking of him because it is rather like that New Testament parable about prayer as a form of importuning. You remember the poor man had to go on knocking at the door of the rich man at the most uncomfortable hours of the night, waking up his chosen benefactor so often that he ordered his servants to give the man at the door what he wanted or he would never get any sleep.'

The response was, I think, to all our tastes. Our lady seemed no longer tense but, with an honest feeling that she must go to the horses as soon as possible, jumped up, kissed us goodbye and went swinging out of the doors into the garden and on to the stables.

We followed about an hour later to the big stadium where the events were to be held, and I had time enough to be instructed in the qualities of horses and riders, who they were, what their records were, the clubs and countries they represented, and their vital statistics of character as well as of the results of their performances. Apart from Paco Goyoago, a number of riders of international fame were competing. The Spanish contingent of men and horses in itself was large and formidable, and as they came out into the stadium one after the other to take part in their various heats, they all looked splendid and glittering in the blue of the day. It looked to me as if any one of them, provided he could stay the course of the six days of jumping that were to follow, could win the race.

I thought so until Paco Goyoago himself appeared – and it was almost superfluous to have him pointed out to me, partly because I knew the horse from its moment of extremity in the pass but mainly because, even if I had not known the horse, I would have recognised the partnership of man and horse. I am not an expert in these matters and could not attempt to report on the technical features of Goyoago's handling of the horse which was part of his achievement. I had come to know, from a vast landscape of years peopled by horses and men, as by reflex, the occasions when a partnership, through natural gift and training, was unique and great. I can just lamely confess that I have never seen so graceful a consummation of natural gifts in horse and man, and they made the sort of impact on me that the story of Bellerephon and Pegasus had had in my childhood. By the end of the day, Paco was marginally ahead in points, which depressed my host but neither me nor our lady.

Blady's heat took place in the early afternoon. It was, of course, not her first experience of these events. She had been amply prepared on many courses in club, intercity and regional competitions, although this was her first entry into what could be compared to international eventing. When she came out of the shadows of the buildings into the light of the ring, there was nothing obvious to mark her out for the horse which our lady believed she was, and which her husband hoped against fear she could be. It was not that Blady was unremarkable but, as I suddenly realised now as I saw her against so strikingly comparative a background, her unusual combination of quality and talent were so proportioned, and her temperament so naturally rounded, that there was no drama of characteristics to single her out. From all that I heard at the place where we went to lay our bets people were more puzzled than impressed by her, and worried that they could not find an angle, as they put it, to sum her up. As a result there was very little betting on her, and I had no difficulty in getting tremendous odds for my modest wager on her, modest compared with the sum which my friend, out of loyalty and I think also to compensate for a feeling of guilt that he could not have greater faith in his horse, bet upon her.

Once upon the course I thought that surely the connoisseurs would see that, whatever they thought about pedigrees and all sorts of other points in horses, what was outstanding was the grace and the ease with which, from point-to-point, Blady took her hazards and her fences. I thought it a deeply satisfying performance and in its way a gem of art; perhaps not the old master that Paco's model was, but nonetheless an impressionist's canvas worth hanging in a connoisseur's gallery of memories. So the fact that Blady had won her race in the beginning with such ease was quickly overlooked or forgotten, because she had taken more time than other winners in their heats, and made the gamblers say to themselves, as my friend did to me quietly with his eyes darkened: '*Ça finira mal*,' to which I replied, '*On verra*.'

Our lady, on the contrary, was delighted, and with the tension all gone could just revel in the delight of the sense of ease and rhythm and harmony that she and the horse between them had achieved for themselves. The moment we met her back at the hotel she took us by the arm and exclaimed: 'She is an angel! She is a miracle! She is a gift from heaven! And now there she stands so modestly in her box as if she had just finished ploughing that diabolical Camargue vineyard.'

We saw Blady in her box, but the moment of translation of which my friend had spoken was not apparent any longer and had been replaced by that sometimes irritating and damnably enigmatic feeling of a something else about her, just waiting as if for something coming from the other side of the universe and perhaps not yet born but about to explode like a supernova in all our lives. What I found perhaps of most significance was the feeling of health and natural reaction about her. Her groom had just brought a bucket full of fresh water, which she sniffed first and then drank like her equivalent of champagne, and then turned about loose to her crib and began munching. It was the kind of munching that had given me such content and reassurance when I first heard it in my childhood, and it did so again now.

We went back to our hostelry and to an evening in which almost everyone was present in the dining-room and there was a growing sense of community, almost of being a family of circumstances together: so much indeed that the Baron had no hesitation at one moment in standing up at his table in the centre of the room and asking permission to tell us something which he would not like us to hear by rumour. We would no doubt have noticed that, although it was getting late, that table by the window was empty. It was the table which was occupied by – and he named two men of some international repute who were notorious rivals. Unfortunately they had quarrelled with each other once again, quarrelled so seriously that if it had happened in the Baron's day it would most certainly have led to a duel. Fortunately in these civilised days, and as befitted the healthy spirit which Castellona always evoked, they had decided it would be better if they and their horses and their grooms went to different hotels and neither of them stayed behind in a way which might suggest he was about to betray the camaraderie of the festival and prejudice the gathering now in the dining-room against the other.

The announcement and the spirit in which it was made was enthusiastically accepted, and the talk returned more objectively to the day's events and its portents for the future, all of which must have led to a loss of such popularity as Blady had enjoyed among the gamblers, because my friend came back with a long face the next morning to tell me that he had increased his wager to nearly double that of the day before, as a result of which I accompanied him to the place of betting and, although I am not inclined to bet, particularly on horses, unless it is absolutely necessary, I doubled my wager too.

He asked me what I meant about betting out of necessity. Surely unless gambling on horses was to a man as spirits are to an alcoholic – and he had known many like that – there was never a necessity to bet?

As we sat on the stands waiting for our lady and Blady to perform and watched another splendid round of jumping, crowned again by a superb performance by Goyoago, I told him how I had always had a special relationship with the Derby; how as an almost penniless young man setting out in life on my own I had drawn a runner in the Derby called 'Blenheim' and won what was to me a small fortune. As I won it I felt, even then, that I must not pursue this luck but just let it happen to me if chance wanted it to. Time went by until the dark days of the 1930s, leading up to the war, and I wanted to have some money to go away and write. I looked at the list of the Derby runners in a restaurant which shall be forever remembered in my chronicle of horses by its name of 'The Welcome Snail'. A friend listening to my certainty that a horse called 'Hyperion' would win the race, and knowing my need, lent me £100 to place on the horse minutes before the Derby was run. Hyperion won and became renowned as the smallest horse ever to have won the Derby, even though it had not only its physical size against it but more white socks on his feet than the proverbial racehorse wisdom in England declared a good horse could ever have. And finally there was a moment when I was flying high over the Arabian Desert out of war in South-East Asia and I drew, in the seaplane's sweepstake, a horse called 'Pearl Diver' which in its turn too won the Derby. Although the financial reward was small, the happening gave me a sense of release and blessing, but at the same time confirmed my resolution not to spoil my relationship with the Derby by consciously exploiting it.

He was profoundly interested and said: 'And do you have this feeling of certainty about Blady?'

'I am afraid I cannot think of Blady in any of these terms. I have a feeling that I must keep my mind, expectations and myself out of it so as not to form part of the intrusion of the world into whatever is happening to the three of you, because already I feel that intrusion is too great.'

I realise I must have sounded pompously oracular, but when you are caught up in so dramatic a series of events, and become so close to people, there are these moments when among the people involved you cease to be as modest as you should be, and I am afraid we all seemed to be more and more involved with the stuff of the oracular by the day.

Happily on this particular day the situation between the horses and men remained unchanged. Paco was maintaining his lead, but Blady was there among the best, although her time was not yet of the best.

By the evening of the Wednesday the situation had begun to change. Some of the horses with the fastest times had fallen behind because of the mistakes they made at their hazards. Others lost out because they made the challenge of hurdles and waterjumps but lost in time, even against Blady. For some reason, we all found the end of the Wednesday night, the central night of divide, disturbing, and I was amazed at the number of people, even the grooms, who did not sleep well or had strange dreams, and one groom who was always on watch at the stables thought the horses had been singularly uneasy.

At breakfast the atmosphere was less of talk and more of preoccupation, almost as if circumstances and the air itself were turning morose. It came to a point when, towards the end of the meal, a groom threw his napkin on the table and startled everybody – at his table where he had sat without speaking and hardly eating and, indeed, in the whole room – by an exclamation that it was really too much. He pushed his chair away wilfully and stood by the table, not looking angry so much as thoroughly upset.

'Friends,' he said, in the kind of voice which writers of horror stories used to call strangled, 'you must please forgive me but I must tell you. Something terrible has happened. Since Monday night my master has refused to speak to me.'

He paused as if the emotion of the fact had utterly overwhelmed him. Instantly one felt the silence and the tension of reaction in the room almost like a gust of wind in the place, and there came several murmurs of 'It is not possible!', at which the groom found his voice again and went on: 'Yes, it is. It started on Monday night when I went to have a last look at my two horses and I found that one horse had kicked the other. His flank was swollen, and felt as if it was still swelling because it was fresh and hot, and the horse, which knows my hand as well as I do, flinched when I touched even the hair on the swelling.'

Again he paused. On such a day and night this was the stuff of great drama, because the master was a rather arrogant young German businessman from the city and both his horses were doing well in the contest.

'He came and we immediately got the doctor. We dressed the swelling and the doctor said it was not serious and would hardly be noticeable in a day or two and it should not handicap the horse much at all. But the moment the doctor had gone, whom he had treated with great politeness and respect and from whom he had parted with gratitude, my master turned on me. He blamed me for carelessness in allowing one horse to kick another. I ask you! I ask you, friends, and please tell me if I am wrong,' and the tears started running down his cheeks, 'where in the world will you find horses – in stables or on prairies – who do not sometimes kick one another? And where in the world could there be a caretaker of horses who, night and day, could keep this from happening? I have spent most of my time in the stables and these two horses were friends! Even a fly could have made one horse lash out at the other. How could I possibly be to blame?'

A growl came from the grooms and protests from other tables.

'I explained this and more to my master, but from that moment on he has refused to speak to me. He will not even reply to my questions or my good-mornings or good-days. I ask you!'

He got no further, because the feeling which in cold reading may seem so little was too much for him, and indeed for his audience. The Baron was instantly on his feet and speaking with a tender authority said: 'Please, my good fellow, do not distress yourself. You have done no wrong. This is a terrible thing to do to you. We know you too well. It is a most unjust and un-*caballero* thing to do to you. I shall have a word or two to say on this matter elsewhere.'

A great sound and feeling of relief came over the room. The disturbed night and all the omens and portents were forgotten, and this small human predicament was given priority until we all went back to the race. But from that moment no one in the hotel, and here I do not mind some anticipation, spoke to the groom's master again. Such were the values of the fiesta at Castellona.

That day, despite forebodings, was one of the best days for Blady because, although Paco Goyoago remained firmly in the lead, Blady was there among the first four, and although our lady was enchanted almost to the point of seeing herself and Blady take over the lead, she had the good sense not to tempt her fate but just looked happily pleased, while her husband began to believe that Blady now would not lose without honour.

On the Friday morning I went down to what appeared a healthy, normal breakfast with happy excited conversation now enriched by recollection and discussion of all the dramatic events of the past days, when suddenly the doors between us and the reception desk opened and the manager came bustling in with a letter which he took to the Baron's table, bowed, apologised for breaking into his breakfast and said he thought he had better give it to him at once because it was marked 'Urgent'. The Baron took it as if he were accustomed all day long to receive letters marked 'Urgent', finished a half-cut portion on his plate, and then opened the letter at his ease. But after the brief history of the breakfast-room, which every day seemed to have produced a drama, all the tables there behaved as if they were warned of something unusual to come. Inside the letter was another letter, apparently handwritten, because the Baron's face suddenly seemed to be full of pleasant anticipation. He opened this letter in haste and began to read, but had not read far when he stopped. All the light went out of his face. He seemed to begin reading the letter again and then, with difficulty, to pursue it to the end. He looked sideways and back into the wall behind him, as if what he had seen in the letter would take it as a sign to go away and vanish from where it had come. But in a moment he looked back and we could all see that he was extremely distressed and fighting within himself for composure and dignity. It was instantly high theatre for all. From the moment of the manager's entry to this moment, the theatre had been in mime, and through mime had filled the air with a sense of tragedy. Now everybody knew the point had been reached when some sound had to come, not to describe but to express what it was that had so distressed the Baron. He stood up slowly at his table and tears were running down his cheeks, unashamed, manly, chivalrous tears and he said:

'I cannot hide this news from you all, because already we have shared so much, and are perhaps about to share more. I have just had this letter from my mistress telling me that she has left me.'

Voices of horror rose from everywhere. Chairs shuffled, and there were people obviously thinking they should rush to the Baron's side and take his hand and say things to make him realise how everyone shared his distress and what a good man he was and how honoured and respected and loved; but there was also a feeling that such a stampede of emotions added to the eruption of emotion in the Baron would not be right or dignified, and so it was left for spontaneous, compassionate words from all across the room to come like starlings to the Baron.

And yet that was not enough. The oldest groom at the grooms' table and a sort of godfather to ours, slowly stood up and said: 'Baron, *caballeros*.'

He said the '*caballeros*' with a sort of city slum accent that made me think of the word as the equivalent of the bright, brave Cockney voices I first heard in London when their greatest term of affection, no matter for wives or friends, was 'mates'. That, anyway, was the feeling in its most direct and human way with which the word came across.

'*Caballeros*, I am going to say now what I was asked to say on behalf of you all on Saturday night. And I'm sure on Saturday night someone else will have better words to say than I can say now. But I must tell the Baron that none of us here who have shared so much with him and know him will ever believe that this unhappiness which has been communicated to him could have been his fault. We would ask him please to remember that already he has proved by the way he has organised this great event – starting with one of the greatest bullfights that I, who have seen a great many, have ever seen, and all this difficult thing of letting men and horses and a vast public gathering compete so happily that he is one of the greatest of the great. We could not honour him more. We could not be more grateful to him, and we can only tell him that he will forever be remembered among us for the welcome he gave us and the affection we have come to feel for him. We are certain too that by now all the world knows him for these things.'

He sat down and the roof of the breakfast-room shuddered under the impact of the '*Olé*'s' that followed. When breakfast broke up in some disorder, with the routine of expectations and feelings broken in their stride by the Baron's grief, our lady and I went to Blady's stables, where our groom was preparing to set out for the stadium. His mind for once was not entirely on our lady, because he had things of his own to get off his chest and, seeing our lady and me, he stamped his foot and said in a clenched, angry kind of way: 'The bitch! The bitch! If it had been me, I would have called her that to everybody's face!'

Our lady, who was very close to her groom, told me afterwards she had never before seen him so angry and, taken aback, she exclaimed: 'But really do you know the woman that you can call her so dreadful a name?'

'No, of course not,' he said, 'I do not know her and I hope I shall never know her, because I know enough of her already.'

'Well, you must please tell us, what do you know?'

With a note of being within himself wiser than anybody in Castellona at that moment he said: 'I know her by her timing.'

'Her timing?' she queried.

'Yes! Yes, by her timing! Only a bitch could know how to make a man feel poor at the moment when he feels perhaps more rich than he has ever felt, as the Baron did.'

And that remains in my mind as the last word on the matter, wondering at the distances the mind can travel and how, just as you cannot judge a book by its cover, you cannot judge a man by his pomaded moustaches, as our groom would be the first to admit.

Although there were no breakfasts without their incidents and special variations, these now seemed trivial. What had happened to the Baron was the climax, and all else at our hostelry by comparison anti-climax, although a singularly happy and resolved anti-climax.

The Friday which was to sort out, as the British Army of my day had it, 'the men from the boys', was a day of almost faultless jumping. Paco Goyoago was one of the first to go and completed a perfect circuit in a very good time, and again widened his lead. But by the afternoon two other horses and their riders had advanced to within two points of his lead and had raised, or troubled, the hopes and expectations of those with a personal commitment to specific horses and men as they had not been stirred before. The spectators could not have been happier; their taste for what they had seen could not have been keener or their appetite for the final to come more eager. Even now I find it difficult to describe the mixture of emotions, and the feeling of the approach towards a height of drama never exceeded at Castellona, when our lady and Blady came to do their turn.

It was extraordinary that no one yet, judging by the betting and the comments at the betting-places, had taken to Blady seriously. The experts there had told us that there was an increase of betting on Blady, but there was no great swell of interest that came with the establishment of real favour or even, one felt, a good outside chance. The sport came mainly from diverse horses backed by the sort of people who would look at a list of the horses and riders and pick a partnership just because they fancied the names, or, what was even more usual, just because they believed in betting on the one with the longest odds. So, apart from the fact that Blady excited a little more interest than usual just because she was there, as it were, among the semifinalists, it was the horse that would come after her and end the day – which had a good record, impeccable breeding and the most experienced German rider – for which the crowd was really waiting.

For the two of us, however, as they came out in the slanting sun of late afternoon, Blady looked all that her experienced, imaginative and sensitive groom had prepared her to be. Now that there were only five of them left and each one of them exposed to the imaginations and wonderings of an excited crowd, all were special. I, who had been an admirer of Blady's from the beginning, thought she had never looked better, and for me she stood as a plenipotentiary of all that the horse had been in the story of man. I was so transported by the spectacle that I could only sit there as still as I had ever sat in my life, and had no mind at all to give to what my friend must have been feeling.

I remember looking at the watch on my wrist without even bending my head and thinking: 'Dear God, how am I going to get through the next few minutes?'

It felt like a vast new landscape of enigmatic time opened out in front of me, and yet when they started the course it was all over sooner than I expected and performed miraculously and faultlessly. The audience was dazed more than impressed by the unexpected result, and my friend beside me overcome, not so much with triumph as dumb and deafened by the crash of mountains of unbelief within him.

It was, as her groom afterwards said, a perfect ride except that at one of the most difficult hurdles our lady's left foot had slipped the wrong way an inch or two in her stirrup and he had feared for a second she would lose it.

'But, of course,' as he said with a shrug and voice of dismissal and a wave of the hand at the crowd, brushing them aside as one might some flies on a cloth over a jug of milk, 'only someone like me would have noticed so small a thing. That lot out there had no idea.'

Our lady and her horse, in jumping those fences, had jumped the gap, and she was now only a point behind Goyoago.

Dinner that night at the hostelry for once was so tense it was almost subdued. For once the strange collective intimacy which had been evolved between us all was not strong enough to contain the emotions and the thoughts for the next day into which everyone was inevitably plunged. There was a certain forced gaiety and rhinestone chat between us all and, for once, a rather refined and just faintly precious character of a Spanish rider, who had lost out with his horse on that day, took a greater part in the talk than ever before because, I think, that sort of forced, polite social manner, so alien to us, was one to which he was more accustomed. It was he who for a moment addressed the groom whose horse had been kicked and said that he hoped that things between him and his master were now improved. But the groom seemed to be taken aback that the matter should be raised again in that way and merely shook his head. I still remember how strange were the cultured tones of the man's voice as he said, rather primly, 'I do think that it would seem rather insensitive and not the thing a gentleman would do.'

The incident might not have stayed in my memory if I were not to hear that voice again in the future.

We dispersed then and all said we were going to bed early, although we knew we would go to bed only to read or to lie awake with our own other selves as we had not done before, and even the sleep that followed might well be uneasy. What I do remember as I lay in the dark was that a poem by a forgotten English poet who loved his horses came to me, and I tried to recall it because once I had known it word for word, and I had recited it to myself again when I was in what appeared then to be a condemned cell in a Japanese prison in Java. The name of the poet was Wilfrid Scawen Blunt, and I made a jumble of the opening of his sonnet and could only remember the last two lines with reasonable precision:

> *Your face my quarry was – for it I rode.*
> *My horse a thing of wings, myself a God.*

I think it came to me because the story of horses, and of Blady in particular, had brought me to a point where I felt the sex of the rider in the poem should be changed, because somewhere in our lady that day it seemed a dominant element had been established which demanded a rare, transported, boy-about-to-become-man face, without masculinisation of the feminine, but which beckoned the woman to a fulfilment uniquely her own.

And so we came to breakfast on the Saturday morning, the last day of the jumping, with Blady now almost neck-to-neck with the great Goyoago horse. That slight lead, if held by any other man but Paco, would have seemed highly unsafe, not only with Blady right behind but with all the rest of the company with which he had to compete. Yet it was against all possible exactions of reason, and a folly of the imagination, to think that there could be a partnership among the others, let alone Blady and our lady, who could beat the horse and the man with the experience and reputation of Goyoago. It was just unthinkable to any reasonable mind among the dedicated followers and lovers of these things.

The excitement in the breakfast-room was so great that I doubt if anyone noticed what food they ate or could even remember what they had said the moment after the words had left their lips. All just wanted the day to begin and, in a strange way, to be over, because they felt something I felt myself, as if unable to endure not so much the excitement as the feeling that the fates themselves had arrived at the festival overnight and were taking personal charge of the day to come. I had no clear-cut intuition to follow, perhaps because, in the deeps, the issue had not been settled yet and at such moments one had not to take the fates for granted; in fact perhaps the most dangerous thing one could do was to ask special favours from creation for any specific and personal thing. It was as if my own experience had taught me that what human beings called luck, or chance, was something beyond human understanding, and that one could not even begin to try and mould it unless at the very least one could answer the question: 'Who was the lucky one, Barabbas or Christ?'

This, I seemed to believe, was something best left to that area of mind which I had told my friend I had put in the keeping of a wise, experienced old prophet called a witchdoctor in the interior of Africa, who would be at that moment somewhere near the cave of a sacred mountain wearing, as his people had bestowed on him, a ring of metal, an instinctive substantiation of the spirit which was visualised as a halo around the heads of saints and sages.

I should leave it there and just wait, devoutly and reverently, as I had often seen Blady wait for someone or something – above all in recent years for our lady – to fetch her.

Whatever the fates were about to do to us, it was clear, the moment we arrived at the stadium to take our seats looking down on that other ring, that they had been kind with their weather. There was a cool air moving from high among the snows on the distant invisible summits of the Pyrenees down over the plateaux and the prairies to the Mediterranean. The air was singularly clear, fresh and healing, and everything seemed to shine and sparkle. The horses had a newly born glitter in their coats, and the atmosphere felt almost as if invisible rain had fallen in the night and the earth and all in it had been subtly refreshed. Above all, whether we knew it or not, we were invested with the knowledge of its being not only the last but the decisive day of a series of days that would never again be repeated in that particular pattern wherein we had known it. It was, as it were, part of the same moon of experience as the first day. The first and the last were joined, so that I seemed, paradoxically, to be seeing both faces of the moon, or perhaps even a moon which had revolved so that the face we never saw had changed places with the one we always see. It was a feeling that in itself was most eventful, and that sense of eventfulness made it one of the longest mornings. Beyond that the detail is not important. When we broke at lunchtime, Blady was still neck and neck with the Goyoago horse, and there were still three other horses left within striking distance. That afternoon there would be a round between all five of them which would be judged for both speed and jumping, and would decide the issue.

I ate no lunch but drank more coffee than even a dedicated coffee-drinker like myself had ever drunk. My friend forced himself to eat, rather like a soldier before battle, trying to repress the fear that most of us feel before going into action by turning to the primordial reassurance that men always find with the consumption of food and the confirmed capacity for survival which accompanies it.

We had only had a brief word with the groom, our lady and Blady. I just had an exchange of looks with Blady, and although we knew each other well and had walked up to our knees on the foreshore of the Mediterranean sea together, I did not put a hand upon her. I just looked and I saw, yes, she was ready and waiting. I quickly embraced our lady, and I do not remember what platitude I fell back upon, as one does on these occasions. I looked at the groom, who looked back at me with a strange kind of Mona Lisa smile at the corner of his lips – and then he gave an enormous lift to the heart with an outrageous wink, which contorted the whole of his face from his left eye, down the cheek to the chin.

There was only one aspect of our brief meeting in between the races that left me uneasy. My friend, as we turned to go, looked hard at our lady and said, almost like someone in a trance and clearly without thinking: 'Don't forget, you have got to get all the speed you can out of Blady. The speed will be decisive!'

Considering its substance, his remark troubled me more perhaps than it should have done, but it suggested to me very strongly that the man in the partnership still felt himself to be in command in an area in which it was clearly the woman who would not only have the doing in her keeping but would also have to endure the consequences. In any case it seemed uncalled for and pointless, because it was none of his or our business and it assumed a control over circumstances which nobody except Blady and our lady could exercise.

By four o'clock in the afternoon, almost on the striking of the clock, the fates had decided that the race was now just between our lady and Goyoago. The rest of the horses had eliminated themselves by patchy performances that both Goyoago and our lady were almost certain to better. The horse that had done best struck me not so much for its performance as its colour. It was what we had always been taught to call an 'Isabella white', after the white dress of the great Queen Isabella of Spain which she wore on the day of her coronation and said she would not change until she had driven the Moors from Spain. Since it took her some fifteen years or more to drive the Moors from Spain, the extent of the 'off-white'ness of the dress must be left to the imagination. To me it would have been a nice gesture of the fates if the decisive race had been between a horse carrying the great Queen's colours and our lady and Blady.

But there it was. For the first time in Castellona, and I think in Spain and perhaps in the world, the best horseman in the world was challenged by a woman, a woman above all on an untried mare. And this woman now was called upon to be the first out into the ring.

I have already confessed my incapacity to describe certain pictures of the moods on these occasions in the ring: first in the ring of the bullfight and now in the ring of horses, surrounded by a ring of men and women, as it were, in a state of complete suspension in a world where the forces of reality, like gravity and levitation, hope and regret, were all abolished and the moment of truth of the six-day drama had come.

I can only say that our lady and Blady took off as if there was no weight in them and no pull of gravity in the earth. They went, it seemed to me, so easily and with such an immense power somewhere on the very edge of rhythm, but never in the least bit beyond containment, hurdle after hurdle, hazard after double-hazard, and totally in the clear until they came to what seemed the easiest and last jump of the course, a straight run at perhaps the lowest hurdle of all with, beyond it, a broad sheet of water that had to be cleared without a touch of a hoof.

I could sense the exultation in my friend beside me and was deeply afraid, because so often I had seen in life the awesome truth of the old English proverb: 'There's many a slip 'twixt cup and lip'.

I remembered the great Odyssean journey when, almost within sight of Ithaka and a glimpse of the smoke coming down at evening over its housetops for which the battered Odysseus had been longing for more than twenty years, the worst of his shipwrecks was inflicted on him. The knowledge of what the equivalent of a shipwreck now on this occasion would do had me by the throat. And then it seemed the shipwreck was upon us, because our lady did something which I had never seen her do in all the years I had followed her and her horses. Blady, it looked to me, was doing all and more that a horse could do to eliminate time and distance when our lady rapped her smartly with a whip on the flanks. It was almost as if I could see – although I am certain it must have been a perception from what excitement had produced in me as a state of mystical participation in horse and rider's spirit out there – a shock going through all of Blady's great system. I say great system because the shock did not become any form of physical impediment. It became the most gigantic physical response to what was being asked of her, but it pushed her timing aside. The effort that came from Blady and our lady was an effort against the time they had to conquer. Blady jumped at least a metre before she had intended to jump. It was an olympian jump, which took horse and rider over the fence at almost twice the height that was necessary and on across the water, greatly extended in length by the untimely take-off, and for a moment it looked as if Blady had cleared it. But on the very verge of success, the edge of the shoe on one of her left hooves just touched the water and made the most imperceptible of splashes.

But a splash, as the judges said, is a splash. No size applied, just as no measure was applied to distinguish between a rail flicked off lightly by a horse's hoof and one demolished by its knees or even its chest.

A low sound of despair came from my friend.

We said nothing but listened to the noise of the crowd swarming like thousands of bees.

Paco Goyoago rode as he had always done and as if what had just happened was something that, one way or another, would never happen to him but only to the scores of people he had vanquished in events all over the world. I am not saying for a moment that he was vain or conceited, just a man caught in the habit of his experience. I am certain that at no time during the last two days when Blady had begun to acquire an identity in the contest did it occur to him that the event could be won by a woman, much as he liked our lady personally and admired her capacities of horsemanship. I just had a feeling that he might be, on this occasion, too tightly buttoned in the success and habit of his remarkable career.

His round was as good as Blady's but no faster as he began that straight run up to the last, low fence, the water jump, and, it seemed, the honours of the race. All hope of his going wrong with the hurdles was abandoned, and the result, one felt in the crowd, became taken for granted as one might take for granted that a letter to some royal destination, already written, folded, in its envelope, completely addressed and with the wax about to seal it, would be safely delivered.

My friend had no doubt about what was to be delivered, and just a very sad, 'Oh, my God, my God' came from him. With his elbows on his knees and his head held between his hands, he watched Goyoago and his horse take to the air.

I do not know how many seconds or fractions of a second it takes a horse to complete the summit of a jump, but I know there is no time too small to be immaterial to the fates. And I do not know what happens on summits, or the false summits that tend to surround them. I do not know how what happened was decided, on the summit of that last hurdle and the water jump. I only knew that something unforeseen was entering the challenge we were watching, and its impact on me was accompanied by a startling visualisation of my haloed old African prophet and his sacred mountain, as well as the memory of the accident to the horsebox with Paco's horse in it in the pass, all there simultaneously. The horse appeared to be safely over the hurdle but then, in my state of heightened emotion, seemed just for an instant to be still, as if enclosed in an aspic of time, before it emerged and the left hoof which in Blady had raised that tiny splash of water appeared to lag, and in the lagging to exceed by the merest millimetre the proportions of the pattern which fate demanded of them. It flicked the hurdle with the most delicate of flicks, and the hurdle appeared to roll and quiver backwards and forwards as if it had a mind not to fall, and then, slowly, went over the edges and came down.

Although the water beyond was untouched, Goyoago and his horse had committed an error which on a narrow point would have been enough to lose the race but, to everyone's amazement, somewhere before that last hurdle and the winning post, they had contrived also to lose in time, so that Blady, who was thought to be rather slow, was a second ahead and the victory was decisive in an area of the race unaided by accident or mis-judgement.

The feeling of unbelief produced an awesome hush in the ring. It would, I knew, precede one of the greatest eruptions of sound that Castellona had ever experienced. I just had time to see that my host seemed stricken with a kind of unearthly joy and an equal and opposite remorse and consequent humility that I had not observed in him before. Something in him too had been fulfilled. I was finding it very hard to keep back my tears, but if asked to tell for what, that was the greatest impossibility of all the impossibilities of the fiesta at Castellona.

And then came the eruption, a chaos of sound – as the first people of Africa would have called it: 'a chaos feeling itself utterly to be chaos'. It must have scared all the birds away for miles, and it went up into the silence of the blue like a great monument. For a moment one felt that no silence, however deep or great in the surround of blue of that incredibly blue afternoon, could ever engulf it, and no wind of time topple it, but the sound would echo and re-echo for ever in Castellona as a memorial of what that woman and horse had achieved between them.

I was pulled sharply out of my own subjective state because I heard a rough 'Excuse me' from my friend beside me and his voice saying, 'I must go to them.' I only knew there was no point in answering then, because I felt that what he was doing this time was pure, instinctive and right. In any case the ascending noise of the crowd and the commotion of horses and men coming into the ring below, and people leaving their seats and hurrying in all sorts of directions like homing pigeons at the end of a week-long flight seeing home at last, reduced what had been, as it were, an ordered script and manifesto of behaviour of the evening to a vast scribble. I left my seat and wandered quietly away, which was difficult with the press of people swirling around and in and out of the ring and the places of the various horses and grooms. I did so not just out of conviction that Blady, our lady and her husband, and for a while perhaps the groom, should be left alone but also because I wanted to be alone myself.

And so for perhaps an hour or more I wandered in and out of the fringes of Castellona to follow an unfolding of my own spirit which somehow demanded a review of something that had started way back with Bird of the Wind and Diamond, and a feeling that somehow Blady had ridden that great race not only for our lady and her man, not only for the horses of Spain and Castellona but in a sense also, by unique proxy, for my Diamond.

With that race I had clearly come to the end of a theme in the sense that it could not be continued in the here and the now. Most of all came a conviction, like a lamp beckoning in the dark, in the window of a house on one of the great prairies, that the conclusion was final. For my friends obviously, as for me, the quality of the conclusion could not have been improved upon, nor anything else made us happier. The fact was that it was the final, like that last hurdle and the water jump where the horses and their riders were submitted to the final test; this conclusion itself was a last hurdle in a point-to-point of life before one could be cleared, as it were, by customs and emigration on the frontier of one's native land and set out for some new world beyond. I thought of how it had taken just a flick of a whip and a flick of a hoof to decide a race which, though run as a sport by men and their horses, nonetheless, consciously or unconsciously, came from some office of re-creation in the cosmos which determines these olympics as a model of greater and more meaningful patterns to come. Without being too solemn about it, it all was there like the white and black feather which the Egyptians believed was laid in the scales of fate to decide whether souls were worthy of immortality or not. If the feather was not balanced in the scales against the soul, the man and the soul were lost.

The answer, it seemed to me, was that at the last fence all the considerations of life, behaviour and character and a wide dimension of complex history of people and horses were added to their performance over a week in the ring, and all together weighed in a moment of truth over the last hurdle, and only then decided. And of the more immediate other factors that seemed to me must have been taken into consideration in our lady's and Blady's favour were the facts first of all of the relationship between them, that was close and continuous and never more so than in her decision to take her horse herself by a road least prone to accident and fatigue to Castellona. By contrast Goyoago did not see his horse until the day before the race at Castellona. He sent his father and his groom with his horse by a shorter but more difficult road, a road which undoubtedly would be more tiresome as well as tiring to horse and man, apart from being sufficiently more prone to a possibility of mishap, however faint, to which our lady was not prepared to expose her Blady.

Then for our lady this was no ordinary race. It was the race of her life, not just of life in the world but of life of the heart and spirit. For her and her horse, who would no doubt race again and again, no race would ever matter as this race had done, because it confirmed a direction of spirit for her. In the world of meaning, it was both a first and a last of its kind.

As I walked there on the leafy fringes of Castellona and the sun began to go more yellow and yellow, the shadows to grow longer and the swallows and the swifts to dive in and out of air limpid as mountain water and soar up to a summit against the sun where they did what pilots in a marathon of the air called a victory roll, I was tempted to call it a fairy tale and Blady a

kind of Cinderella, but it was really more than that. Its conclusion established as a fact that there is something in life, in
men and women and their horses, which does not need terrible
apprenticeships in the kitchens of fate, polishing its containers
with the ashes of burnt-out hopes and energies, and scraping
the black pots and pans of jealousies and envies of lesser people
and a ruthlessly competitive world, graced only by a chance at
the equivalent of an occasion where one is presented and seen,
beautifully dressed *à la mode* of the moment, as a princess at the
ball. One can understand and be glad that there is in fate far
more possibility of this kind of recognition of quality and honest endeavour and potential than one normally supposes, but it
is not to be compared to what I think happened between our
lady and Blady and was proved so delicately and yet so decisively
at the last hurdle of all: that there is a greater something which
recognises Cinderella not at the ball but before. It is easy
enough to recognise beauty when it is on exhibition as in Cinderella's story, but what had happened that day was validation
of the spirit which recognises the rejected and averted face of
the feminine in life long before the ball was ever imagined.

It may not seem to be an earth-shattering conclusion, yet at
that moment it appeared to me that this trail, on which I had
begun with Bird of the Wind and Diamond, had led me to a
place where I could bear witness to this unique manifestation
and affirmation of the feeling, the caring, the discerning feminine elements of life so long denied by the world and by men,
and even on this fateful day nearly defeated by the intrusion of
the masculine at a moment where it was intended to be helpful
and loving with that ruinous interruption: 'Don't forget, you
have got to get all the speed you can out of Blady. The speed
will be decisive!'

I had no doubt then that it was the memory of that intrusion
of the man she loved that made our lady use a whip she had
never used before, like a hardened jockey.

As for Goyoago, should he ever come across this account of
a race that he has probably forgotten, I am certain he will not
even read it to the end, because it would seem a lot of convol-
uted nonsense. That does not diminish him as a great horseman

and indeed a chivalrous competitor. It is an honour that the world owes him, and as honours go it will not vanish from the world which bestowed it. But it seems to me that the honour of our lady and Blady, at the very least, is an honour that was bestowed by life, and the example they set in the disguise of a sport will remain in life as long as life is left to answer the grave questions which the love that created it in the beginning gave it to answer.

I turned about to make for home – that was the word that came to me now for our hostelry – and as I turned I recalled the music of a ballad from my childhood, as sung by the voices of our coloured and Hottentot people in my home in the interior of Africa to the sound of concertina, banjo and mouth organ. Rendered into English it would be something like:

> *I rode through the night,*
> *I rode through the moonlight,*
> *And in the far, far distance I found a fire,*
> *And by the fire someone who had waited long.*

I do not know how long and how far I had walked before I came to the end of these sorts of things, but it was nearly dark when I came to our hostelry. Wherever there were lights they were turned on and there were people and their voices, those voices of Spain, loud, energetic and vigorous, with no one silent for long and sometimes five or six voices all saying the same things together and just in a constant and uplifting vigour creating a feeling of what the Chinese call 'togetherness' and others 'all-belonging' that made one feel welcome even before one became oneself one of the voices.

Behind me all round Castellona great drums began to beat, bugles resounded in one quarter, trumpets in another, bands struck up and music, still faint and far, began to converge as if towards the centre of the town. The tunes were Spanish versions of the kind of music military bands all over the world play after the funerals of those killed in battle or service to their country, and was full of thrust, spirit and hope, as if life had not been interrupted and was streaming on like a river from a mountain to the sea of the future. But behind this generic resemblance, it was a sound peculiar to Spain and, in addition, a sound that had the underlying tone and character that came with the Moors from the fringes of central Asia over the places where Babylon, Thebes and Nineveh and the temples of the pharaohs had stood. It expressed a sort of longing whose origin may have vanished but which still lived on to be at one with the long and wandering story of what had gone before.

But I lost the sound as I walked in the main door and found both the reception hall and the dining-room full of people celebrating. Almost all were people who had been active participants in the concourse and organisation of the fiesta, but they were all out of their professional clothes, as it were, grooms and all, and mainly in sober blacks. I had not far to look for our lady and her husband, because they came out of the crowd to meet me and clearly had been anxious for my return. One look was enough to know that their relationship had what one might easily have called 'changed' or been 'rediscovered' but to me was confirmed, rather, and transformed. They had both gone through the same retort of circumstances of fate and through the fire and heat of a subtle metamorphosis. I had never doubted that they loved each other, but now for the first time they had discovered the totality of that love. I cannot find words to say how happy that made me and, in a sense, it had an impact that changed the climate of the evening for all.

But I was not able to, nor indeed did I want to, start on another trail of introspective exploration of that complex happening, and was only too glad to be told that I must hurry to my room and come down quickly because, one and all, we were going to the square to participate in the penultimate act of fiesta.

Within minutes we were all gathered in the hall and in a group made for the square. As we came near it, the music of which I spoke converged, and suddenly the bells of the cathedral let out a storm of sound that not only swept through the night like the first winds of sound but was an almost substantial something that jumped and leapt into the great curving peaks of silence and broke there like tidal waves of the sea dissolving in foam and spray of music.

From then on it was useless to try and speak, because if there was a gap in between the ringing and booming of the bells there were drums, trumpets, bugles and other brass instruments and masses of freelance accordions joining in and making for the same centre. But as we came to the square the music stopped suddenly and the bells were silent and, far away, we heard a crackle that sounded to me almost like the faint sound of rifle fire one had heard on the edge of hearing as one made one's way with one's heart in one's throat towards battle. That sound too was coming from all directions, as the music had done, closing in rapidly and ever more loudly towards us, and was suddenly joined by the voices of hundreds of young men cheering the crackles on. When it ultimately arrived, loud, quick and now almost like the sound of machine-gun fire, it was accompanied by hordes of young men and women carrying torches whose flames fluttered high into the centre of the square. The hundreds of crackles and sparkles led to the great pile of fireworks I had seen in the square on my day of entry. As the crowd of young joined the older people and made way for the crackling fires to approach the centre, and the bands to gather in the square, each crackle was accompanied by sparks from the fuses, so that it seemed as if thousands of fireflies were going joyfully upwards to join in the defeat of silence and darkness which is the inheritance of the night. When the sparks finally arrived at the centre one was almost deafened by the explosion, which was like the heart of whatever makes the spirit of fiesta burst out of bondage of the breast and take wing to where the harmony of the spheres is made.

No one there, not even the deaf (because they had sight), not even the blind (because they had ears), could not have been uplifted and, in a sense, taken wing.

The associations within me were many and, though some were sombre, they were not sad but had a kind of delicacy and tenderness that so strong, gigantic and robust an ending needed. One of the many associations which came to me was that of a great friend, Lilian Bowes-Lyon, who loved horses. Indeed she wrote a beautiful poem about a black horse of mine called Duchess, and later, when she was dying, much too young, wrote the opening lines of another poem. One had merely to read the lines to know that only an awareness beyond the here and now could have continued them. She died alone and, I am told, with great peace in her home in a quiet square in London, and on an occasional table there was something which showed that her last thoughts too had been of horses and a kind of apotheosis of the horse. These were the lines:

O Pegasus, my dazzler, bend your knees
So that I may mount you with ease.

At that moment it was as if all of us there, myself, my host, his lady, our groom, the moustachioed Baron and, I am certain, many others at this consecration of the concourse of horses, had struck the earth of Spain with hoof and sandal, as once the Dazzler had struck Mount Helicon, and this Hippocrene of eventfulnesses had risen, fountain-wise, at Castellona in the passion of the fiesta.

Back at our hostelry, although it was nearly midnight, a meal of meals was waiting for us. Just before we went to our table, our beautiful sixteen-year-old rushed in with a handsome, rather dark and singularly Mediterranean-looking young man, tall and elegant and for his age unusually manly.

She embraced our lady again and again, and the words and the tears of happiness seemed to meet on her lips. She introduced the young man, but what he said and what our host and hostess said to them I could not follow because it was fast and all in Catalan. But just before she left she told our lady, with perhaps a hint of shyness: 'He has promised to ride that horse of mine.' Clearly our lady had taken her into her confidence and told her how once, at that age herself, she had felt she must give a special horse to the man of her choice to ride and see if he knew how to manage it, before she let out any feelings from her locked-in self in his direction.

As they left I asked our lady how the girl had done in the trials and was told that she had not done badly, but not of her best. As she said that, she looked after the young couple going through the door and remarked: 'We have not seen much of her this time. I think she was swept off by the Duke and her friends who were at the bullfight the other day.'

She paused before adding, rather questioning her thought: 'She is a natural rider and could go far, but . . .'

At which our groom, who had joined us briefly on his way to the Baron's table, seized on the pause and delivered the stable judgement: 'She will not go much further.'

'Oh! You are truly incorrigible,' our lady exclaimed, 'the way you talk about women nowadays as if you knew all about them!'

'No, there is not a man on earth who can ever know what goes on in the heart of a woman. I can only speak of women through horses, and I can tell you I have known others like her. They seem to be full of the love of horses but then, just when you think they will never be without horses again in their lives, they go off and get married and the horse is left in its stable with chaps like me.'

He said all this with a kind of stableyard irony and, what with the triumph of his lady and Blady, was rather pleased with himself and could not resist the temptation also to be prophetic, which is perhaps the ultimate hubris of all men.

'She will be married before long and that spoilt old horse of hers forgotten. She is not of the world of horses like you, my lady. You couldn't have got married unless you had included horses, or at least a horse like Blady, in the partnership.'

He was suddenly abashed and shy of the emotion that came over him in a way which I would not have expected, and he hurried away. Our lady was silent, but her expression and her eyes said much, while her husband uttered a truly, but totally uncritical and astonished: 'Well, well I never! Out of the mouths of babes and grooms . . . !' and wisely left it there.

So there we were, back in the room where our life in the hostelry had started, on the last night of our allotted little span in Castellona, and even for my eyes – let alone all that goes on behind the eyes, the hearing and the other physical senses – the distance we had travelled in relation to its so-called inanimate objects was hardly credible.

I remembered that the first time, as we approached our table, everything, however neat and attractive, had seemed strange to me, so strange that I had a kind of feeling which would have had us submit our calling cards first to the room, and then come back at a time when it was 'at home' to alien people, properly introduced and only then arranged a date for dinner. As it happened, we were precipitated into it, and one took to one's table with a feeling of having been presumptuous and over-familiar. Putting one's hand on a chair to pull it out towards one seemed like putting one's arm on a stranger's and rudely turning him about and engaging in intimate conversation. But here one went further, and was so familiar as to sit immediately in the lap of the stranger, adjust everything to one's convenience, and then proceed to talk over it and to eat.

But in the course of the week there had been a profound transformation in my feelings about the visual scene. By day it had looked more attractive and welcoming, and on this night it went far beyond that to a conviction that nowhere else could all that had happened have had its consummation.

We were all at our old tables, but the Baron's table had been enlarged to include all the grooms. I was touched to see that at his side on the right, in the place of honour, was the groom who had suffered so much by being put into the purdah of the arrogant young German businessman's mind. Now he was transformed. The truly dedicated caretaker of horses, although remorseful that his own charges had not done better, was out of the area of hurt into which an archaic Teutonic sense of masterdom had pushed him, because it had led him into the affections of such a company, and such a place of honour.

Another result of the extension of the Baron's little parish of the borough of Castellona, which our hostelry had become, was that it included also the table of the gentleman whom I have already indicated was somewhat more refined, if not precise, than any of the other riders in the contest. Indeed, it brought him so near that he could have touched the groom with whom he had sympathised and, if he dared, even the Baron.

We too were closer, and we began at our table with the nicest of possible beginnings for, as our lady stepped forward to take her place at our table, she made a very young sound of delight and exclaimed: 'How wonderful!' And there was a shining silver tray, shining as if Cinderella herself might have polished it as one of the more precious items in her kitchen.

In the middle of the tray was a vase with a single, beautiful white rose in it. I believe it was called *Gloire de Castille*, and round the rose was a wreath of wild laurel, true *Daphne laureola*, a kind which only the Mediterranean grows, with a sort of glow of the first pewter to come out of the dark of the past, interwoven like the wreath of laurel placed around the heads of winners of the first Olympic races in Greece. There was no card to explain it, no particular name to put to it, but whoever prompted it seemed to me to have perfected the ultimate sensitivities needed on these occasions, implying that it came from a general state of wonder which included also the wonder of life.

In the centre of the table there were two vases, one of white and one of rose carnations of Spain, fresh, large and each curved petal precise, and above all with that scent of an ultimate of spice. Beside them was a card which, translated literally into English, read: 'With all my homages to a wonderful and most graceful rider. Paco Goyoago.' This card was to play a small but dynamic role in the mind of the Baron, who, as we were about to discover, was not at that moment totally pleased with Paco Goyoago.

It was interesting to see that at the Baron's table there were already all sorts of the deep-sea *hors d'oeuvres* in which the Mediterranean part of Spain delights and specialises. All kinds of beautiful fried fish in dry little bits and pieces, not delicate and saucy as *hors d'oeuvres* of France, but forthright, real and bold as the heart of Spain. There was squid, done in a very special batter, shrimps, prawns, bits of lobster, crab and crayfish, fragments of 'wolf of the sea', and both succulent green olives and their black and more common cousins, smaller but more favoured by a general taste; bread still hot and smelling fresh from the oven, but no other intrusion from any product of the land.

There immediately the scene was of eager consumption, sip-

ping of a wine that, when a glass came into the light, was transparent like the finest rubies from Mysore, and an atmosphere
which all in all was singularly alive and set the room almost
sensually throbbing, as if there were somewhere very close in
the arteries of the earth a tribal Dionysian drum beginning to
beat and summon all that there was of carnival on land, in sea
and heaven.

The three of us sat down, then arose instantly, looking for
our groom. He was sitting at the end of the Baron's big table,
near enough for us to see his face sideways, and our lady and
her man could hear, too, his outbursts of bold and original
pronouncement which were, at that moment, interrupted by the
Baron, who rose from his chair, no longer, as he might have
had to do at the beginning, awaiting or demanding silence.
Conversation instantly stopped, and he looked over the room
and at the way everything had been arranged. One is even
inclined to say that, with great modesty yet undoubted conviction, he found something of his own creation and found it good.
We all felt an impression of almost messianic mission on his
face, of great wellbeing, good will and, for a moment, unre-
served inner happiness. It was almost like a background light
everywhere in the room which became, I believe, subliminal in
all who watched.

He smiled gently, and said: 'Please do not be alarmed. I am
not here to make a speech and interrupt what is happening, nor,
above all, to spread alarm in the kitchen and chefs who have
been so generous to us. I just want to say welcome to this feast
of farewell from Castellona and thank you all who have created
so good a feeling among everyone who has been here, that I am
certain it was like a leaven in honest bread on which the fiesta
was nourished and became the best fiesta I have known.

'In this very room at this moment something has happened
which people may think trivial and hardly worth mentioning
but to me is like evidence of that tiny seed of which we have
heard, that grew into a power that moved mountains. Look
around you, please, friends, and you will see that all the tables
in this room are full. There is not a chair or a place vacant, and
it is exactly as it was when we had our first night here, a first

night which was sadly followed by a table suddenly vacated. This table has stood vacant, although spread for a welcome, all the time and every day drew my eye to it and induced a certain feeling of sorrow that it had to be so, however well I understood the reasons. Tonight it is occupied by the gentlemen who occupied it at the beginning. They have rejoined us and they make our original circle complete, and they must have done it because the *caballero* in them is alive and great and still rides. For this, and for the way they have ridden in the trial of strength that was the eventing, they are welcome, and I would suggest that we all raise a glass to them as a token of what we feel.'

The response from all was a response, judging by its immediacy and sound, that might have marked the end rather than the beginning of the feast, and it was hardly over and the grooms again ready to take on the conversation where they had left it as the most urgent of unfinished business, when at that moment the kitchen doors swung open and there came in a platter, a great earthenware platter patterned on the sides with a light and a dark blue and a seductive yellow. It was so heavy that two men carried it, high above their heads, and it was piled almost to the ceiling with a monumental *paella*, and almost immediately the room was full of the smell of saffron.

The world of spice has many complex and subtle scents and variations of smells that come from all over the world, adding nuances to men's food that transform not only their food but in some intangible way affect their thinking. For me, although it is not a classical spice and I know that it comes from the pollen of a European flower, it is nonetheless the spice of spices in colour, in scent and power of evocation.

The platter was carried through the room almost like a kind of effigy of the miraculous, and we could all but be silent in the face of such an achievement and such abundance; and in the silence, it must be said, however much it defies one's wish to go on being lyrical about so unique a manifestation, everyone began to water shamelessly at the tongue. It was placed in the centre of the Baron's table and received a loud cheer, and then there could be no doubt that the real foundation stone of the feast to come was in place and men could now drink and eat at will with only the limitation of their own capacities to inhibit them.

Nonetheless the grooms at the Baron's table still wanted to settle something and were back examining our groom like a witness before a special court pronouncing on the merits of the cases for Goyoago and our lady. It soon became clear that they were all trying to find a rational explanation of what had happened at the last fence. It was delicately and not at all judgmentally agreed that our lady might have avoided doing what she had done by that flick of a whip on Blady's flank. They all agreed they had witnessed the consequences, and many of them said that they did not regret the whip because they had seen a jump for which the course and the nature of the contest had not provided, and therefore also could never be in the records, but which must have been one of the greatest jumps ever witnessed by human eyes.

Our groom responded, as if this sort of question diminished the performance of 'his' horse and its lady: 'Our lady won the race on time alone, so what we are talking about is really irrelevant.'

At which the voice of the refined rider came over his shoulder from behind: 'I do not wish to intrude, gentlemen, but it is a question that is purely academic now and yet of great interest to all of us, compelled as we are by our calling to study carefully the best techniques of riding, and in no sense whatsoever a reflection on a most gifted rider and a great horse, obviously so well groomed.'

Our lady smiled and, almost giggling at the intervention, whispered to us: 'He is not a bad fellow and really rather a good rider. He did very well in the contest, but . . . you promise not to tell? I think his trouble is a little bit the same as his manner of speaking. He rides as he talks, with the equivalent of an Oxford accent.'

The groom, however, refusing to be diverted, continued without being disloyal and without departing from his bluff, honest way. 'My lady and my master and I have discussed the matter honestly. We all feel that it was a mistake on our part. This mistake, of course, made no difference to the result, and we all three acknowledge that it was unfair to Blady. She had no need of it, and I should have warned my master and lady not to take any notice of all this popular criticism about Blady being rather slow. Slow!' His voice was just one great exclamation mark in sound: 'Slow! Blady is the greatest horse in every department.'

The word, so obviously not his own but borrowed from the grooms' bible, *The Horsebreeders' Weekly of Spain*, sounded oddly official and perhaps inappropriate because of its smell of cities. He just lifted his glass where he sat and muttered as if it did not concern him whether anybody joined in or not: 'Blady and my lady – champions of the world!'

The light over the Baron's table went ruby from all the glasses raised as one, followed by a gulp that was audible at our table.

There was then a lull before someone remarked: 'I find it easy to understand the Blady incident, but the real mystery for me is what happened to Goyoago and his horse.'

There seemed to be no offers of a definite and illuminating explanation at the table. I could see that our groom was fighting back an impulse to explain, but he held it down successfully with an effort that showed clearly in his face.

Then suddenly he was asked a direct question and so was released from the weakening effort not to volunteer, and he said: 'I think it was due to something which happened before the race – a trifle perhaps, but something no one with our experience of horses would have put on the bill!'

He told them all about the incident in the pass, and how the Goyoago horse had been forced to stand in a horsebox tilted dangerously over the edge of the road. Although the horse had seemingly come out of the trial without damage to its temperament, he felt that a horse placed in that position, so unnatural, for so long, must somewhere have strained a delicate nerve or sinew or something in those incredibly complicated organisms of theirs that had not fully recovered, and had at the summit of the last jump, in a succession of jumps at the utmost speed, just failed to react to its fullest extent, and it had been rather like the proverbial straw that broke the camel's back.

'But even so,' he ended belligerently, 'even if the horse had come by archangel to Castellona, Blady would still have won, whipped or unwhipped!'

Thereupon another voice spoke from a different angle but still, like all imaginations there, rooted in the events of the afternoon, when it said to the Baron: 'Sir, we're also glad that it was at Castellona, and particularly a fiesta that you personally fathered so well, that world history was made today and there is now a lady rider champion of the world. Some of these educated gentlemen here may know better than I, but I think it is the first time anywhere in history that a woman rider has done so much better than a man.'

At this the refined voice, again asking to be excused for intruding, interjected with a politeness stretched to the tentative: 'Gentlemen, we must not forget Queen Isabella of Spain.'

We saw a look on our groom's face which showed that he felt forewarned and, for some non-rational reason we could not understand, was mobilising his powers of indignation, which could be fearsome.

A groom suspected of being somewhat left-wing and radical, very largely because there was a rumour, however unconfirmed, that his reading went beyond the *Horsebreeders' Weekly* and that he had been seen to have rather big books in his luggage, and known to be deeply anti-royalist, demanded in rather a querulous voice: 'What has that Isabella got to do with this?'

The rumours seemed to be confirmed by his tone, and people were quite happy to hear the refined voice insist: 'If you would allow me, I believe she has everything to do with this because she, where all the other men and kings of Spain had failed, drove the Moors from Spain. I feel it does not boggle the imagination of man to see some parallel there with what happened today,' and as he said that, he half rose in his seat and bowed in our direction, 'thanks to that lady we are honoured to have in our midst tonight.'

As he relaxed in his seat, various sounds, not of disapproval but of qualification rose, including our groom who muttered: 'I'm tired of hearing about the Moors.'

Another complained: 'Why do people always talk as if the

only thing we have ever done in history was to drive the Moors out of Spain?'

'You are quite right,' another observed. 'When you come to think of it, there were Spaniards in Spain long before the Moors came.'

The Baron, scenting cause of dissent with almost parental concern, remarked: 'Yes, it is good always to acknowledge all of our ancient history, but to remember that history does not detract from the very great achievements of our blessed Isabella.'

Whereupon the voice of culture was heard again: 'Thank you, sir. Because, as you know better than any of us, that was not the whole of Isabella's achievement. Had it not been for her inspiration to support Columbus, there would have been no America today.'

This was too much for our groom. His instinct seemed to think that this trend in the conversation was a clear warning of all the dangers that too much culture and education could bring to men of horses. In a voice that was clearly abandoning irony for sarcasm he said, rather gruffly, avoiding the eyes of all by looking firmly at a piece of squid on his plate: 'There are people not exactly a thousand metres from here who may well think it a pity.'

How right his presentiments might have been seemed suddenly confirmed. The words had hardly left his lips when the groom suspected of a heresy, if not hubris, of education let out a very strange noise, a kind of grunt, not meant to be a grunt but was a scramble of all the letters that in an ordered way might have spelt out the words with a great exclamation mark: 'Hear, hear!'

At this moment the Baron – clearly afraid that what was starting as a scuffle at his table might become a riot of the opinionated minds you always find in a group, as proved by the fact that already the voice of culture was rising in its seat and some sort of orchestration of the theme would be inevitable once he spoke – intervened:

'Friends, for myself I always like to think of Columbus's achievement not merely as the discovery of America. Whatever people may feel about the Americas today, the name all of Europe first gave it, with no thought of labelling it with the name of a lesser, however meritorious discoverer, was that of the New World, a new way for the West to go East, a new world which – as I look at it today when it too, like all of us, is becoming old – is a world full of horses and bulls that have come from Spain and has spires and great cathedrals inspired by Spain and has an imperishable background of Spain and the Mediterranean which, however confused and troubled, is rediscovered every year in fiestas and bullfights such as we have seen in Castellona this week. Everywhere, from the Argentine to Peru and Mexico there is another world of horses and bulls and cathedrals and men that is forever Spain and is rooted somewhere in earth that is in a sense, however far and foreign, forever some kind of Castellona.

'So our friend here on my right has done well to make us think also of our great Queen Isabella who did better in her day than any man had done, and also pointed men to the discovery of a new world.

'I think it would be good now for us to drink to the lady, to the horse, to his groom here at our table and to our lady's husband – who clearly is also a man of horses – and record the fact that history was made here in Castellona today.

'I have been told that somewhere today, gentlemen, the deposed world champion, deposed for however short or long a time but properly and demonstrably deposed by this lady, said that he thought that the lady who had beaten him rode a wonderful race, indeed series of races, morning and afternoon for a whole week, without blemish, and he could not honour her more. He was saying that there were a surprising number of people who thought already that, in losing that day, he had started to fail them. But, he said, these occasional little provincial mishaps were inevitabilities . . .'

Whereupon, before the Baron could carry on, our groom snorted. He had his own reasons for feeling affronted.

'Inevitabilities, my foot! Necessities, yes! And no "mishap"! He was beaten fair and square!'

The Baron swept on to express his own susceptibilities: 'We

all honour and respect Señor Goyoago, and he was obviously talking in a moment of haste and pressure and said something which his chivalrous soul, as those flowers on the lady's table so amply reveal, would never normally have allowed to pass his lips. I repeat it now only because some newspapers of the great cities have sometimes taken this view, and I would like to refute that approach once and for all tonight!'

Here the tinge of colour in the Baron's shining cheeks became redder, his eyes reflected fire and he banged the table so that the tips of moustaches, never so long and pointed and carefully pomaded, quivered like the antennae of a troubled butterfly.

'This event at Castellona,' he thundered, 'is never and can never be called provincial. There is no other event like it in the whole of Spain, or the world. It confers honour on all that participate that is unique and cannot be repeated anywhere else.

'I would ask you, therefore, to drink to Castellona which, out of its own heart, has attracted to it this unique, historic event, and a breakthrough in history which is a triumph of woman over man in the world of our horses. On behalf of you all and, indeed, on behalf of Spain, I would thank the lady, and above all thank Castellona for what it has given us and will go on giving the world.'

His emotion was by now showing through unashamedly, as the tears started coming down his cheeks, no doubt because of the finality to which the words were so rapidly leading him and the thought that he would have to wait at least a year, if not forever, for his next fiesta, rather as a sensitive and imaginative child at the end of a great and abundant birthday of gifts and love wonders how it will ever get through all the days and weeks and months before the next. Whatever the emotions, which are always swifter than the swiftest thought, and the thought, swifter than the words which must express it, they inflicted a helplessness on him that overwhelmed all capacity for expressing the more that was left unspoken in his spirit. He stood there with a face that was suddenly a face of a child of history, inhibitions and self-consciousness shed, all heart and innocence, and then around him everyone at all the tables stood up and applauded with hands clapping, with 'Bravo's!' with '*Olé*'s!'

and only the gods know what other sounds and gestures, and officially the end of the fiesta was a something of feelings, moods and all the complex and subtle variations of which the human spirit is capable, raging like a storm on the other side of the proportion and laws of harmony.

The Baron paused here for so long that everyone may well have thought he had ended with that last sentence, not unsuitable for the final words of his address, but the theme was obviously not exhausted in him. It was obvious to everyone looking at him that he was, as it were, almost trapped in emotions that were the products of a lifetime, and this, plus the difficulties of trying to express the inexpressible which was in his heart and mind, showed itself clearly on his features, and above all in his eyes, where there was a look still close to tears.

And so we were not surprised that he seemed, in a sense, a small example of the predicament of even the greatest of composers, like Beethoven or Schubert, who at moments seem reluctant to end their great testaments of music, perhaps because they are afraid of the moments of emptiness that would face them after the end.

But he did find words at last, and he said: 'Forgive me if I sound too personal, but we have brought questions of time and place into this discussion, and a world far beyond this place, and Spain. I know something of that world that is called things like 'wide' and 'great', because it was part of my education, as the tradition of my family had it, to go out into that world as a young man and to travel it at length – Americas, Philippines and all. Ultimately, though, it was not a way of life but a form of distraction for me. I thought it was my fault that all the travelling did not seem to broaden my mind, which was supposed to be the whole object and purpose of travel. I began, slowly, to experience an increasing longing in my heart for glimpses of the hills and the prairies and the places of Spain; places not only of olives and vineyards, ilexes and oranges, but, above all, bulls and horses, and the so-called ordinary people at home.

'As I thought "at home", I realised that I had not used the words in my mind for years; that it was a thought almost forbidden for its banality, and yet suddenly it seemed full of magic, and the people around it were not ordinary but everyone extraordinary, and far more interesting than anyone I had met on my journeys – and I met numbers of good, decent and interesting people. I came back immediately to Castellona and not only thought I never wanted to see the world again, but it has seemed to me the longer I have been here, with every year marked by a fiesta bringing people from everywhere together, that this is the best of life I have ever encountered.

'Even as we talked tonight and there briefly came in references to the Americas and a new world, I thought how strange that, although in many ways it is obviously far greater and far more important than this little place where we are here on earth, and is undoubtedly a wide, wide world which Castellona is not, yet Castellona, for us who go through the years which seem so long in the living but so short when we look back, Castellona is greater because it is not the world: it is, at this moment, the universe.'

In the course of this moving and convincing demonstration of respect and gratitude one saw the tears, as it were, withdrawing from the Baron's cheeks, rather than being dispersed by the warmth of the applause and of the room. The impact of their disappearance on me was that of the wet on his face withdrawing gently to its source, rather like the great river at my home in Africa after the rains which, though my head knew it was making for the sea, yet to my eyes and my heart was like the withdrawal and a sinking in to the faraway place in the earth where it bubbled up as a mere fountain; and that brought me to the mystery of tears.

There are, obviously, many things that distinguish the human race from the animal kingdoms of life. I have known animals to howl and complain but I have never met an animal capable of tears, or of their partner, laughter. There is a hyena, I know, referred to as the 'laughing hyena'. I knew it well at a younger time and another place. What is called laughter there is a kind of hysteria of sound in the depths of the African night from one of the most highly strung creatures of bush and veld and desert. I have looked hyenas in the eyes in the crepuscules of dawn and evening, and there is great sadness there, but I have never seen a tear.

I have ridden, as I have told, on Diamond with lambs separated from their mothers bleating so that they were nothing but an instrument of bleat; all the rest of their being vanished. I have stroked their heads to comfort them and I have looked into their eyes, and there were no tears.

I once looked through leaves into the eyes of an old elephant, eyes that do not see, it is said, very far, not because they are weak eyes, as people believe, but because, ultimately, the look of the elephant more than any other animal on earth is directed within. And this old elephant was a great elephant at the end of his days, and as he first came over the horizon and stood there in the wind and colour of morning and paused, he looked like a monument to all the elephants there had ever been. When he came near I looked into his eyes, and there was a strangely wise-old-man-look, a profoundly human look which startled me out of my senses because of so close a feeling of kinship which, despite my love of elephants, I had never expected. And yet, in spite of this kinship, there were no tears.

I could go on with examples from the natural world of this absence of tears and the way in which tears come to the human race, not on demand but of their own accord. In this there is expressed the deep and inexpressible mystery that is in the keeping of human flesh and blood, and there are moments when the frail and vulnerable creature can be hurt in a way in which the mystery within us seeks to convey its fellow feeling with us and so, when we are deeply, and in the terms of our contract with life, full of a valid joy, tears of laughter will come; and when, in a grief which is part of the sorrows of life and creation, it sends tears to tell us that it is with us. This is the great comfort and proof of companionship always of the mystery and caringness of life, and to me, for that moment, among all these animal visions – above all the lone old elephant dominating the scene of Africa where he stood, great as he was in physique yet so small, wrapped in the great blanket of the blue of the central African morning – the Baron was like a child and happy because not only was the mystery there to comfort him with tears, but also he had the company of the extraordinary, ordinary men of his chosen world.

The room was now silent. The Baron was still on his feet but the expression on his face had changed, and where he had been in a winter of himself, it was now in full anticipation of another spring. A smile like that on the face of a child who had been inconsolable with grief suddenly appeared and was allied to the look in his eyes which clearly demanded that he could not express Castellona's sense of farewell on so sombre a note. Indeed he felt this so deeply that, in a voice of command, which must have come back from his youth when he was doing his statutory service as a soldier in Spain, he said: 'Gentlemen!', and there was added a something of mischief to the word as well, 'You must please all come back to Castellona! But on one condition . . .' He paused like an experienced actor about to establish the point of the play, and then continued: 'You are not to come without your horses!'

The thought that he, at the end of all that had happened, could think them guilty of the unthinkable was so unthinkable to his hearers that he was rewarded with sustained and affectionate laughter, and I felt free to give way to the wish once again to be on my own. I could not contribute or digest any more, and what followed had no need of a grain of what was not Spanish.

I walked slowly down through the garden to the stables. I went straight to Blady's loosebox. The half-door was opened and there she was; and instantly she knew there was someone leaning on the lower half of her door. I could just see her head coming out of her halter crunching food. Clearly her physical hunger had already been assuaged and she was ready to take notice of the outside world. I could not be sure but I thought she knew me, because she continued to look, and I looked back, for a long time without saying anything or her shifting from one foot to the other or even shaking her head or whisking her tail. It was a moment of great stillness between us, contained in the half-sound of distant voices and celebration of Castellona. I thought I recognised what I had come to call her classical stillness, the stillness and the quiet that Keats had found once beneath the rim of a Greek urn, and I asked myself what it was that obsessed this mare in her waiting and made me so obsessed with this quality in her and attach an importance to it which I could not express.

As I confessed my inability and my puzzlement to myself and to Blady and the night, it came to me. She was waiting for readiness, for a readiness in time which would be joined to the readiness of a spirit devoted, and not questioning, to the waiting in between the other readinesses of providence and creation, and another need of life would come instantly for the immediacy such waiting had given her. It seemed to me that, in the course of that week at Castellona, that readiness was being promoted in everyone and everything, even of history and future, and the readiness came and joined all the other readinesses and became invincible, despite all the odds, in that last point-to-point.

And there precisely, as so often, my imagination found itself at home and confirmed by the master of all who write in English: 'there's a special providence in the fall of a sparrow. If it be now, 'tis not to come; if it be not to come, it will be now; if it be not now, yet it will come; the readiness is all.'

Hamlet's words show how, though the time and all the 'here and nows' are always out of date – and there would be no point in creation if there was not always a need to make them immediate and contemporary – yet in between the soul of man is stricken with a 'to be, or not to be' moment until the darkness lifts and the light of a far-off dawn comes through.

Inwardly a great 'thank you' went out to Blady, and also to our lady, and then soared out into space beyond my favourite nebula, Andromeda, where perhaps something of my Diamond and Windvoel, this mysterious starling of creation, born of man and woman of the first people of Africa, were being re-breathed in a whiff of breath of smoke and fire of the stars out there, and – I was startled that I had not ever seen it before, because it was so relevant – in a vast arc of stars and black holes and mist and other constellations I saw, to the northwest, low in the sky, the Plough itself.

I felt strangely excited by this for Blady and all of us, by the sign that there was no rejection or abuse in her bondage to a plough on the edge of the hot Camargue and that it too was, in some sort, part of the great process of translation in which heaven and earth are constantly engaged – a process to which the great constellation seemed to bear witness just then. I almost went back to fetch Blady and show her that other plough, but I realised that it would be an indulgence of myself rather than a service to Blady.

With a heart full of nostalgia I was about to turn away as for the last time, listening for her to cease her watching and waiting and resume her munching, and let me hear it loud, clear and authoritative as the munching with which I first began to wonder about these things in the deep interior of Africa.

Then suddenly I knew it. I knew with an uttermost feeling of resolution and a compulsion to lay my hand upon my heart for not having known what it was before: Blady's waiting was the waiting of the feminine, the waiting of the feminine not just after a thousand million years of neglect to be recognised by man but a waiting that was utterly for waiting's sake, a waiting in which the longing which moves all creation is born, a waiting which is not the waiting of man. Man has his own kind of waiting, but it is a waiting imposed on him by his quest in the external world; it is more conscious in its beginning, and it develops as an instrument of will and experience and character and outer necessities. The waiting of the feminine is there and was there always, born with the feminine, always alive in the feminine. It was the waiting of creation itself, the waiting which is at the heart of time where out of a longing the stars are made and the child is formed and born. How could one not have known that all the living and growing and all the light and shining things coming out of the darkness at the beginning were made out of this waiting, which neither the darkness could quench nor any sun, however great, burn away? It was as if a seed that had not fallen by the wayside had found some dark, still place in the earth of human life, in the earth of the feminine being, where it could slowly uncurl and begin to reach out to where it could grow and achieve in the full light of the new-born day the flower that beckoned it in its heart.

It was at that moment of illumination and resolution that

Blady spoke in a way that Diamond always spoke to me when
he was excited and full of an anticipation of some special horse's
joy. It was a sound of breath expelled through the delicately
carved nostrils and long sensitive lips that horses possess, and
was like a gust of air shaking a branch of young leaves in the
spring. And then it was gone almost as quickly as it had come;
and yet, short as these lines are in the writing, in less time than
the writing takes Blady was back at her food and I heard her
munching. The reassurance and the feeling of fulfilment made
me almost lightheaded, and I was thinking, perhaps with a smile
in the dark: 'Oh Blady, Blady, munch on. You are a great lady.
You are a great lady in waiting. Munch on.'

I went back to the hotel where our lady and her man were
looking for me, because everyone was pouring back to the
square. We went to the square, and there I saw the climax of the
fiesta's aspirations, its seeking to bring light and fire to the
utmost pitch and summit of the night. Scores of fireworks all
at once exploded and roared into the night. I have never seen a
display so incessant. There was not a minute in which, at the
summit of darkness, a rocket did not penetrate and explode, and
all about it lights at lesser and greater heights rain down in
incredible patterns of colours and shapes and flames, and the
whole night become an endless fountain of soaring and falling
light. And in between the light the great cathedral bells started
ringing, reminding all that what had happened at Castellona
and on this night had to submit itself to the ultimate eucharist
where men lay down their powers of mind and reason, their
sense of achievement and their ambitions for the future and go
on their knees for help from something beyond all, for a pardon
and a blessing for making their triumphs as well as their sorrows
a source of blessing and a chance of receiving grace.

And then the tumult of light and sound diminished into one
rocket, soaring towards Sirius, and the echo of one peal of
cathedral bells. It was black and it was still. The fiesta was over.
It went away suddenly as if a wind had come on the first night
of spring and moved all of sound before dawn out to sea.

It was in this mood that I stood for the last time at the window
of my room contemplating the sky above the rooftops, so clear

and packed with stars, and the smell of the garden coming up like a bouquet of the wine of morning, and I heard voices, low but clear, coming from the balcony next door. I had no balcony but the voices were distinct and they were speaking in English. Our lady and her husband never discontinued the endearing habit which had grown up between them of speaking English when they had things to say which were not for the public, knowing that their English would give them perfect protection even for the most delicate intimacies.

He was saying: 'I keep on thinking, every time I am not thinking of you and Blady and all that happened today, of that first day of the war when you decided in Scotland that you had to come immediately to Spain and join me.'

He spoke in a tone that was new to me, and she likewise answered in a tone that was unfamiliar, although I thought I had heard it once or twice when she was alone with Blady and unaware of my presence.

'Why?' she asked. 'Does it trouble you?'

'Oh, goodness me, no!' he answered – I am certain, although I could not see, with a smile of affection. 'Nothing troubles me now. It is just that I find myself full of a kind of wondering, and wondering in particular about that day, wondering what connection there can be between that day and us here tonight, except of course gratitude that if it had not been for that day we would not be here tonight.'

'Indeed,' she said, 'there is for me a very clear, unbroken connection.'

'But it was, if I remember rightly, a sudden decision?'

'Yes,' she replied quietly. 'Chamberlain's words about Britain being in a state of war had hardly been uttered when there and then I knew I must come to find you.'

I had no need to be with them to know that there would be a look on her face which would say more and, indeed, pose the everlasting question of woman to man: that although woman knows, sadly and gratefully, in the depths of her heart how feminine love needs male armour and therefore understood there could be a valid need for the man to go to war, did the man know how much he needed the spirit of woman and her responsibility for life coming out of life and laid upon her for maintaining the link between beginning and end, so necessary to give them both their meaning?

She was back in a moment when the whole of the civilised world seemed to be crumbling around her, with nothing but death and destruction ahead, and the line of duty and contract laid by life on her as a woman lay direct and clear to him in Spain. I knew this by the fact that she said, almost as if afraid of so big a declaration, almost frightened by the world of emotion from which it came: 'You see, I knew at that moment that life had presupposed you for me.'

There was a long pause. She, perhaps, to make certain that there was nothing more to be said and no necessity that she should retrack long years between the now and the then, and he, I think, deeply moved that she could have known to what he referred, as it were, like lightning. He remembered that first Sunday in September, which was beautiful and still and so full of the sense of fulfilment of summer, and then already the next morning a chill of autumn and a world suddenly fragmenting and losing its established cohesion of mind and spirit, communications and travel. She had reappeared with astonishing speed, without stain of travel or any kind of perturbation, in his life. All this went through him swiftly and he said:

'So the thing that made you decide, thank God, and brought you back to Spain . . . was it the same thing that made you take Blady out of the plough, and so on to this afternoon in the stadium?'

'Yes. I would not say it was the same thing so much as that both those things originated in the same area of myself. But ultimately it was you, and all I felt with you, that led me to Blady. It was my love of you that precipitated, in my general love of horses, the coming of Blady. I kept on feeling all along that it was through my first love of horses, and a horse of horses, that I could really prove the love that was so instantly born between the two of us. All along I was training Blady and I rode her and I shall always continue to ride her because of this enlargement of the love of man I seem to feel – all around us, this evening, from the garden growing things down below us, and up above the trees and that spire of the cathedral, up, up to beyond the furthest of the furthest stars – it encompasses it all.'

There was a moment when I felt the depth of feeling that these beloved friends had reached at that moment, and the walls between us almost transparent with the light in which they were seeing themselves. And none of this was diminished but heightened by a note of masculine tenderness which in matters of life and death can be a tenderness as delicate, if not even more penetrating, as that of the best of the more rounded feeling of the woman, and all the more delicate and tender because it was uttered on the frontier of laughter and tears, those tears which my native countrymen in Africa say one must take as beads and arrange on a string of feeling and so make a necklace which one can hang around one's heart before one can find joy again.

'One thing I promise you. I will never again make you feel you have to use a whip on anything. Never again will I ask you, or myself, to go faster. I shall learn to hasten slowly and so contain ourselves always for always within our own ration and measure of time.'

At that I turned quickly away. I knew that what was still to be said could only be between two, and to listen on with intent would be a kind of sacrilege. In that honest, straightforward, unfussy, unpretentious Spanish room, I closed the window gently and then went slowly over into a steady and untroubled discussion within all that I knew of parts of myself.

It was again an Odyssean moment, like the moment when he realised that one should not seek favours from the gods themselves, because favours and the divine patronage which the gods bestowed were only ever gifts of the lesser gods, and hence the sources of great envies and jealousies in heaven and, inevitably, divided men against themselves, and groups of men against one another, so that the thunder and lightning of Zeus and the retribution of fate for excess of its laws of proportion – indeed, all forms of divine as well as human hubris – are thrown at the trespassers to restore them to harmony and order.

It was only then that Odysseus realised not just that he had to sacrifice things of great value to the gods who favoured him, or as appeasements to the gods whose jealousy and envy had been aroused, but that the sacrifice had to be to every one of them, to whatever was valid and proportionate in them. Only then was he promised and certain that he would lead what was left of his life in wisdom and that, at the end of all his journeying, death would come to him gently like a mist of the sea.

I do not suggest that at that moment I was engaged in anything quite so uplifted and sombre, but merely – on these nights in that honest little room and its window on the garden – reviewing all that there was of totality from the beginning, and all that followed from then on to Castellona.

As I prepared for my bed, I went meticulously over the journey of mind that had brought me to this point, and how it had obscurely started the search in a state of spirit and an immediate appearance of reality which could not possibly, on the surface, have foreshadowed and foretold the journey to follow and the way it would go, but brought me safely through darkness in a prison of war and moments of condemnation to death, miraculous release and another kind of search in bush and desert of Africa and rediscovery of my own native heart of land; and so on through a sense of the sickness of time and the valley of the shadow of cancer in my own family life and that of the most special of friends; on and on to a return to the Mediterranean wherein I had first sat down seriously to follow my own trade of spirit to write and so rediscover a Mediterranean heart in myself; on and on to this moment, to this happiest of happy moments, concluding in a way, and not chronologically as we know it in our measurements of time but following another kind of chronology of meaning, a pursuit of the order and the measure in which meaning evolves in a human life to a pattern that is not so much in time as carved out of moments of time, all reintegrated and reunited in one transcendent knowledge, a knowledge not absolute and static but eruptive and dynamic in the lava and blood within ourselves; a knowledge forever enlarging itself through the seasons and emerging greater out of decay. Within myself a knowledge that expanded with that expanding universe, brilliant with stars over Castellona, that brought me back just then to the window on the garden just as, far, far away on the verges of the classical little city of Spain the first Castellona cock began to crow, long before there was a glimmer of the day, and to look out and up beyond the still, silent leaves, again up and up until I found the belted and sworded constellations and followed the course of the foam and spray of light that is the Milky Way – which in all mythologies, even that of the first man of Africa, is an expression of feminine being and doing – to the certainty that all stories in the short run may have to go through darkness and death and the most profound of sorrows; that we too, like Chiron who walks in our mind wrapped in a robe of stars, a god of great sorrows and great goodness, will be joined inevitably with the last great story of all, and its happy ending.